Campaign '72

Campaign '72

The Managers Speak

Edited by Ernest R. May
and Janet Fraser

Harvard University Press
Cambridge, Massachusetts
1973

Contents

The Authors

The authors were discussants in the conference on campaign decision-making which was held in Cambridge, Massachusetts, on January 5 and 6, 1973, and sponsored jointly by the Institute of Politics in the John Fitzgerald Kennedy School of Government, Harvard University, Ernest R. May, Director, and the Nieman Foundation for Journalism, Harvard University, James C. Thomson, Jr., Curator.

DAVID S. BRODER, political correspondent and columnist for the *Washington Post*

PATRICK H. CADDELL, president of Cambridge Survey Research, which handled survey work for Senator George McGovern through the primaries and the 1972 general election

BILLY JOE CAMP, press secretary for Governor George Wallace

JACK L. CHESTNUT, 1972 national campaign manager for Senator Hubert Humphrey; attorney, partner in the Minneapolis firm of Chestnut, Brooks and Burkard

The Authors

PETER H. DAILEY, president of the November Group, the advertising agency organized to handle the 1972 re-election campaign of President Richard Nixon; president of Dailey and Associates Advertising in Los Angeles

MORRIS S. DEES, JR., direct-mail chairman for Senator George McGovern in 1972; attorney, co-founder (with Julian Bond) of the Southern Poverty Law Center in Montgomery, Alabama

CHARLES GUGGENHEIM, media adviser to Senator George McGovern in the 1972 campaign; documentary film-maker based in Washington, D.C.

GARY W. HART, 1972 national campaign director for Senator George McGovern; Denver attorney

THOMAS J. HOUSER, chairman of the Illinois Committee to Re-elect President Nixon; attorney, partner in the Chicago firm of Sidley and Austin

MAX M. KAMPELMAN, adviser to Senator Hubert Humphrey; attorney, partner in the New York and Washington firm of Fried, Frank, Harris, Shriver and Kampelman

ROBERT J. KEEFE, consultant to the AFL-CIO; national political director for Senator Birch Bayh

JEB S. MAGRUDER, deputy campaign director of the Committee for the Re-election of the President; from 1969 to 1971, a member of the White House staff

JAMES M. NAUGHTON, political correspondent for the *New York Times*

The Authors

JAMES G. O'HARA, chairman of the rules committee at the 1972 Democratic convention; U.S. congressman from the 12th district of Michigan

ALAN L. OTTEN, Washington bureau chief of the *Wall Street Journal*

JAMES M. PERRY, senior editor of the *National Observer*

J. PHILIP REBERGER, executive assistant to deputy chairman Ed DeBolt of the Republican National Committee

ROBIN SCHMIDT, campaign manager for Congressman Paul McCloskey; also administrative assistant to McCloskey

RICK G. STEARNS, deputy campaign manager for Senator George McGovern; formerly a staff member of the McGovern Commission on Delegate Selection and Party Structure

RICHARD H. STEWART, press secretary for Senator Edmund Muskie; formerly Washington correspondent for the *Boston Globe*

BEN J. WATTENBERG, adviser to Senator Henry Jackson; co-author (with Richard Scammon) of *The Real Majority*

ANNE WEXLER, director of the national voter-registration drive for the Democratic National Committee; from January to April 1972, national director of Citizens for Muskie; from April to July 1972, coordinator of uncommitted delegates for Senator George McGovern

Campaign '72

Company 72

Introduction

BY ERNEST R. MAY

In the literature on American politics, this book is unique. Word for word, it reproduces discussion among backstage managers of a Presidential campaign. The reader can hear the number two man in President Nixon's campaign organization compare notes with the national campaign director for Senator McGovern. The latter in turn trades reminiscences with people who fought his candidate in the primaries. Other Republicans and Democrats comment frankly and often eloquently on preparing television material, getting out letters to voters, and raising the millions of dollars which a Presidential campaign consumes. All the while, skillful reporters are trying to learn what they had been unable to learn when the performances were staged.

For no other campaign in American history is there a comparable document. Newspaper coverage focuses on the candidates. Since historians depend heavily on newspaper sources, what they write also concentrates on candidates and thus on appearances projected for public consumption. As a rule, neither reporters nor historians learn how the drama on stage was produced or directed or how the scenery was set. This book gives us glimpses of the planning, calculation, contrivance, miscalculation, and mischance that determined what the electorate saw.

1

When investigations of the Watergate bugging and related episodes have been completed, we will know a great deal more about dark aspects of the campaign. Since the discussion here took place before much evidence surfaced, it scarcely touched on criminal acts or even on methods used for collecting hordes of secret cash. It dealt only with normal, aboveboard scheming.

At the moment, we can guess that the election of 1972 will be remembered because of its scandals. Otherwise, we cannot estimate whether it will seem significant to later generations. One candidate challenged and overcame his own party's established leadership. He then lost by a landslide in the general election. In these respects, the election is reminiscent of 1872, and it may later be remembered as of no more moment than Horace Greeley's drubbing by Grant. On the other hand, the 1972 election could turn out to seem like the election of 1896. Then, William Jennings Bryan, another evangelical Westerner, captured the Democratic nomination. A wholly new element took over the party's leadership and committed it to a new program of reform. For practical purposes, the party remained dedicated to this program until its final accomplishment in the era of the New Deal. In retrospect, McGovern may seem a second Bryan.

If so, Nixon may seem a second McKinley. After having for many years interpreted the 1896 election as primarily a stage in progress toward reform, historians have recently begun to note that large numbers of Lutherans, Roman Catholics, and urban workers switched party and that, as a result, a new Republican coalition retained control of the Presidency and Congress for most of the next three and a half decades. Insofar as the discussants in this volume edge toward prophecy, they deal with the question of whether or not the Nixon victory of 1972 augurs such a future.

The value of this book does not depend on 1972 turn-ing out to have been a critical election, for it casts light on aspects of politics not peculiar to the one campaign. Nevertheless, readers need to be reminded of the specific events discussed. Hence, it is well here to set down some essentials of the piece played on the public stage.

On the backdrop throughout were images from the war in Vietnam. Abating but still going on, that war had been the dominant issue in American politics ever since the mid-1960's. In 1968 Senators Eugene J. McCarthy and Robert F. Kennedy had both challenged President Johnson in Democratic primaries, running as antiwar candidates with fervent backing from youthful volunteers. Johnson dropped out of the race. A narrow victory in the Cali-fornia primary gave Robert Kennedy a lead over Mc-Carthy. Then a madman shot and killed him. At the party's convention in Chicago, the rebels had no effective candidate to pit against Vice President Hubert Humphrey, who had President Johnson's backing. As the convention proceeded to nominate Humphrey, police clashed with antiwar protesters in the streets and parks outside, and scenes of bloodshed spread over American television screens. Leading a disunited party, Humphrey then lost narrowly to Richard Nixon.

As President, Nixon gradually disengaged from the ground war in Vietnam while continuing every effort to prevent a communist victory. Violent antiwar protest resumed and rose past previous levels. The high point, indeed, came in the spring of 1970 when the President temporarily enlarged the war by ordering a ground attack on communist sanctuaries in Cambodia. Afterward, anti-war demonstrations diminished. Polls, however, showed desire for an end of the war to be mounting among the general public.

In the Democratic Party, one result of the turmoil of

1968 had been a vote by the Chicago convention for reforms in the party. Commissions undertook the task. One preparing new procedures for selecting delegates was headed by Senator McGovern and later by Congressman Donald Fraser of Minnesota. One charged with rewriting convention rules had as chairman Congressman James G. O'Hara of Michigan (a participant in the discussions recorded in this book). With most professional politicians paying scant attention, the McGovern commission devised and won acceptance of rules requiring that all delegates be elected at least in open conventions; that not less than three-quarters of all delegates from any state be chosen at a level no higher than the congressional district; and that young people, women, and minority groups be represented in a "reasonable" relationship to their proportions in a state's population. Democratic National Committee chairman Lawrence F. O'Brien said, "It's the greatest goddamn change since the two-party system."

Early in 1971 McGovern formally announced his candidacy for the Democratic nomination. In retrospect, it is easy to see that he had formidable advantages. As one of the earliest and most outspoken opponents of the Vietnam war, he could attract much of the following of McCarthy and Robert Kennedy. The new rules of the party and a new constitutional amendment giving eighteen-year-olds the vote meant that such a following would give a candidate more strength in 1972 than four years earlier. At the time, however, McGovern was scarcely thought a serious contender. He did not project a captivating personality to television viewers. On the screen his tense smile seemed that of a man holding fast to false teeth. He delivered speeches in the dry, monotonous style of a small-town parson. Preference polls among Democrats in the winter of 1971–72 showed only 2 to 5 per cent choosing him. Election analyst Richard Scammon, surveying Democratic prospects in January 1972, ticked off a number of possible nominees but omitted even to mention McGovern's name.

Journalists and politicians agreed that the front-runner was Senator Edmund Muskie of Maine. Frequently characterized as "Lincolnesque," Muskie had been Humphrey's running mate in 1968 and an effective party spokesman during the mid-term elections of 1970. Identified less with the antiwar movement than with efforts to curb pollution, he was regarded as a candidate who could unify the party.

During 1971 many men talked of challenging Muskie but then decided not to do so. Senator Birch Bayh of Indiana, Fred Harris of Oklahoma, Harold Hughes of Iowa, and William Proxmire of Wisconsin all launched campaigns and then abandoned them for want of support or money or both. Bayh's departure from the race happened to occur in October. Some participants in this symposium refer to Bayh's withdrawal announcement as coinciding with the point when the campaign began in earnest.

After this juncture, there remained plenty of entrants. Some ran without any expectation of winning, among them Sam Yorty, the pronouncedly conservative Mayor of Los Angeles, and Shirley Chisholm, a black member of Congress from New York. Some entered as long-shots, hoping perhaps to end up as Vice Presidential prospects. Chief among these were Senator Vance Hartke of Indiana and Congressman Wilbur Mills of Arkansas. As chairman of the Ways and Means Committee, which handled all tax revenue legislation, Mills was reputed to be the most powerful man in the House. (A veteran politician said to me in early 1972, "Mills hasn't got a chance, but, God, how I'd love to be in his boiler room. The phone would be ringing all the time with corporations asking if the chairman couldn't use a little more money today!")

One candidate given at least an outside chance of winning was Senator Henry M. Jackson of Washington. Known as "Scoop" because of his background as a newspaperman, he had a down-the-line Democratic record on domestic issues but at the same time defended the war in Vietnam and supported heavy defense spending. He was expected to have some appeal for conservative Democrats and organized labor. Because he advocated that the United States give firm support to Israel against the Arab states, he was also thought attractive to Jews. *Time* reported, "His deep conviction is that . . . the other Democratic candidates are running away from the great middle ground of American politics." Readers of this volume will find that his campaign adviser, Ben Wattenberg, retained such a conviction all through and even after the election.

Another candidate emerged to vie for the party's left and left-center. This was Mayor John Lindsay of New York, who had only recently resigned from the Republican Party and become a Democrat. With the looks and build of a country club tennis pro, he had an appealing television image. A strong critic of the war with a record of concern for minority groups, he seemed a more likely heir than McGovern to the mantle of Robert Kennedy. When he entered the race, a McGovern aide said, "I don't think Lindsay kills us, but he certainly hurts us."

Throughout 1970 and 1971, there had been speculation as to whether Hubert Humphrey would run again. Many party leaders had concluded that he would not and committed themselves to Muskie. In the course of 1971, however, Humphrey made up his mind to run.

The former Vice President had liabilities. His name called up memories of the violent Chicago convention. Antiwar Democrats remained antipathetic to him. Although his clothing and hair length were in the latest styles and he showed as much energy and buoyancy as ever, he was past sixty, and many of the young thought him an old-fashioned politician. He was notorious for giving speeches at breathless speed but inordinate length. (In 1968, Henry Kissinger, subsequently Nixon's chief foreign policy adviser, intoned to me sardonically, "If Humphrey is elected, we will hear announced on an afternoon, 'The President will address the nation tonight from 8 until 11.' ")

On the other hand, Humphrey had assets. More than any other candidate, he had a claim on the loyalty of labor unions and blacks. He had helped to write much of the nation's social welfare legislation. Although he had been defeated in 1968, he had garnered almost as many votes as Nixon. And he was a zealous campaigner. He loved "armpit politics." Describing his wooing of voters at a factory gate in Omaha, a *Newsweek* reporter captured his style: " 'Man-oh-shevitz! They're really coming through!' He grabs, shakes, taps, pokes, beams. 'Hello hello hi there good to see you thank you friend thank you honeybunch.' A lull between the waves. 'By God!' the candidate says, 'I've only missed four.' " In the end, such old-style politics could pull in votes. With Humphrey in the race, commentators could no longer concede Muskie a shoo-in nomination.

A question which reporters continually raised was whether Senator Edward M. Kennedy of Massachusetts would appear in the lists. The youngest and most charismatic of the brothers, he was certain to win a fervent following if he did so. On the other hand, his luster as a candidate was clouded. In the aftermath of a social affair in the summer of 1969, Kennedy had driven off a bridge into Chappaquiddick Pond. The girl whom he was chauffeuring died in the submerged car. The fact that he consulted lawyers before revealing full details to the police led to ugly speculation that never quite died down. It seemed almost a certainty that the incident would be exploited against him if he ran. In addition, his family and friends feared that some lunatic would see another Kennedy as a logical target for an assassination. Talk about his possible candidacy nevertheless continued. Less than two months before the actual nominating convention, *Time* reported a number of Democratic politicians to be fantasizing "that stalemated delegates from all factions of the party will send up a cry from the floor, 'Kennedy! Kennedy!' "

A final element of uncertainty was contributed by Governor George Wallace of Alabama. First coming to prominence as an opponent of school desegregation in the South, Wallace had run as a third-party candidate in 1968 and obtained the electoral votes of five Southern states. In 1972 he announced that he would not revive the third party but would instead run for the Democratic nomination. No one felt able to forecast what the effect would be or whether Wallace would not later change his position and mount a new third-party effort.

Instead of clarifying matters, the early primaries of 1972 made confusion worse. New Hampshire came first —on March 7. Since Humphrey had not filed, Muskie's chief opponent there was McGovern. The press therefore took the position that the primary would principally test Muskie's strength. The question was not whether he would win but by how much.

A little more than a week before the voting, Muskie made a special daytime public appearance to protest a personal attack upon him and his wife appearing in the fiercely conservative *Manchester Union Leader*. Standing on the flatbed of a truck in driving snow, Muskie denounced the *Union Leader*'s publisher, William Loeb. "He has lied to you. He has lied to you about me . . . By attacking me and my wife, he has proven himself a gutless coward." While shouting these words, he broke into tears. The merciless lenses of television recorded the spectacle for every citizen who watched that evening's news. Afterward, daily and weekly press coverage asked whether Muskie was proving that he could not stand the pressure.

Meanwhile, the New Hampshire polls showed McGovern climbing. When the ballots were finally cast, Muskie led but had less than 47 per cent. The press interpreted these results as indicating a flagging in the Muskie campaign. Reporters expressed surprise at the unexpectedly large vote for McGovern, but very few concluded that he had made himself a real challenger.

Only a week later came the Florida primary. While New Hampshire was a small state with a total Democratic primary vote of less than 90,000, Florida's primary was expected to bring more than a million and a quarter Democrats to the polls. Floridians, moreover, would choose among almost the whole field of candidates, for Humphrey, Lindsay, Jackson, Wallace, and others were on the ballot. Because of the make-up of the state, the outcome might indicate national trends. As Jackson observed, "Northern Florida is Southern and southern Florida is Northern." Wallace said more pithily, "Florida is an *all*-state." Hence, with the exception of McGovern, who had concentrated on New Hampshire, the serious contenders deployed all the resources they could muster.

Early polls showed Wallace seizing a lead. As in several other states, Florida had at the time some school districts in which court-ordered desegregation could be achieved only by transporting children to other neighborhoods. Parent and citizen groups were protesting this "forced busing," and Wallace took up their cry. He also denounced "welfare loafing" and a federal tax system that, he alleged, favored the rich over the working man. A characteristic line in his speeches attacked the "pointy-headed pseudo-intellectual who can't even park his bicycle straight." His campaign was aimed, said one of Wallace's media advisers, at "the guy selling groceries or shoes or driving a truck."

Lindsay attempted to challenge Wallace and turn the primary into a two-man race. In particular, he defended the objective of school desegregation and charged Wallace with appealing to racism. Toward the end, Muskie adopted the same tactic. He attacked Wallace as "a preacher of prejudice."

In the upshot, however, Wallace won a decisive victory. He received almost twice as many votes as his nearest rival, Humphrey. Jackson came in third, and Muskie a poor fourth, with only half as many votes as Humphrey. Lindsay pulled up fifth, with only 7 per cent of the vote. McGovern was sixth, but commentators hardly took note of the fact, in part because he had campaigned little in Florida, but even more because most of them had not yet begun to take him seriously. Predicting eventual success for Humphrey, Stewart Alsop wrote in *Newsweek* that Jackson's "nomination seems almost as improbable as McGovern's."

It was Muskie's vote in Florida which received most attention. The press asserted that Muskie had lost his position as a clear front-runner. Reporters and columnists described the race as wide open. Although they discounted Wallace's prospects for winning the nomination, they began to interpret his success in Florida as indicating that the electorate was much more responsive than most politicians had assumed to protests against busing and welfare and appeals for tax reform.

Between mid-March and early April, the only primary was that in Illinois. Governed by confusing legislation, it permitted no clear choice among the major candidates.

The fact that Muskie emerged with the largest number of delegates did little to repair his fading image. The next race on which the press concentrated was that in Wisconsin, where a million or more Democrats would, as in Florida, choose among all the major contenders.

Just as New Hampshire had been regarded as a proving ground for New Englander Muskie, so Wisconsin was taken to be a gauge of Minnesotan Humphrey's strength. It was not Humphrey, however, but McGovern who came in first. The former Vice President not only trailed by almost 100,000 votes but came in third behind Wallace. Muskie was a poor fourth. Jackson was fifth, and Lindsay was almost out of the running. When reminded that he had once called Lindsay "the wild card in the campaign," a Muskie man said, "He turned out to be a deuce."

The Wisconsin results caused Lindsay to abandon the race. The press exclaimed that there was now a three-way contest (some said two and three-quarters) among McGovern, Humphrey, and Muskie. For the first time, the media began to speculate that McGovern just might win the nomination.

News programs and newspapers buzzed with questions. Would the opposition to McGovern coalesce behind Humphrey? Could Muskie make a comeback? Would Ted Kennedy change his mind and become a candidate? What would be the effect if Wallace made an even stronger showing in other Northern states? Few professed to have answers.

In the last week of April, simultaneous primaries in two Eastern states produced a further winnowing. Humphrey charged to victory in Pennsylvania with a 200,000 vote lead, as McGovern and Wallace almost tied for second place. In Massachusetts, meanwhile, McGovern won a clear majority over all his opponents. These results seemed to prove that Muskie had lost most of whatever following he once had. Although the Maine Senator did not withdraw from the remaining primaries, he announced regretfully that he would cease campaigning. He did not, however, release his delegates or give his endorsement to another candidate. "Put it this way," said one of his aides. "We're in a holding pattern."

About this time the press began to notice that McGovern was gaining a lead in states where delegates were chosen through conventions rather than primaries. Attempting to explain both this fact and the surprising primary results, commentators offered three observations. First, they noted that, like McCarthy and Kennedy in 1968, McGovern had legions of enthusiastic young people and women voluntarily telephoning and making door-to-door calls in his behalf. Second, they said that he had succeeded in putting together an extraordinarily hard-headed professional campaign organization. Some came close to characterizing as geniuses the top McGovern managers, Frank Mankiewicz, a veteran of the Robert Kennedy campaign, and young Gary Hart. They spoke similarly of Charles Guggenheim, who prepared the Senator's television material, and pollster Pat Caddell who, though only a year out of college, was producing forecasts more accurate than those of established national polling organizations. Third, commentators pointed out that, while McGovern and Wallace appeared to stand at opposite ends of the party spectrum, both attracted "alienated" voters. In surveys for the *New York Times,* Daniel Yankelovich found McGovern to be a strong second choice among Wisconsinites who had voted for Wallace. The combined strength of the two men was said therefore to indicate that the whole electorate might be in a rebellious mood.

The primaries of early May produced no significant changes. Humphrey won in Indiana, Ohio, and West

Virginia, while McGovern won in Nebraska, and Wallace decisively defeated his chief opponent in North Carolina, popular former Governor Terry Sanford. Up to this point, Jackson had continued campaigning. Now, like Muskie, he retreated to a holding pattern.

Press attention turned to the mid-May primary in Michigan. There, some communities had recently seen citizens' demonstrations against "forced busing." Because of the automobile manufacture concentrated in the state, its Democratic primary vote was ordinarily read as indicative of sentiment among all blue-collar workers. Early opinion polls showed surprisingly strong support for Wallace.

A primary was to occur simultaneously in Maryland. Polls also showed Wallace well ahead in that state. On the last day before the voting, Wallace campaigned there. At a shopping center in Laurel, a suburb of Baltimore, a psychotic youngster with a vacant grin pointed a pistol at him and fired five shots. Wallace dropped, gravely wounded, and was hurried to a hospital. Voters in Michigan and Maryland went to the polls the next day not knowing whether the Governor was alive or dead.

Wallace nevertheless emerged as the overwhelming victor in both states. In Maryland he had 38.5 per cent to Humphrey's 26.7 per cent and McGovern's 22.3 per cent. In Michigan he received more than half the total vote, with McGovern pulling up a poor second and Humphrey even farther behind.

Doctors meanwhile managed to save Wallace's life. It seemed probable, however, that he would need a long convalescence and might never recover use of his lower body. As a candidate, he ceased to figure in the pre-convention campaign. As a symbol, however, he continued to do so, for none of the remaining candidates could overlook the fact that in total popular vote in primaries he had outstripped them all, pulling in 3.4 million to Humphrey's 2.7 million and McGovern's 2.2 million.

For practical purposes, the contest for Democratic delegates thereafter became one between McGovern and Humphrey. Primaries in Oregon and Rhode Island gave McGovern a lead. Victories in convention states extended it. Humphrey's one remaining opportunity to check the South Dakotan lay in the largest of the head-to-head primaries, that in California.

Both candidates threw themselves into the struggle in California, using all the time, money, and volunteer labor they could muster. The television networks provided time for live confrontations. Theretofore, Humphrey and McGovern had generally refrained from attacking one another. In their first joint television appearance, on Sunday, May 28, however, the former Vice President threw questions and charges like a fighter trying for a first-round knockout. He assailed McGovern's proposal to cut defense spending by one-third, arguing that the national security might be gravely jeopardized. Also, he attacked McGovern's plan of replacing the existing welfare system with an income-maintenance program that would involve paying $1,000 a year to every adult. Although a sophisticated economist might have defended the plan, McGovern proved unable to do so. He seemed confused. He had to concede that he did not know what it might cost. (On the following day, a colleague exclaimed to me, "What are the Democrats going to do? One of their candidates can't keep his mouth shut. The other can't add!" This proved to be a not untypical reaction.)

McGovern won the June 6 California primary by a margin much closer than had been indicated by polls taken prior to the television debates. Indeed, McGovern ran only 5 per cent ahead of Humphrey. Since California had a winner-take-all primary, he nevertheless won all the state's convention votes. On the same day, McGovern won primaries in New Mexico, New Jersey, and his home state of South Dakota. Two weeks later he emerged as victor in a contest with Humphrey for delegates from New York. McGovern seemed to have the nomination almost in his grasp.

The national convention was scheduled to begin on July 10. As the date approached, a credentials committee chaired by Patricia Roberts Harris conducted hearings on challenges. There were some eighty-two cases, raising questions about the eligibility of more than 40 per cent of the people requesting recognition as delegates. In many instances, the issue was whether a delegation was sufficiently representative or the procedure of its election sufficiently democratic to satisfy the letter and spirit of the reform commission reports.

The two most noteworthy challenges concerned California and Illinois. In the former case, the challenge was brought by Humphrey partisans who argued that the winner-take-all principle produced an unfair result, failing to reflect the fact that Humphrey had carried almost 40 per cent of the popular vote. In the Illinois case, an insurgent group claimed that a delegation of fifty-nine from Cook County, led and largely handpicked by Chicago's powerful Mayor Richard J. Daley, had been chosen undemocratically and lacked adequate proportions of women and members of minority groups. The challenge had first been made at the time of the Illinois primary, and some of Daley's lieutenants had warned their boss that he might not be seated at the convention. The Mayor was skeptical. "In a pig's ass," he observed.

On June 29 the credentials committee made headline news by deciding the California appeal in favor of the challengers. By a 72–66 vote, it awarded 151 of California's 271 delegates to Humphrey, leaving the remainder with McGovern. On the following day, it achieved headlines again by ruling 71–61 to support also the challengers from Illinois. The first decision threatened to injure McGovern. Since Mayor Daley and his adherents were believed to be opponents of the South Dakotan while their challengers were mostly his supporters, the Illinois decision had the reverse effect. The California case, however, involved almost three times as many delegates. The combined result was to throw into question McGovern's ability to win a first-ballot nomination and to make it certain that preliminary convention votes to uphold or overrule the credentials committee would serve as key tests of strength. Congressman Wayne Hays of Ohio lamented, "The Democratic Party is in a shambles, and this isn't going to make it a better shambles."

When the convention assembled in Miami Beach, the preliminary ceremonies were followed by credentials battles that continued through much of the night. The first concerned neither California nor Illinois but South Carolina, whose delegation the credentials committee had approved in spite of a challenge asserting that it contained an inadequate number of women. Many people active in the McGovern campaign were ardent supporters of the South Carolina challenge. As the state roll call proceeded, almost all of McGovern's adherents lined up with them. The outcome seemed likely therefore to measure the strength of the contending forces.

As television commentators pointed out, the McGovern camp stood to benefit from a ruling already delivered by the convention parliamentarian. On most issues, a motion would not be deemed to have a majority without 1,509 votes. After first holding that challenges were not exempt from this rule, the parliamentarian had reversed himself and declared that, in such cases, the requisite total would be a majority of the votes that could be cast. Since the 151 challenged Humphrey delegates would be ineligible to vote on the California issue, this meant that the McGovern camp would have to muster only 1,433 votes to unseat them. If the South Carolina challenge should win by less than 1,509 votes, however, the Humphrey forces might demand a convention vote on the parliamentarian's general ruling. If they succeeded in overturning it, McGovern's aides would have to round up 1,509 votes to win on the California issue. Or so reporters said. As readers of this volume will discover, neither reporters nor most professional politicians understood fully what was happening or might have happened during this balloting.

The South Carolina challenge went down to defeat. Most reporters perceived that this result was brought about by switches on the part of McGovern delegates. They reasoned that the McGovern managers had decided to disappoint supporters of the challenge rather than to risk a victory in which the majority fell below 1,509. Some concluded that there might be question as to whether McGovern had the 1,433 necessary to win in California. Their saying so persuaded some millions of viewers to continue watching as the balloting on California progressed.

By 1:15 in the morning (Eastern Daylight Time) the vote of the New York delegation gave McGovern a victory on California. The convention overruled the credentials committee and unseated the Humphrey delegates. Since this appeared to make a first-ballot nomination certain, many commentators predicted that McGovern's managers would appease the opposition by agreeing to seat Mayor Daley and his Illinois delegates. This did not happen. Instead, McGovern delegates upheld the credentials committee. What the Mayor had scoffed at in April had come to pass. He no longer had any official standing at the convention.

Subsequent proceedings were anticlimactic. Humphrey, Muskie, and Mills all formally withdrew as candidates. The second session again lasted through most of the night. Governor Wallace arrived in a wheelchair to speak in favor of alternative platform planks. His motions were quickly voted down. The convention approved the platform drawn up by its platform committee. McGovern then easily won the nomination. He had more than the requisite 1,509 votes by the time Illinois was polled. In the final count, he had a total of 1,864.95; Jackson had 485.65; Wallace had 377.5; Chisholm had 101.45; and 186.45 were scattered among other candidates or recorded as abstentions.

On the next day, McGovern selected his running mate. He was rumored to be approaching Muskie. Then reports circulated that he had in mind Boston Mayor Kevin White. His choice turned out to be Senator Thomas F. Eagleton of Missouri. Although the only business of the convention's final session was to ratify this verdict and hear acceptance speeches, hours went into balloting on other names proposed for the Vice Presidency. As a result, the culminating moment of McGovern's campaign for the nomination was postponed till the early hours of the morning. His acceptance oration, with the refrain, "Come home, America," was delivered after most Americans had gone to bed.

Within two weeks after the convention, the Democrats suffered a calamity. Reporters turned up the fact that Vice Presidential nominee Eagleton had three times been hospitalized on account of mental depression. When questioned by McGovern and his aides as to whether he had any "skeletons in the closet," he had withheld this fact.

At first, the South Dakota Senator declared that he supported his running mate "1,000 per cent." Soon, however, McGovern turned around, allowed Eagleton to resign the nomination, and arranged for the Democratic National Committee to substitute R. Sargent Shriver, a brother-in-law of the Kennedys.

Up to this juncture, preparations for the election on the Republican side had attracted much less attention. Two years earlier, President Nixon had been judged by politicians and pollsters as likely to have difficulty winning re-election. The public demonstration following the brief invasion of Cambodia had suggested that the war issue might cripple him as it had done Johnson. Significant Republican losses in the 1970 congressional elections, occurring despite strenuous White House support of Republican candidates, reinforced the common opinion that Nixon faced an uphill battle.

The subsequent eighteen months, however, brought marked changes. Antiwar agitation seemed to die down almost as a direct function of reductions in American casualties and draft calls and a reform of the draft which enabled nineteen-year-olds to learn with some certainty whether or not they would be called. In February 1971, when the United States provided air support for a South Vietnamese invasion of Laos, the public uproar only faintly resembled that provoked by the earlier invasion of Cambodia. A year later, when Nixon announced renewed and enlarged bombing of North Vietnam and then a blockade of North Vietnamese ports, protest demonstrations were few and small. Public-opinion polls, while still showing strong public desire for an end to the war, recorded majority approval of what the President was doing.

Meanwhile, Nixon startled the country again and again with unexpected new departures in foreign and domestic policy. Abandoning a two-decade-old tradition of uncompromising hostility to communist China, Nixon suddenly shifted posture. Astonishing most of his own aides no less than his nationwide audience, he announced on television in July 1971 that Kissinger had visited Peking on his behalf and that he himself would travel to the Chinese capital! While the Democrats were grappling with one another in spring primaries, Nixon made this trip, affording the American public an opportunity to follow it through full, live, color television reportage.

Nixon also built up a better relationship with the Soviet Union. Negotiations for mutual limitations on strategic nuclear weapons had been under way for some time. When the President went to China, it was announced that he would soon afterward go to Moscow to conclude the first of a series of arms limitation agreements. The subsequent stepping-up of the war against North Vietnam caused many commentators to predict a crisis with the Russians. Instead, the visit to Moscow and the signing of an arms limitation accord proceeded on schedule. Nixon seemed to be making real progress toward the "era of peace" that he had promised.

At home, Nixon had drawn criticism for failing to carry out earlier promises to clean up "the welfare mess" and to cut back federal spending. He also faced evidence of growing public concern about inflation and the weakness of the dollar on world exchanges.

As a partial counter to criticism, he pressed on Congress a proposal for a family assistance plan seemingly designed to reduce the numbers needing welfare support. He also proposed sharing some federal tax revenues with states and localities so that agencies allegedly nearer to the people could take on more of the tasks of government.

In August 1971, suddenly reversing a long-held position, Nixon announced a temporary freeze on prices and wages and the imposition of longer-term controls. Almost simultaneously, he devalued the dollar. Taken together with his initiatives in foreign policy and his proposals for a family assistance plan and general revenue-sharing, these decisive actions produced an impression of strong leadership, and public-opinion polls showed Nixon's popularity rising.

Some opposition to the President nevertheless crystallized within his own party. Criticizing him for continuing the war in Vietnam, Congressman Paul N. ("Pete") McCloskey of California proclaimed in July 1971 that he would run against Nixon in the 1972 Republican primaries. Later in the year a dozen conservatives led by columnist William F. Buckley announced that they were "suspending" support of the President on account of his politics abroad and at home. By December, the conservatives had found someone to carry their banner in the primaries. Congressman John M. Ashbrook of Ohio declared that he would stand as a candidate so that conservatives could express their dissatisfaction.

Although some columnists reported the White House to be concerned lest Ashbrook poll a large vote, neither challenger proved strong. In the New Hampshire primary, McCloskey ran a poor second to the President, and Ashbrook trailed still farther behind. Not long afterward, McCloskey withdrew as an active candidate, pleading inability to finance other campaigns. Though Ashbrook stayed in the race till the end, he seldom obtained in any primary even 10 per cent as many votes as Nixon.

Whatever fire might have lingered in the conservative opposition was quenched a month before the Republican convention when Nixon announced that the pronouncedly conservative Vice President, Spiro T. Agnew, would again be his running mate.

The summer months, however, produced incidents troubling for Republicans. To begin with, the party decided belatedly to move its convention from San Diego, California, to Miami Beach, Florida. One reason among many was the fact that Miami Beach, as an island, offered better security against riots. Reporters' inquiries into the shift of site, however, turned up the fact that the International Telephone and Telegraph Company had offered to put up a large subsidy for the convention. ITT officers explained that the convention was expected to provide business for hotels in its subsidiary Sheraton chain. Editors, columnists, and Democratic politicians hastened to suggest an alternative explanation, for ITT had recently settled with the Justice Department a potentially expensive antitrust suit. The Attorney General then had been John Mitchell, who resigned in order to direct President Nixon's re-election campaign. The charge made or implied was that ITT's contribution represented a pay-off.

Hardly had this sordid rumor ceased to be a staple in the press when television news programs and newspaper headlines turned to the Watergate affair. Five men, including the security director of the Committee to Re-elect the President, were apprehended at the Watergate office building in Washington inside the offices of the Democratic National Committee. Police caught them in the act of burglarizing the files and planting electronic eavesdropping devices.

Within days it had become evident that the criminals had acted on orders from at least low-ranking officials of the Nixon campaign organization.

With columns and newspaper and television editorials still speculating on whether high figures in the Nixon campaign might be implicated in the Watergate case, it was disclosed that some large companies had taken in huge, unexpected profits from wheat sales to the Soviet Union. Democratic politicians alleged that the companies had had advance tips from government insiders.

Coming one on top of another, these incidents opened the prospect that the Democrats might center their fire not on the President's record but on alleged scandals.

The Republican convention in late August nevertheless appeared that of a party confident of victory. Most Republicans regarded McGovern as the Democrat whom it would be easiest to defeat. After McGovern's nomination had become likely, John Mitchell made a tongue-in-cheek denial that the Committee to Re-elect the President had been engaged in choosing the Democratic nominee. During the California primary, a Humphrey aide had predicted, "McGovern will go into the campaign against Nixon with those Tinkertoy proposals of his . . . and Nixon will blow him right out of the water." Most Republicans believed this prophecy.

In contrast to the Democrats six weeks earlier, the Republicans staged all major convention events during the hours when the majority of citizens were awake. The only contest of the three days concerned proposed rule changes designed to give the populous urban states larger representation in future conventions. Insisting that past Republican vote remain a major consideration in determining how many convention votes a state would have, Southern and Midwestern party leaders defeated the challenge. Otherwise, the convention merely ratified the platform the President had approved and renominated the Nixon-Agnew ticket.

The subsequent contest between Nixon and McGovern proved uneventful. The President seldom appeared in public, relying instead on surrogate campaigners. This tactic became so obvious as to become the subject of jokes. Marlette drew a cartoon for the *Charlotte Observer* which portrayed exasperated Democratic strategists watching a television set from which issued the announcement, "In response to Senator McGovern's charge that the President does not care enough about Israel, White House gardener Saul Sternberg said today . . . ."

Industriously stumping the country, McGovern and Shriver encountered small and listless audiences. Their attacks against the Administration on account of Vietnam lost some force when negotiations with the North Vietnamese resumed and the President's chief adviser and representative, Kissinger, told the press, "Peace is at hand." Even references to ITT, Watergate, and the alleged wheat deal aroused little response. In 1973, when Watergate became the focus of a national crisis, it was to be explained that the people had turned a deaf ear to Democratic campaign charges because they were so predisposed against McGovern that they did not want to hear any argument on his side. Public-opinion polls showed the Democrats far behind and gaining little ground. According to a Yankelovich survey for the *New York Times*, McGovern lost most in the states where he worked hardest.

The race could not be characterized as one between two popular idols. Nixon's wary-eyed, wide-jowled face had been familiar to the public at least since his first Vice Presidential candidacy in 1952. During an earlier campaign, Democrats had circulated pictures of him with the caption, "Would you buy a used car from this man?" While respect for his abilities had grown during his Presidency, affection for and trust in him had not noticeably increased.

In this regard, however, McGovern was the President's match. The California primary, the convention, and the

Eagleton affair impaired his image. According to Yanke-lovich, people who had once judged him a "strong liberal" began to see him as a "weak radical." Some of his early advocates had argued that the electorate would view him, in contrast to Nixon, as simple, straightforward, and honest. Unfortunately for his candidacy, it was the sim-plicity that registered. Columnist Art Buchwald remarked that, if Nixon resembled a used-car salesman, McGovern looked like one of his customers.

Although samplings found relatively few voters who identified passionately with either candidate, they un-covered much more support for Nixon than for his oppo-nent. The Gallup and Harris polls reported him leading 64–30 and 63–28 as of Labor Day. Their last tallies be-fore the election forecast Nixon victories of 62–38 and 61–39. Election night proved them almost on the mark, for Nixon won 60.7 per cent of the vote to McGovern's 37.7 per cent. Nixon polled 46 million votes to Mc-Govern's 28.5 million and carried every electoral vote ex-cept those of Massachusetts and the District of Columbia.

As was remarked earlier, this book casts light not only on this particular outcome and what led up to it but also on questions relating to all modern Presidential cam-paigns, including those of the future. Since the record concerns only one campaign, it obviously does not answer these questions. It does, however, expose issues which scholars and journalists would do well to explore further.

How, for example, are constituencies perceived by cam-paign managers? We can easily discover what the con-stituencies turned out to be. Computers and survey re-search can tell us the age, sex, ethnic background, religion, residence, and social and economic status of those who preferred one candidate over another. But we seldom have any sense of how well the campaign strate-gists anticipated these results or how they expected to influence them. Which groups did they assume to be solidly in the candidate's camp? Which had to be wooed, and how? Histories of past elections tend to take it for granted that debates between Presidential candidates mirrored accurately the cares of the public. In explaining why candidates took differing positions, most histories waver between two assumptions: on the one hand, that the candidates said what they truly believed and, on the other hand, that they cynically selected the words most likely to win votes.

The record here points to additional hypotheses. It suggests, for example, that positions on issues may reflect neither principle nor calculation but be products instead of problems within the campaign organization or accidental results of the way the organization works, the prearranged schedule, or sheer coincidence. A speech taking a particular line on a particular subject may seem necessary from the manager's standpoint in order to appease some factions at headquarters that do not necessarily have any large counterpart in the electorate. The speech may have a certain character because some ghostwriters happen to be on the scene when others are not; the pressure of time permits their text to be used without clearance at headquarters; and the candidate becomes committed to a posture that he might otherwise not have adopted. A long-prearranged schedule may put the candidate in front of an audience with a special interest at a time when what he says attracts more attention than the managers had anticipated. Addressing a veterans organization, for example, he has to say something about defense policy. If defense issues happen to have sprung onto the front page, his managers may find that they have inadvertently made defense policy seem one of the candidate's major concerns. A Presidential campaign offers choices to the electorate, but this book suggests that we have a great deal yet to learn about how these choices take shape.

Another question highlighted by this record concerns the role in campaigns of the media and especially of television. The selection of issues seems often to be determined by judgments as to what will capture front-page space and even more as to what might gain time on the evening network news. Speeches are written and public appearances are staged not for their effect on the audience at hand but for their potential visual impact on television watchers. Major statements must be made not before live audiences at evening affairs but before small crowds in mornings or early afternoons because anything said after 3 P.M. (EDT) is unlikely to show up on the screen between 6 and 7. This transcript sometimes provokes an uncomfortable suspicion that candidates and their managers often cease to think of reporters, commentators, and cameramen as agents through which to reach the people but instead conduct their campaigns as if the media were the whole electorate.

One further question which this book underlines has to do with the role of money in campaigns. Accounts of elections seldom if ever pay adequate attention to the persistent and omnipresent pressure of financial need. This pressure may sometimes determine where the candidate goes, the issues he seems to choose, and what he says about them. In "The Political Campaign as an Organization," a pathbreaking essay in a 1973 issue of *Public Policy* which elaborates many of the points mentioned here, Xandra Kayden reports that McGovern gave three major speeches on Vietnam late in the campaign, not because he judged the war his best issue against Nixon but because the speeches would bring in large contributions from individuals and groups already committed to him. The discussion among managers recorded here indicates that lack of, need for, or hope for money was a constant preoccupation, shaping critical decisions in all camps. Clearly, we need a better appreciation of the extent to which this has been so in the past and will be so in the future.

The idea of holding this symposium originated with three long-time associates of the Institute of Politics: Evan S. Dobelle and James B. King, assistants respectively to Massachusetts's two Senators, Edward W. Brooke and Edward M. Kennedy, and Helen Keyes of the John F. Kennedy Library Corporation.

James C. Thomson, Jr., the Curator of the Nieman Foundation for Journalism at Harvard, agreed to be a joint sponsor. Janet Fraser, the Institute's omnicompetent Assistant Director, undertook to serve as manager and to edit the transcript. Some former Fellows of the Institute pitched in, among them Robert E. Bradford, an assistant to Senator William E. Brock of Tennessee, and David S. Broder of the *Washington Post*. Roland J. Cole, the rapporteur for an Institute faculty study group concerned with the dynamics of political campaigns, lent aid, as did several Nieman Fellows and a number of undergraduates and graduate students from the Institute's invaluable Student Advisory Committee.

Not everyone invited agreed to come, but most did so. Not everyone who wanted to come could make the date on which we finally fixed—the weekend of January 5–6, 1973. There are therefore some lacunae. For example, no one was present who had been involved in Ashbrook's campaign. Perhaps most conspicuously, no one present had special knowledge of either Republican or Democratic efforts to attract black voters. Nevertheless, the participants represented a wide spectrum of campaign organizations and specialties.

The symposium took place around a square table in the

library of the Harvard Faculty Club. Along the walls sat an audience of about a hundred or so faculty, students, Institute Fellows, Nieman Fellows, and invited guests. In addition to the four moderators, a number of newspaper and television reporters were present. All agreed to treat the proceedings as off-the-record until a transcript was ready for publication. We are grateful to them for holding to this agreement, and to their editors and station managers for permitting them to do so.

Above all, we are grateful to the moderators and the participants in the symposium for their willingness to take part, their candor, and their interest in teaching us outsiders just what goes on in Presidential campaigns. We believe that our sense of gratitude will be shared by readers both now and in years to come.

1
Before the Primaries

JAMES M. PERRY (*National Observer*). I thought we'd just arbitrarily pick January of 1971 as the beginning of the pre-primary phase. To refresh your memory, I'll outline how things looked to the press in that month. There were still 280,000 American troops in Vietnam. President Nixon said in January: "We can see the end of America's combat role." The American casualties through the end of December totaled 44,000 killed. B-52's at that time were striking heavily in Cambodia, Laos, and South Vietnam. The peace negotiators met in Paris on January 7, 14, and 21. The meeting on January 21 was the hundredth since the talks had begun in January of '69. As the month ended, a news embargo was declared in Vietnam and the so-called incursion [into Laos] had begun at that time. Unemployment in December was at 6 per cent, which was the highest since December of '61. The 1971 deficit was admitted to be $18.6 billion, from an earlier projected surplus of $1.3 billion. The Gallup poll reported that 74 per cent of Americans were pessimistic about the general economic situation, and in an interview that month with network correspondents Nixon said: "I do not plan to ask for wage or price controls." In his second State of the Union message delivered in January, the President called for "a new American Revolution" involving $16 billion in revenue-sharing and a sweeping revision of Cabinet departments. "The nation," he said, "is ready for the lift of a driving dream." Wilbur Mills said the program was defective. Robert Dole succeeded Thruston Morton as chairman of the Republican National Committee. On January 15 Edmund Muskie was meeting Alexei Kosygin in Moscow. On January 18 George McGovern declared his candidacy, pledging to withdraw every American soldier from Vietnam and to shift the nation's resources to domestic rebuilding. "The kind of campaign I intend to run will rest on candor and reason," he said. Then he charged that the Nixon Administration had deepened the sense of depression and despair throughout the land. On January 7, in a little noted move, McGovern had resigned as chairman of his party's reform commission [McGovern Commission on Delegate Selection and Party Structure]. He said that reforms would mean the 1972 convention would be the least boss-ridden and the most democratic in the party's history. On January 21 Edward Kennedy lost his Senate post [as Majority Whip] to Robert Byrd; and Ed Muskie, George McGovern, and Birch Bayh showed up to address the California Democratic convention; and the Colts beat the Cowboys 16–13 in the Super Bowl. And that's about how it looked to most of us at that time.

We'd like to start this discussion, I think, by asking representatives of the candidates, including the President, to describe for two or three minutes how things seemed to them in January of 1971. There are obviously some questions we'd like to consider. Why did McGovern start so early and what effect might his early start have had on others in the race for the Democratic nomination? Why was Muskie's position perceived as centrist? What had to happen to allow Hubert Humphrey to become a candidate, or to make him become a candidate? When and why did George Wallace decide to seek the Democratic nomination and when and why did he decide to run in the primaries, even in the Northern primaries? When Wallace's decision was known, how did it influence the strategy of other candidates? There are, of course, other questions that I don't have to list here. We'll start with Jeb Magruder, who would soon join the President's re-election committee.

JEB S. MAGRUDER (Committee for the Re-election of the President). In popularity, we were at the trough of the President's four-year term. I think the Gallup and Harris polls were showing us in the mid-forties, which was about the lowest point of popularity the President had during the last four years. All of us who were later in the campaign were still on the White House staff, and there was a considerable degree of concern that the President would have a very difficult time being re-elected. We felt that things were not coming around as quickly as we had hoped in the economy, and certainly relating to the war. Consequently, by January we already had a task force set up in the White House to start looking at the campaign; and then by mid-spring, we opened up our campaign headquarters across the street from the White House and actually started in operation. We felt it was going to be a very difficult race; we thought that if the Democratic Party was able to put itself together, it would be formidable. We felt that a centrist candidate would be the most difficult to beat, and we all felt that Senator Muskie would be the most difficult candidate for us to run against. At that time, as I recall, he was the favorite, and all the polls showed him running either ahead of or certainly even with the President. So we were concerned and we started early for that reason.

PERRY. Gary Hart, for Senator George McGovern.

GARY W. HART (campaign director for McGovern). To understand the McGovern campaign, we should start in 1970. Prior to the announcement in January of '71, we had done six or eight months of work that laid the base for that announcement and for our later campaign. Certainly, the strategy which we had decided to pursue had been determined a number of months before that announcement; and, to a surprising degree, it proved out and was followed in the year and a half after that announcement. This was a period in which we were concentrating very much on getting the nomination. We've been criticized since then for not paying more attention to the incumbent candidate, for not concentrating our efforts more on the Republicans, for not preparing for the fall, and so forth. But I would like to emphasize that we were very much the underdog. What limited resources we had during this period were almost totally and continually devoted to getting that nomination. Over the six-month or eight-month period prior to the announcement in January of '71, Rick Stearns [later, McGovern's deputy campaign manager], myself, Yancey Martin [McGovern's minority-affairs director], and one or two others had traveled throughout the country, both on behalf of other Democratic candidates and on our own, into both primary and non-primary states, to determine whether or not a base for a McGovern campaign did exist. We satisfied ourselves that it did. Regardless of the polls and the odds and prognostications at that time, it was in fact an open contest; someone other than Senator Muskie could get the nomination.

At a fairly important meeting in July of 1970, the basic strategy of the campaign was laid, and the rationale for an early announcement was brought forward, primarily by the Senator himself. There were three reasons for an early announcement. First of all, it would illustrate—dramatize, if you will—the element of candor in the McGovern campaign. The Senator found it very uncomfortable to go around the country in the fall of '70 being asked by reporters whether or not he was running, and saying, "Well, I'm thinking about it, or some of my friends are urging me to think about it." He felt much more at home just coming out and saying very early, "Yes, I am a candidate for the nomination. It's an unprecedentedly early time to do so, but that's just the way I am." Second, because he was so little known in the country, he felt that the year and a half—or extra year, really—of exposure as an announced candidate for the Presidency would be extremely important in getting the campaign off the ground. And then, third, as a strategic matter, we felt very strongly that it would permit him to take a leadership role in defining the issues in the nomination race and perhaps even the general-election race—in a peculiar sense, to carry the brunt of issue definition in that year. As an announced candidate, early on, he could forcefully state what he stood for and then hopefully bring the other candidates around to respond to those statements and either be with him on those issues or define a separate role. I think those three reasons were behind the early announcement.

PERRY. Dick Stewart is under a little disadvantage because he didn't join the Muskie campaign as press secretary until April of '71, but he was reporting on Muskie early in '71, and so I'll let him try to go back as far as that.

RICHARD H. STEWART (press secretary for Muskie).

The omen of the future may have been the fact that I joined the Muskie campaign and agreed to go on April Fool's Day. Two days later I took my family out for Chinese food, opened a fortune cookie, and found a little label that said, "Wait for a better opportunity."

As I viewed it then, I should be right now [January 5, 1973] about two weeks away from my own chauffeur-driven car—but it didn't work out that way. Nixon was low in the polls or even with Muskie, and the history of Nixon in political campaigns had been that he had traditionally needed an early lead to win—fourteen or fifteen percentage points. He had an early lead of fourteen or fifteen percentage points in the races against both Jack Kennedy [for President] and Pat Brown [for governor of California]; he blew those leads, and very nearly blew the lead against Humphrey in 1968. So, from that point of view, I thought Muskie was in awfully good shape. The money was flowing in fairly well in keeping with Muskie's standing in the polls. I figured that all we had to do was sit and wait, and that it was only a matter of a few months before Muskie would win the nomination and then we'd have a race for the Presidency which I thought Muskie could win. When I joined the campaign, there was money and there was high standing in the polls. There was also a press corps telling the nation that unless something extraordinary happened, Muskie appeared to be the likely candidate for the nomination—and I had no reason at that point to disbelieve them. I do now.

PERRY. Jack Chestnut was for Senator Hubert Humphrey, and he might not have believed them.

JACK L. CHESTNUT (campaign manager for Humphrey). In January of 1971 Humphrey's posture was probably a little different from that of most of the other candidates-to-be. He had been out of national politics for several years following the 1968 elections. He had returned to the college campus and had only re-entered politics in the 1970 Minnesota Senate race. In January of '71 he was back in the U.S. Senate after the largest win in the history of his career in Minnesota. Senator Humphrey recognized the vulnerability of the President at the time, particularly in the area of domestic issues. But he also recognized the power that an incumbent President has in running for re-election and was not at all convinced in January that he should be a candidate. It was a period of quiet organization, watchful waiting, and testing. We felt that it was necessary to test to see whether or not Humphrey was acceptable to the youth of this country, whether or not he could go on college campuses and speak with freedom—as he was not permitted to do in the 1968 Presidential election. We found that he was very acceptable on the college campuses. We made a number of political speeches, and non-political speeches, during the early stages of 1971. We did feel that Muskie's position was not so strong as it was being described by the press during the early phase of 1971. We detected some slippage—some rather substantial slippage in the period of November 1970 until January 1971, which continued on through the first six months of that year. As a consequence, we felt that should Muskie slip to the point where it did not appear that he would be the consensus candidate of the Democratic Party, we should attempt to ensure that Humphrey would be in a position to step in to fill that void.

PERRY. Billy Joe Camp was, and is, Governor George Wallace's press secretary.

BILLY JOE CAMP (press secretary for Wallace). In January of 1971 Governor Wallace was just taking office for his second term as governor of Alabama and had made no firm decision to run. As others have mentioned, he was aware that President Nixon's popularity was down to a low point. But he also realized that the President had a considerable amount of time to bring this back up through the power of his office. There had not been any —or very little—discussion about running as a Democrat. In January of '71 the decision was made to have a series of dinners throughout the country to gain some press coverage and put Governor Wallace back on the national scene. These dinners took him to Dallas, Nashville, Houston, Jacksonville, and Chicago, reflecting considerable support and assisting fund-raising. But at that time the major problem or objective of Governor Wallace was to get back control of the state government of Alabama. He faced a legislature in which a majority of the representatives and senators had opposed his re-election for governor. The decision to run for President as a Democrat came a year later.

PERRY. Bob Keefe, at that time, was with Senator Birch Bayh.

ROBERT J. KEEFE (consultant to the AFL-CIO). I think if we're saying anything here, we're saying that campaigns are long-term things. Today is the third anniversary of the first finance-strategy meeting of the Bayh campaign for '72 in the basement of his home. And two years ago we felt that there was great opportunity in the Democratic Party for someone other than Ed Muskie or, frankly, any of the candidates previously discussed. We had been around the country for a year and a half—very actively around the country during the '70 campaign—and we felt among Democrats across the country a real desire to have a younger, charismatic candidate come out of the wood-work. Of course, that fit us. In January of '71 we were opening the Bayh committee office. We went out to California late that month and took on our two rivals at the time, who were actively out on the hustings—Mr. Muskie and Mr. McGovern—and we thought we came off first best out there and really had some momentum generated. We thought we had something going, and we all still wish we'd been able to find out if we did.

PERRY. Finally, we have Ben Wattenberg to speak for Senator Henry Jackson.

BEN J. WATTENBERG (adviser to Jackson). I would echo what most everybody has said: by January of 1971 most Democrats felt that there was a great opportunity to beat Richard Nixon. I still feel that way—there was a great opportunity to beat Richard Nixon, but it didn't quite work out that way. I myself did not actively join Senator Jackson's campaign until several months after January. I had just come off working Senator Humphrey's campaign with Jack Chestnut. Senator Jackson had just won his Senate race in Washington with an 84 per cent vote, the largest majority in any two-party race in the country. We looked ahead, for example, to the Florida primary and which candidates were positioning themselves where. At that point, the line-up of Democrats in Florida looked something like: John Lindsay, George McGovern, Fred Harris, Ed Muskie, Birch Bayh, and Harold Hughes, with very much of a question mark about whether Senator Humphrey was going to be in those early primaries or in any primaries at all. Given that line-up, exclusive of Senator Humphrey's candidacy for a moment, there appeared to be a field well to the left of center; and a candidate who represented what we might call a centrist view might have a golden opportunity. He could pick up any votes to the right of center without actively campaigning for them, which would enable him to maintain all sorts of credibility with centrist, and even somewhat left of centrist, constituencies. Governor Wallace, of course, came into that race and markedly changed its whole complexion.

I think we all understood from the very beginning that Senator Jackson's candidacy was a long-shot. It was a long-shot for one basic reason: he was not a well-known political personage. To become well known as a political personage in this country, you have to win something in this primary system. This is what happened once Senator McGovern started winning things; that's when all the press came and that's when national identity came. We had hoped to win or come in a close second in the Florida primary, and that didn't happen. What did happen in the course of the primaries was that the party itself fell well to the left of any center view of American politics, and this ultimately came back to haunt the party. In point of fact, it is still haunting it.

PERRY. We have Robin Schmidt, who was with Congressman Pete McCloskey. We don't have anyone here representing Congressman Ashbrook, but we do have Robin.

ROBIN SCHMIDT (campaign manager for McCloskey). January '71 is easy for Pete McCloskey. He was a third-term congressman who had been elected as an antiwar candidate and had been searching for some way to get Congress or the President to act, and couldn't find it. Just about January, he had come to the conclusion that probably only one strategy would work, and that was to find a name Republican to take on the President in the primaries and focus on the issue of the war. He was not a Presidential candidate, nor even close at that time.

PERRY. On January 18 we have McGovern in the race. What effect did that have on anyone else? Did anyone take that seriously? Did anyone think much about party reform and what that might mean to the McGovern candidacy at that time? [To Gary Hart] What did you think that party reform was going to do at that time?

HART. There has been a lot of misinterpretation of the last political year, suggestions that McGovern somehow squirreled through some bizarre procedures which he then turned around and took advantage of. Party reform was more a product of the time and the political mentality of the country than of any one man or any small set of people. I never really calculated it as an ace in the hole [for McGovern]. A lot of commentators have thought that we had this as a card up our sleeves, one that no one else was really thinking about. People like Rick Stearns and myself realized from '68 that there were enough states that were open enough already—that if you did it right and you started early enough, you could get a helluva lot of delegates without changing any rules. Then, when the rule changes came in and they began to be accepted state after state and by the national party, we realized even more that the procedures that were available already in '68 were just being expanded into more states. And we always felt that the best organization was going to win.

KEEFE. Because we [in the Bayh campaign] had members on the reform commission, we were aware of what was going on and paid attention to what was going on. But I think many campaigns got very far down the road without ever stopping to figure out exactly what the procedures were that were going to get us to the convention.

DAVID S. BRODER (*Washington Post*) [to Anne Wexler]. When you joined the Muskie campaign, did you have the feeling that they were unaware of the effects of the party reforms?

ANNE WEXLER (Democratic voter-registration director). I had the feeling right through until the very end that they were not unaware of them; but simply because of the nature of the campaign itself, they didn't know how to handle the thing.

KEEFE. It was not awareness; it was thinking through how each state was going to do it and how to get done what you had to get done there. I don't think that we did that in the Humphrey campaign—not filing in New York [in the primary], for example.

HART. The Muskie strategy was to win big in the two early non-primary states to start the so-called bandwagon psychology going into New Hampshire. Iowa and Arizona were staffed up—Muskie people were in those states at those caucuses. As I recall, the unannounced strategy was to show great Muskie strength in the two early non-primary states in January.

WEXLER. The difference was that the McGovern staff in Iowa and Arizona was geared up six months in advance. The Muskie staff went into those states three weeks before the caucuses were held, and that made a substantial difference.

RICK G. STEARNS (deputy campaign manager for McGovern). That's not true. I managed our campaign in

Arizona. The first presence we had in Arizona was in mid-December. I didn't go to the state until the 19th of January for the caucuses on the 29th.

WEXLER. But you had a substantial number of supporters there who were working before you ever got there.

STEARNS. As it turned out, we did. But we were unaware of a lot of the work that was going on, and I think you can exaggerate this, too.

CHESTNUT [to Robert Keefe]. You mentioned that the Bayh campaign had members on the reform commission. I think that was particularly important. It seems to me that the Democratic National Committee did not even put out the manual on various rules and guidelines for the particular states until December of 1971—maybe just a few days before you had to do certain things to qualify in some states, or at least the process was starting. In the Humphrey campaign, for example, where the decision to go ahead wasn't made until December of 1971, it became a very difficult problem to cope with.

KEEFE. With a lot of high-ranking advisers who had gone through it four years ago but were coming into a completely new structure and didn't know it.

STEWART. Is my recollection correct? Wasn't George Mitchell [of the Muskie campaign] a member of that reform commission?

WEXLER. So was I.

STEWART. So was Anne Wexler. And Mitchell was in the campaign as the deputy campaign director for Muskie earlier than Anne, and he was very cognizant of the rules and procedures of the reform commission.

HART. Jack Chestnut's point is ironic, because the movement which led to party reform was based upon the fact that procedures prior to '68 started too early and that delegates were being selected in '67 and even in '66; that's what led to the uproar at Chicago which led to party reform. That is, that delegates were being selected in an untimely way.

KEEFE. Birch Bayh spoke at the 1970 Wyoming convention in May at which the first delegates to '72 were to be selected. That was the opening gun, had reforms not been instituted; that was before the party accepted them. But we were the only ones who paid any attention to Wyoming in 1970. I think that's because Birch Bayh was on the commission, and he made us pay attention to it.

BRODER. Did Wallace have any mechanism for keeping up with party reforms and the effect of party reforms?

CAMP. For the Democratic Party, the answer is no. The Wallace campaign can fault no one except the Wallace campaign for that, either. I will say, in defense of the reforms, that I think they could have been used to the advantage of any candidate represented here. I feel that we proved this in Texas, where we did get into the precinct caucuses, the district caucuses. Probably Texas came to the Democratic convention with the most representative delegation of all as to delegates committed to the particular candidates. I think it pretty well reflected the feeling of the Democrats in Texas.

KEEFE. By that time, everybody had figured it out.

CAMP. That's right.

PERRY. When did Wallace decide that he would go through the Democratic primaries?

CAMP. The final decision came in January of 1972.

BRODER. How and why did he make that decision?

CAMP. I think basically he had been watching the political scene. He felt that there was probably a great void among Democratic prospects of centrist and right-of-center candidates and that there were a great number of Americans who did not have a candidate. I think he felt that he probably had a better feel for the issues at that time than did the other candidates. In defense of this, I would point to Florida, where I think he changed the issues of the campaign around, or defined the issues.

ALAN L. OTTEN (*Wall Street Journal*). What was wrong with Muskie that each of the other candidates perceived? When the consensus among a lot of the politicians and the press was that he was so far out in front, why did all these people—Bayh, Jackson, McGovern, and so forth—think that they still had a chance? What was the weakness that they perceived? Was it philosophical? Was it personal?

CHESTNUT. One of the things was that the press itself was not accurate in forecasting Muskie's position. In many cases, you were giving him credit for delegates in states where delegates hadn't even been selected yet. I remember a program called "60 Minutes" where he was everything, I think, but crowned as the nominee of the Democratic Party before a single Democratic delegate had been selected. When we [Humphrey people] went into the states and started talking with the people who appeared most likely to either be the delegates or have something to say about who the delegates would be, we didn't find this depth of feeling or depth of support. There was an extreme shallowness as far as Senator Muskie was concerned.

KEEFE. Muskie also relied on other people for his organization, and he didn't build his own. He had governors and so forth and relied on them to do his organization work, and you can't do that.

JAMES M. NAUGHTON (*New York Times*) [to Jack Chestnut]. You mentioned a Muskie slippage early in 1971, which would have been not terribly long after a performance that everybody credited him with on television [in November 1970]. What kind of slippage were you talking about, and how was it measured?

CHESTNUT. I was talking on the polls. We were charting the three leading polls at that time, and it appeared that the high point in Muskie's popularity was the after-election speech in November 1970. Then it started to slip, and it was a gradual but steady decline all the way through May of 1971. It seemed that the more exposure he got, the more damaging it became to him in terms of these particular public-opinion polls. Part of this may have been the fact that the press had put him so far out ahead as the leader that they were giving him a measure that was far too high in the eyes of the public.

WATTENBERG. At about that time I heard the Muskie strategy articulated by some of the Muskie people. It was one of style, center; substance, left. While he was perceived of as the great American middle man, he apparently also felt that there was a real threat of a left-wing veto in this country and that he would have to trim his substantive positions to diffuse it. This strategy, of course, proceeds on the assumption that voters aren't terribly smart and that they can't perceive this game. Muskie went ahead with a whole series of actions that attempted to placate the far-left wing of the party. It reached the point, finally, a year later, just before the Wisconsin primary, where Jack English [of the Muskie campaign] said that Muskie's strategy would be to be the last surviving candidate on the left, which in point of fact he was. McGovern was moving into the center with the speed of light; Muskie was going out there to capture a relatively small left-of-center constituency. People came to feel that he had gone over that way completely, or else that nobody really knew where he stood. It was such a blurred sort of an image that he became just a professional middle man. They said, "Oh, well, he's in the center, whatever that means," without having any substance to attach to that image. I think ultimately this eroded a potentially very successful candidacy.

PERRY. Pat Caddell is a professional pollster who was taking polls later on in this period.

PATRICK H. CADDELL (Cambridge Survey Research—McGovern). In December of 1971 I did a memo pulling together a number of things that we'd been looking at for a couple of years. We had been trying to figure out what was going on in the country. I wasn't too concerned with public surveys in terms of what they were showing about the primary races, because those tend to be just a function of recognition. But rather we were looking at the potential involved. We had for some time, starting in '68, begun to really study the phenomenon of "alienation," getting into the feeling of discontent and national decline that was a totally different sort of experience in this country. In December 1971 our analysis of the situation was that Senator Muskie, outside of Senator Humphrey, was the best known of the candidates, but that sometime in the summer and fall there had been a change in public perception of him. A lot of people who had perceived him after the '70 speech as being a very decisive individual, a person who had some substance, began to get the feeling that there wasn't much there—that he was not taking stands and was all over the place. Our feeling by late December was that he was in very serious trouble.

I interviewed a lady in Jacksonville, Florida, in October of '71. She had voted for George Wallace in '68 and said she didn't want to vote for Wallace again but wanted to vote for a real candidate. She had started off very strong for Ed Muskie because he was different from other politicians and stood up for what he believed; she thought he could really heal the country. But she had been very disillusioned with him in the last six months because he seemed to be like other politicians and wasn't taking any stands. She did not like Richard Nixon at all, and I asked her what she was going to do if it came down to Muskie and Nixon in '72. And she said, "In that case, I guess I'll just vote for Nixon, because it's just not worth the moving expense."

For Humphrey, a serious problem all the way throughout the primaries was the fact that he'd been around for a long time. John Lindsay had a serious problem because of being from New York and being very well known; and glamor was not exactly a great trait this year. Actually, the person I thought had the best potential, other than George McGovern, by late '71 was Scoop Jackson, because he was unknown, which was a tremendous plus.

WATTENBERG. This is very accurate. There is a great advantage for a politician, at a certain time, in not being too well known. I spoke recently to a congressman who said that, looking back on it, the ideal candidate for the Democrats in 1972 would have been Governor Richard Kneip [of South Dakota]. I said, "Governor Richard Kneip? Nobody knows him." He said, "That's the whole idea." A man running just as a Democrat who nobody knew very much about would have done very well.

CADDELL. I think the point is that people were at a juncture where they felt that all these people had been in before and just screwed up things, and that they had to do something differently. I'm not sure they exactly knew what they were doing. I thought Senator Jackson's major problem would be that he would become a champion of the past rather than advocating any real changes and being very specific. All the candidates were well known, and Muskie, by this time, suffered the problem of appearing to be like all the rest. What you had going in January in the country was an extremely unstable situation, the kind that was open to anybody who could emerge —who could be that new face, who was different, who seemed non-political in a sense.

MAGRUDER. Looking at it from our standpoint [in the Committee for the Re-election of the President], an important thing happened the day of the '70 election—the famous filming of the President at Phoenix, Arizona, when he gave his great speech in a hangar, which almost hanged us. Muskie came on afterwards, and Muskie at that time seemed to have one characteristic trait which we were really afraid of in any frontal contest—and that was that he seemed Presidential. One of the things we forget about is that the public is quite intelligent, and the public is voting for a President, and they want somebody they feel can be President. When Muskie gave that fifteen minutes up in Maine looking across the lake, or wherever it was, he was fantastic, and he gave a tremendous impression of substance. And he was Presidential. Then when he started campaigning, he started making all of the mistakes that a guy running for President can't make. He was a great campaigner in Maine for the Senate; but when he got in the big picture, he was lacking.

At least from our viewpoint, the only person, when it was all said and done, who had the characteristics to be President was Hubert Humphrey. We thought he started too late, didn't plan, didn't have the time or the effort to plan the campaign correctly. But he was the only candidate, according to our polls, who was perceived by the public as being a legitimate Presidential candidate. I think George McGovern was the most effective planner, without question, in the beginning in the primaries. He had the right strategy and the right planning for the primaries; but when it came down to it, when he had to face a Presidential election as against a primary situation, he was found lacking by the public in Presidential caliber. I think there's a tremendous difference between a Senate race and a Presidential race.

BRODER [to Jeb Magruder]. What are the elements that go into making somebody Presidential, as far as you can define them?

MAGRUDER. The public can be critical of the President in many ways, in the sense that all sorts of things have been said about him over the past twenty-five years of public service. But Richard Nixon has performed in such a manner that the public, even those who might not like him on all issues or be with him philosophically or in party orientation, feels quite comfortable with him running the country. I think that this is also true of Hubert Humphrey. He built a reputation over the years. At first, it was probably a little weak, but his issue orientation changed considerably in the last four to six or eight years and he became, I think, the most articulate spokesman of what I would call reasonable Democratic thought and articulated it very well. Whereas the other candidates were either off on the right or on the left, in positions that were untenable for the general electorate, in not only issues but approaches.

THOMAS J. HOUSER (Committee for the Re-election of the President, Illinois). But you agree that the elements that Dave Broder is searching for are experience, competence, and an aura of professionalism?

MAGRUDER. It's much more than just liking a person, which is sometimes one of the things we forget in politics, I think. We look at polls and we think, "Do you like the candidate?" I don't think the public is really interested in whether they like the candidate; they're interested in whether that candidate will perform effectively as President. This is where Richard Nixon has always done very well, and I think the Democratic candidates just did not measure up in this election.

BRODER. Is it the general feeling that there is a special set of qualifications that apply to a Presidential candidate and that you somehow have to get your man up to that level if he's going to have a chance? Does this consciously affect the way you employ your time in the pre-Presidential year?

STEWART. I think the American people always look to

a President to be better than themselves—somebody with dignity, someone with the kind of grace that we always ascribe to Jack Kennedy. I remember saying that very thing to Muskie one time when I first went to work for him.

Pat Caddell's polls and our polls showed actually the same thing. In the several polls we had done in different places, almost without exception the phrase "wishy-washy" showed up—not necessarily the first thing the public was conscious of, but there in each one of the polls. The other thing that created a problem for Muskie was that at the very outset he was surrounded by press. He was under a microscope from the very outset, whereas McGovern did not have the problem while he was organizing and putting things together. McGovern got it late when it was harmful to him; we got it earlier when it was harmful to us. The press covering you too closely was a problem; but at the same time, the press paid for the airplane.

PERRY [to Jeb Magruder]. There must have been a time along in here when you decided how you would make the President look even more Presidential.

MAGRUDER. Another factor in the political ball game today, which people don't realize, is that it is big business. A man running for the Senate of the United States in a state that he's quite familiar with can run a good campaign many times without doing the proper preparatory work. I don't think you can do that for President in this country: there are too many states; there are too many variables; and the electorate is much more difficult to read than we would like to believe. One of the characteristics of the McGovern activity was its fantastically effective planning—at least, from what we [in the Committee for Re-election] could see. On the other hand, there was a fantastic lack of planning on the part of almost every other Democratic candidate, right down the line from Governor Wallace to Senator Humphrey to Senator Muskie. In Muskie's case, I felt they just misread it. I think they did some planning, quite a bit of it, but I think it was incorrect planning. But you can't go into a Presidential race and expect to do it in six months or three months. You've got to go in and spend a year and a half and do the kind of preparatory work so you'll know what you're going to do when that candidate gets out there. We did an awful lot of this, and we used the polls to find the strengths.

PETER H. DAILEY (The November Group—Nixon). Reflecting on the essential difference between the 1968 and 1972 elections, you get back to the question of how you can be Presidential and still a candidate. In 1968 you dealt with two people, Richard Nixon and Hubert Humphrey, who were both candidates for the office of President. The one thing that we felt was critical in the development of our public presentation in 1972 was that we never allow the public to get the impression that there were two candidates for the office of President. We always wanted to project that there was only one candidate, and that was whoever the nominee of the Democratic Party was going to be; and then there was the President. So we were almost trying to keep it like a referendum, a vote of confidence in the President.

STEWART. You did it very well.

DAILEY. I think it poses an interesting question as to how you can be a candidate for the opposition when there is already a President in office, how you can do an effective job of running for the nomination within your own party and still maintain your stance as Presidential to the public. It was a very difficult problem for Muskie. He tried to be Presidential and all of a sudden started getting great competition from within his own area. And you can't help but be scarred by it.

STEWART. There are those who thought that if Muskie had immediately moved aggressively for both money and support after the election-night speech in 1970, he could have locked it up and kept others out. Muskie's position was, "Let them stay in, they serve a purpose." But the more people you have in, the more problems you have. It doesn't seem to me that he took advantage of the publicity and public acclaim that resulted from the speech.

HART. He moved in a way that was in line with his own strategy, to lock up endorsements. But if there was anything that was proved ineffective in this political year, it was the political endorsement. Muskie convinced the governors, the senators, and a lot of congressmen that because of that speech and other things he was the likely nominee and that they ought to support him. That was the beginning of that sort of bandwagon thing. Senator Phil Hart [of Michigan] on election night was so carried away by his own election and this Muskie speech that he just came on television and said, "This is the man that's got to lead our party." The only other way you can move is the way we moved [for McGovern], and that is to begin to identify the unknown people out there who are going to do the work.

KEEFE. The only other way you can get the other candidates out of the race, I think, would be to take away all the money in the world.

WATTENBERG. Ultimately you have to run in some primaries; and if you're going to lose in primaries, no matter what you do, it's going to destroy the candidacy.

KEEFE. The only way you're going to take the ambition bug out of most candidates is to not let them be able to finance their ambition.

OTTEN. It seems to me that we haven't yet touched on what I think were the most important political developments in 1971, which were the President's decision to put on wage-price controls, his decision to go to China, his decision to go to Russia. And I remember we were all writing at that time how this pulled the rug out from under the Democrats—by adopting the Democratic program. What changes were dictated in the position of the Democratic candidates as a result of this? Did it make a difference? Did you just keep on running for your own primaries, or did you have to readjust your strategy?

STEWART. I'm not aware of any readjustment in the Muskie strategy because of that. As a matter of fact, it strikes me that it wasn't long after the trip to China [February 1972] was over that the polls came out again and showed Nixon had not picked up any measurable amount.

CADDELL. Yes, I think the Moscow trip [May 1972] was more help than the China trip.

HART. This whole subject of what appears to be Presidential is so interesting and complex. When you run for the Presidency against an incumbent, you're running two different races. First, you're running for a contested nomination—in the McGovern case, in an insurgency kind of uphill campaign. All of our energies were directed toward beating Muskie and then Humphrey. Then, it is almost as if you wake up the next day saying, "Well, now we have a whole different race." It's awfully hard to run against Democrats to get the nomination and, at the same time, be waging a campaign against the President as well. Different factors are called for, different characteristics. I couldn't agree more with what Jeb Magruder and Dave Broder and Pat Caddell have said about competence; in my judgment the whole race in the fall was waged on one issue alone, and that was apparent competence to be President.

WATTENBERG. May I comment on the notion that what wins elections is to be "Presidential," and that "trust" is what counts most? It seems to me that there is a strange feeling there that you can run in a vacuum if "people trust you." Senator Muskie did this for a while, and there was a period when Senator McGovern was also saying, "Well, you know, you can trust Senator McGovern and you can't trust Richard Nixon." The real issue, it seems to me, to the mind of the voter is not trust, but *what* do you trust a candidate to do? There were a lot of people by November 1972 who trusted that Senator McGovern, in point of fact, would be an isolationist and would turn over Israel to the Arabs and would legalize marijuana and would do a whole lot of strange things. They trusted, implicitly, that this is what he would do.

What I'm saying is that the notion of trust is superseded by a substantive notion of what you trust a candidate to do, and that to talk just about a person's being "Presidential" is very misleading. After all, all of the candidates who were involved in this election were professionals; they were for the most part U.S. senators; they were not making the very elementary gaffes. Ultimately, the public sorted out these candidates in some almost mystical way, but on the basis of substance, not on the basis of character. I would argue to Mr. Magruder that Richard Nixon is not the embodiment of all things Presidential in this country, because our polls showed that he is not regarded as a man imbued with this great quality of trust. There are many people in this country who are still deeply suspicious of Richard Nixon and his motives.

MAGRUDER. I don't think the question is whether there are many such people. I think the question is what the majority thinks, because the election is won or lost on the majority vote. I think there is a basis of substance behind the feeling as to whether a person is or isn't Presidential, and in this case, we had that basis of substance, grounded on the issues. August was the beginning of the turn-around in '71 with the price and wage situation, and it continued; after China we moved up a little bit in the polls, and then Russia came along and we moved further along. I think it is true that 35 or 40 per cent of the public did not feel comfortable with Richard Nixon, but a far greater number felt and do feel very comfortable with him, and felt very comfortable with him even at the trough. Even at the trough we were only down, as I recall, at 47 or 48 per cent on Gallup on approval. Actually, for a person without the personal characteristics that Eisenhower possibly had, or Kennedy possibly had, he has maintained a remarkably stable public-approval rate.

Another factor which many people fail to remember is that the Republican Party in this country is by far the second party, with a very weak base of support in the states. In state after state, in the big states like California, New York, Texas, Illinois, it's running three to two, three to one against us on registration. The fact that a Republican candidate can win a Presidency in these decades is, I think, a factor of basic issue differences that are not reflected in party registration.

[To Ben Wattenberg] I agree with you on the issue background, but I think this overall feeling of comfortableness—if that's a better word than trust—is very important. At election time the country felt very comfortable with Richard Nixon; and I don't think that McGovern was the only candidate who would have been beaten badly. Almost any candidate, with the exception, I would say, of Senator Humphrey, would have been beaten badly this time by President Nixon.

NAUGHTON [to Jeb Magruder]. Would you describe, if you can, how the political calculations were factored into the President's decisions to go to China, to go to the Soviet Union, to adopt wage and price controls, and precisely how that all developed politically?

MAGRUDER. In the famous Camp David meeting [in mid-August 1971], which is maybe the best example of the decision process on the wage and price controls, there were two opposing sides—George Shultz [Office of Management and Budget] was basically against wage and price controls, and John Connally [Secretary of the Treasury] was for price and wage controls. I think the President basically had made up his mind by that time that he was going to do something, and the question was what. They went up to Camp David and had it all out around the table. I don't think that the decision was made only for political purposes; but certainly you would have to be a fool, if you wanted to be re-elected, not to consider the consequences of not moving in the area of the economy. I think that though the President felt George Shultz was philosophically right, he realized that things weren't working at the time and that we had to make a change. It was obviously a political decision in the sense that we hoped that it would work and that we would recover some of the lost ground. But we also hoped, and I think John Connally felt very strongly, that it was the right decision. The public, at least, felt that it did work.

As for China and Moscow, I myself was not involved in those decisions, but from what I can gather they were made on the basis of much of what the President had set out in his Inaugural Address in 1969. If you go back and read his 1969 Inaugural Address, you'll find that he talked about rapprochement with China, arms treaties, and other things of this kind. So these decisions were part of his overall plan, and he was consistent from the beginning.

BRODER. Pete Dailey has talked about the advantage of having a President as your candidate. Is there any problem of getting political decisions made because you're dealing with the President rather than somebody who is seeking the office? For example, as a reporter, I had the feeling that a lot of Republicans tried to send a message to the President in 1970 and the first half of 1971 that he was in political trouble because of the economic policies, but that it seemed to take an awful long time for that message to get a response. [To Philip Reberger] Was that the perception, say, from the Republican National Committee?

J. PHILIP REBERGER (Republican National Committee). I think that happened at times, but we met with Jeb Magruder during early '71, worked closely with him, and, at his suggestion, started working on our research and political organization plans. While we had pressures from party members around the country on various issues, having an incumbent President pretty much resolved a lot of decisions; if we'd been sitting like Ray Bliss [former RNC chairman] prior to '68, having to work with the many candidate groups, we couldn't have acted. We went ahead without getting too much into the issue side of things, other than in research. We did our political organizational homework just because we had an incumbent President, and decisions were essentially made for us. We just went out and marched, so to speak.

CHESTNUT. I don't think any of us who ran campaigns have really responded to the question of how the President's activities affect the operations of a campaign and how we respond to them. I think we were placed in a somewhat difficult position with an incumbent President, from the standpoint that he's always able to hand you your words the next day. I think we recognized many of the President's activities as the activities of a very skillful political leader who was President and understood how to handle that power. I think Senator Humphrey was particularly sensitive to that as a result of having been in the executive. He was in a position several times to respond to the President on China, to encourage him immediately to go to Russia, to encourage him immediately to mend fences with Japan, for example, which the President did. Probably the President had this plan at any rate, but it did permit Humphrey, because of his experience, to play a little bit of quick counterpoint. But as far as programs were concerned, if Senator Humphrey came out with a particularly good program or pointed out a need that ought to be acted on and the President recognized it as such, he could do it. And it wasn't Senator Humphrey that received the credit for it, or Senator McGovern who received the credit for it; it was then the President's program.

OTTEN. How was Senator Kennedy perceived by each

of the other Democratic candidates during this period, and by the White House? I remember, certainly in the early period, that the McGovern people were constantly having to combat the "stalking horse" thing. Did Humphrey, Muskie, and McGovern see Kennedy as coming in, or were you absolutely convinced he was out?

HART. I don't think we ever seriously thought he'd be a candidate. Senator McGovern was in almost constant contact with him and was constantly being assured and reassured that he did not intend to seek the nomination. Our biggest problem was the reporters. I felt that the press had an inordinate interest in speculating on what Senator Kennedy was up to, what his motives were, and what he was really going to do. It got very frustrating to constantly pick up the papers and read a column or an article saying, "Now, here's what Senator Kennedy's really going to do." I don't know whether he was getting information out, or whether people were leaking information to try to get him to run, or what was going on, but we had the line directly from him to Senator McGovern that he was not running. The constant press attention was to some degree a credit to his stature in the party and in the nation, but it was a constant harassment to us—this business of the "stalking horse" and the speculation that our campaign was the spring-training camp for the Kennedy campaign. There were periods when it hurt us financially—that is, we were not able to raise funds that we were later able to raise when people really believed that Kennedy was not in the race.

CHESTNUT [to Gary Hart]. Our experience [in the Humphrey campaign] was the same as yours, 100 per cent. We always had a clear indication direct from Kennedy that he definitely was not in it. But hundreds of rumors kept cropping up, press speculations that seemed to lend credibility over the months that perhaps he would be in it at some point.

KEEFE. There was nothing anybody else could do about it. He was either going to run or not going to run; you couldn't plan your life around how to handle that problem.

STEWART. I never heard any discussions about the prospect that he would run. I think everybody in the Muskie campaign was convinced that he was not a candidate.

OTTEN. At what point did the other Democrats begin to take Wallace seriously?

STEWART. The Florida primary [in March 1972].

HART. Florida.

OTTEN. Not in '71? Toward the end of '71 the Florida noises were beginning to come fairly strongly.

HART. I think they conditioned our decision [in the McGovern camp] to back off from the Florida primary. I think we saw, maybe better than some of the others, what was going to happen to that one.

OTTEN. That was in '72.

HART. Well, we made the decision late in '71.

KEEFE. But the '71 factor was that Wallace was going to help beat Richard Nixon in the fall, presumably with a third-party candidacy.

CAMP. Toward the end of '71 we began leaking to the press the possibility of Wallace's running in Florida as a Democrat. When feedback came, it looked pretty good —not only in Florida but in other places too. The longer we looked at it, the better it looked.

WATTENBERG. Right through to the end of December, there was still talk as to whether he would be allowed on the ballot in Florida. The Secretary of State had to make a ruling.

CAMP. Oh, yes, there was that talk, not only in Florida but in other states also.

STEWART. Muskie had been put in such a position as the front-runner that he felt he had to prove himself the front-runner by running in as many primaries as he could. In retrospect, he believed that as soon as Wallace got into the Florida campaign, he should have pulled out.

WATTENBERG. Senator Jackson certainly would have run in the New Hampshire primary had he known that Governor Wallace was going to be in the Florida primary. There were many who thought that he ought to have anyway.

MORRIS S. DEES, JR. (direct-mail chairman for McGovern) [to Billy Joe Camp]. Let me ask you a question about Wallace. He had just gotten through with the governor's race in Alabama against Albert Brewer and won it by only 25,000 votes with virtually the whole Senate and House against him. When he had run for President in 1968 on the Independent ticket, just about the entire legislature had packed up and shipped out around the nation to help him set up his third-party organization.

Do you think that George Wallace could have, in fact, run third party in 1972? Do you think he could have gotten the base of support that he needed in Alabama to go out and do all this organizing and get him on the ballot in all these states? Do you think that the Democratic primary was the only place he could have run effectively?

CAMP. I think he could have run as a third-party candidate. Maybe the base of financial support would have been a little more difficult as far as Alabama was concerned, but he probably had more of it in other states than he had in '68.

DEES. I didn't mean financial support; I meant legs and arms to do the work.

CAMP. The same is true of the legs and arms. There were more of them in other states, too, that were ready to help him in a third-party campaign. I think what surprised all of us was the willingness of these same people to help him with the Democratic campaign, because it was a point of concern as to how the American Party folks who had been his supporters would take to the Democratic campaign. We didn't know if they were going to say, "To hell with you," or come in and help. We had, of course, contacted many of them and talked with them about it; and they said, "Sure, we'll help Governor Wallace —whatever he runs on, we'll be for him." I suppose there were some—a small number, percentagewise—that got mad and didn't care to have anything to do with him, but not a large number at all. I think he could have had considerable support from the Alabama legislators, as well as other state politicians, but not as much as in '68.

HART. You said that Governor Wallace made his decision to get into the Democratic race because he didn't feel that the issues he was concerned about had a spokesman. What about Senator Jackson?

CAMP. It appeared to us that Senator Jackson was trying to champion the centrist and right elements in Florida— probably a good state in which to do so. We knew that Senator Jackson had voted for legislation which supported busing—or against legislation which was against busing—and we felt that in Florida he was weak on this issue. Also, we didn't think he was a particularly powerful man on the stump.

HART. So it wasn't totally ideological.

CAMP. Right.

OTTEN. What were the White House relations with Wallace during this period? What was the Attorney General [John Mitchell] doing to keep him out of a third party?

MAGRUDER. We, of course, kept cordial relations with all people who wanted to keep contact with us. We kept contact during the campaign with all sorts of people in both parties. As you know, we felt we had an extremely effective Democrats for Nixon operation.

OTTEN. But what I'm talking about is 1971, when there were a number of stories that the Attorney General, or John Connally, was making contact with Wallace to persuade him not to go the third-party route.

MAGRUDER. We hoped he would not go the third-party route. We felt that it would have been a mistake, from the standpoint of the electorate, to have a third-party candidate whose views were so closely associated with the views of the President in many domestic issues and foreign policy, too. I think if you go down the issue orientation of Governor Wallace, in most cases you'll find it very close to the President's. Practically speaking, we did not want a third-party candidate, and I think that was quite clear from the beginning. There was a lot of talk by the press at that time—[to Gary Hart] maybe you were supporting it—that Wallace supporters were really McGovern supporters. But the Wallace supporters turned out to be Nixon supporters by a huge majority, and I think we felt that from the beginning. There were some people, like Bob Mardian [political coordinator of the re-election committee], who thought it would be better to have Wallace in the race. But I could not see—none of the rest of us could see—how those numbers could come out any way but for the President. That's why I could never understand the talk that came through the press to the effect that groups in the Democratic Party were thinking that the Wallace vote was gettable for them. I don't think it was gettable for any of those candidates except maybe Senator Jackson if he had won, and we didn't think he would win.

NAUGHTON. Granting for the moment at least that there was no compact between the President and the Governor, how did you go about letting Wallace know directly or indirectly that it would be just peachy if he'd stay out of a third-party race?

MAGRUDER. I don't know of any direct communication myself. Maybe Billy Joe Camp does.

CAMP. To my knowledge, there was absolutely none, except on the official state business that you normally conduct with the White House or the executive. I recall one incident that got pretty widespread play in the press. The President came to Mobile sometime in '71 for the dedication announcement of the Tennessee Tombigbee Waterway, a joint venture among the states of Alabama, Tennessee, Florida, Mississippi, and Kentucky. All of the governors from those states rode on the airplane—Air Force I—from Mobile to Birmingham, where the President made another speech. Columnist Jack Anderson took this flight as a reason to write that Wallace and the President had made a deal. Well, on the airplane, Governor Wallace was seated with the other governors, including Governor Nunn of Kentucky, Governor Askew of Florida, and maybe Governor Williams [of Mississippi]. They had lunch, and then the President came up and spoke to them briefly—probably a matter of two or three minutes. One reporter asked Governor Wallace about it later: "What kind of deal went on?" He said, "Well, we were sitting there and the President came up to us," and he named the governors and then said, "If you wanted to make a deal, what kind of deal could you make with those folks around?" The idea of communication between the President and Governor Wallace, or even their staff aides, is just erroneous. It didn't exist.

MAGRUDER. I think that we, on many occasions, made it quite clear publicly that we hoped the Governor would not run as a third-party candidate. I don't think we made any secret of it in '71 or '72.

PERRY. Is it true that in your plans all along you figured that you could have the Wallace vote and that you did plan on that basis through '71?

MAGRUDER. Except for the gentleman I mentioned [Bob

Mardian], I don't recall anyone in the White House—
Bob Haldeman [Assistant to the President] or anyone else
—or in our re-election committee—from John Mitchell
down—who didn't feel that the Wallace vote was primarily a vote that could be gotten by the President in a
race with any Democrat, with possibly the exception of
Senator Jackson. Maybe also excepting Senator Humphrey, because he did position himself very, very effectively in the campaign on the issues. Humphrey could
possibly have done well with some of that vote because
it was a Democratic registration: these people are Democrats—they register Democrat and they are used to voting
Democrat, and if they can vote Democrat, I think they
like to. But we felt they were our voters, and they can
continue to be voters for a position similar to the President's position in coming elections also.

WATTENBERG. It was very interesting what Jeb Magruder said about the possibility of Jackson's attracting
some of the Wallace vote. In the middle of 1971 the
Christian Science Monitor ran a mail poll of Republican
chairmen around the country asking which Democrat
would be the most difficult to beat. At that time Jackson
probably was not known by 15 per cent of the American
people, and the Republican professionals said that Jackson would be the most difficult for precisely that reason,
I think. The use of the phrase in the Democratic Party
now somehow suggests that the something called the
"Wallace vote" is something very dirty and difficult and
racist and a whole lot of other things. In point of fact,
when you're talking about the "Wallace vote," you're also
talking about "resurrecting the FDR coalition." Every
Democratic President in recent years—Roosevelt, Truman, Kennedy, and Johnson—won because they were able
to attract the Wallace vote. That is a very cold fact of

electoral politics in the United States. I would agree with Jeb Magruder that Jackson could have gotten a hunk of it; Humphrey might have gotten a piece of it; and beyond that it was lost. Therein lies one of the major problems in the Democratic Party right now.

HART. Did John Kennedy get it?

WATTENBERG. Yes, sir. He sure did.

CAMP. I do not think that the '68 Wallace vote would have been equally split. I personally feel that the majority of it would have gone to Senator Humphrey, because these voters were traditionally Democratic—they had voted for Kennedy and they had voted for Roosevelt. When they voted for Kennedy in '60, they had voted against Richard Nixon, and it was the same man running again in '68. So I think Senator Humphrey's chances of getting the majority of them in '68 were probably good.

WATTENBERG. The retrospective polling in '68, asking Wallace voters who they would have voted for had Wallace not run in '68, shows that by somewhere between two to one or three to one they would have voted for Nixon.

CAMP. Probably so, from retrospect.

CADDELL. I want to touch on that some because we [Cambridge Survey Research] spent a great deal of time —long before we got involved in the campaign—looking at the Wallace vote, particularly in the South. First of all, the Wallace vote is much more complex than is often thought. It's clear that the '68 Wallace voters and the '72 Wallace voters were really different blocs. The '72 bloc was much more expanded. There are two parts to the Wallace coalition, one of which is a very ideological, racial bloc. But by '72, most Wallace voters were people who tended to be a great deal less ideological and extremely alienated from the political process. They were people who were very strong in favor of things like expanded health care and a number of social-welfare programs. The Wallace vote in '68 in the industrial cities of Ohio, for instance, broke heavily for Jack Gilligan in his Senate race against William Saxbe—in very large numbers. Gilligan tended to outrun Humphrey in most precincts in Cleveland, Youngstown, Toledo, and those areas. In '70 the Wallace vote in the South overwhelmingly went, on almost every occasion, into either more moderate or more populist Democrats, like Dale Bumpers, Reuben Askew, Lawton Chiles, and Jimmy Carter, while throwing out establishment conservatives.

Taking that non-ideological Wallace vote, as distinguished from the racial vote, was a very key part of what we were trying to do from late '71 on. Those people had those strong indications of alienation. The decision [for McGovern] to go to Ohio, when he was running with only half the vote that Humphrey had, was premised on the fact that most Wallace voters were in the undecided column and weren't sure where they were going. And certainly in Kenosha and Milwaukee it was a tremendous battle, especially among young blue-collar workers, between Wallace and McGovern. I think you have to look at the Wallace vote on a very broad spectrum. The CBS survey on Election Day, with a massive 18,000 interviews, showed that the Southern Wallace voter went very heavily for Nixon but that in the North it was much closer.

BRODER. Before we finish this section, I'd like to direct a question to Bob Keefe. Dick Stewart asked whether it was possible for Muskie to have locked it up in '71. We know that he did very well in terms of support from state party leaders—governors, state chairmen, senators. If the leaders of organized labor had come in behind Muskie strongly, before the primaries opened, would that have locked it up? What was their thinking at that point, and why did they choose not to get behind a candidate?

KEEFE. If they had moved in full force, they could have given Ed Muskie the organizational base he lacked. I think he later failed because he didn't have an organizational base to do the organizational work. That assumes that they would have gotten the job done. It would have meant a full-fledged, very expensive kind of campaign on their part, but one which they were capable of doing. I think they didn't do it for several reasons. One, probably the most important, was that traditionally they hadn't gotten deeply involved in Presidential primaries until much later. With the exception of the Humphrey thing in '68, which of course started very late, they were never in primaries heavily from the beginning. Secondly, the constituency to which the president of the Federation reacts is the executive committee of the AFL-CIO. In that group you had some of Hubert Humphrey's best friends in the world, some of Scoop Jackson's best friends in the world. There was no way, at the time, for George Meany or any other labor leader to get cohesion in that group behind Ed Muskie or any other single candidate. Without that cohesion, their support would not have made that much difference. You can argue whether or not they should have discussed it at that time, but they did not. Perhaps their great error was in not sitting down in December [1971] in an executive committee meeting of some sort and thrashing that whole thing out and doing what was suggested earlier—all move one way and get the rest of the guys out. Perhaps that's what they should have done, but they didn't do it. And they consequently had very little impact on the nominating process.

CHESTNUT. Had they done that, it might have had two effects: I doubt very much that Hubert Humphrey would have become a candidate; I also doubt very much that Scoop Jackson would have become a candidate.

HART. I'd be interested to know whether there was substantial support on that board for Ted Kennedy also. Not support maybe, but a desire to wait and see what Senator Kennedy was going to do.

KEEFE. No, not too much. We're talking about thirty-five or forty guys with whom Hubert Humphrey has met and eaten and drunk for twenty-five years, and likewise Scoop Jackson. They're very legislatively oriented guys who have lived with these senators for years, and it's a personal friendship. The friends that these guys have are just close personal friends, and there's an awful lot of policy made on that basis as opposed to logic and polls and all that sort of thing.

BRODER. Can we assume that it was a major objective of Humphrey and Jackson at this point to keep them from deciding on one candidate?

KEEFE. It seemed that way from the Federation.

WATTENBERG. I think that both Humphrey and Jackson were trying to get as much support from organized labor as they could possibly get, and in part what eliminated the possibility of organized labor going solidly behind Muskie was the influence that Humphrey and Jackson had. But far more significantly, the ideological positions that Muskie was taking tended to alienate those guys in great degree.

KEEFE. Muskie never had the magic with that crowd. At the '71 executive committee meeting—they meet every February in Miami—several of the candidates came by: Ed Muskie, Scoop Jackson, Hubert Humphrey. And Birch Bayh was there. I don't think George McGovern made it. The one guy in the crowd who didn't have any chemistry with these thirty-six guys was Ed Muskie. He'd never been there before. He made his own date and went out and played golf with Mr. Meany—let Mr. Meany pick up the tab and things like that.

PERRY. To wind this first session up, we could just go around the table and ask the same people where they stood as of January 1, 1972. Was there much change in anyone's position?

KEEFE. Birch Bayh's was drastically changed—an interesting phenomenon. The day before Mrs. Bayh went to the hospital, we had had an appropriation meeting where we appropriated funds through March 15 [of '72]. We had an allocation somewhere in the order of $1.4 million and had about half of it on the table. So Birch Bayh did not run out of money.

HART. Were you going to run in New Hampshire [in March of '72]?

KEEFE. Sure were, and we would've beaten you [McGovern] bad.

HART. I doubt that, but I wish we'd had some of that $1.4 million.

MAGRUDER. We [Nixon] were getting better by January of '72.

STEWART. We [Muskie] were getting worse.

HART. We [McGovern] had just begun to fight. January of '72 was sort of the Valley Forge of our campaign. We had almost no money—we were almost completely destitute. It was a very, very low period. We knew that if we could just scrape through into that first primary, we were going to do very well. We needed to get into New Hampshire and we needed to get into Wisconsin, and we were desperately trying to figure out financially how to do that. All the way through, our premise was that when you come to a nomination in the Democratic Party, there is, for all practical purposes, no center. Our strategy was always to co-opt the left, become the candidate of the liberal wing of the party, and then eventually get it down to a two-man race. It might be that Senator Muskie would opt for the right and successfully get it, and we would run against him in the later primaries. Or if Senator Humphrey beat Muskie, which is what happened in our judgment, we would run against Humphrey. We always knew it would be a two-man race between a liberal and a conservative. There was, in fact, no center, and it was just a question of whether or not we could win on our side and who would win on the other. We wanted Humphrey to emerge on the right.

CHESTNUT. Our situation, of course, had changed quite a bit by January of 1972. Humphrey was now a Presidential candidate, whereas in January of 1971 very few people considered him to be a Presidential candidate for 1972. As Jeb Magruder so very accurately pointed out, the fatal weakness in the Hubert Humphrey campaign was that we did not start early enough. Even three or four months more would have made a tremendous difference in the organizational ability of the campaign to do the necessary things in many states which, as a consequence of the late start, had to be practically abandoned. Some of this delay was due to the psychology of the candidate himself in making up his mind as to whether or not he even wanted to be a Presidential candidate, whether or not Muskie in fact was weakening to the point where it was dangerous, whether or not he could beat Richard Nixon. The decision should have been made in July [of '71], and unfortunately it was made in December.

CAMP. In the first full week of January '72, Governor Wallace had returned from a short vacation in Key Biscayne, Florida, which is a little distance away from the other place down there [President Nixon's Florida home]. We had our first meeting of what was to become the nucleus of the '72 campaign staff, and the Governor gave us his decision to run as a Democrat. The first state we'd go into was Florida. We lacked two things—organization and money—and in that meeting we discussed how to get both. From that meeting we moved into Florida; the Governor announced on January 13. We felt, by the way, at that time that the two people to beat in Florida were Senator Humphrey and Senator Muskie, and probably in that order.

WATTENBERG. Our polls—the Quayle polls—were already showing Jackson ahead of Muskie in Florida. We had put a lot of time and a lot of money into Florida and had gone from just about no identification at all to a point where Jackson was running, as I recall it, only behind Senator Humphrey. When our polls were showing that in early December or late November, we figured that it wouldn't be long before Senator Humphrey decided to come into Florida. There was an upward curve for Jackson, both of identification and of voter support, which was ultimately deeply eroded when Governor Wallace came in.

2
The
Primaries

DAVID S. BRODER (*Washington Post*). I suggest that first of all we deal with the Republican primary races, which you had to look at very quickly to see occurring, and then switch to the Democratic primaries. My proposal, if it's agreeable to you all, would be that we take the period in three chunks: first of all, reviewing the early and middle-ground primaries, running through Maryland and Michigan and the shooting of Governor Wallace, when it became essentially a two-man race; then taking a look at what happened and why in the non-primary states; and finally, coming down to the shoot-out at OK Corral in California. I hope we will have time at the end for some general comments about what happened in the primaries, and why it happened, and what, if anything, it has to say about the kind of decisions that proved to be critical in this peculiar form of political combat. By way of launching the discussion, I'd like to pick up exactly where Jim Perry left off—in January of 1972—and ask each of the campaigns how and why the decisions were made to enter the primaries that were entered. I would hope that you would try to touch on the considerations and the effects of the availability of money, of organization, and your estimate of what the competition looked like in those primaries; and to talk about how those three factors, and any others that were part of your thinking, shaped your choice of where to run and where not to run. Robin Schmidt, for the McCloskey campaign.

ROBIN SCHMIDT (campaign manager for McCloskey). McCloskey had finally gotten into the primaries because he had been unable to find any Republican with "more stature" than he to do it. He still felt that the challenge was very important to make because it gave a chance for debate on the war in the Republican Party before the Democrats would ever be able to focus the issue. As of December '71, the McCloskey campaign was all but broke. Sometime in August the White House had announced Phase I, which essentially dried up the money that we had been finding up to that time. That greatly changed the strategy of what we were going to try to do because we were aiming for the debate rather than for the election. We were trying to keep McCloskey viable nationally so that we could get the TV and press coverage on the Vietnam war issue and wanted to look at the primaries to see where he could do best and improve his position. When money ran out, roughly October 1 [of '71], it was his assessment that unless he concentrated everything on the New Hampshire primary [March 7, 1972] and did fairly well there, he would disappear as a national figure and therefore lose the effect of this debate. As of October, the staff in Washington and most of the national press activity was discontinued, and a small staff was put into New Hampshire with the hope that the campaign could be continued on a voluntary basis. And there, of course, we ran straight into the McGovern campaign and were essentially competing for the same workers. Also, with the announcement from the White House concerning visits to China and so on, we knew that unless we could afford some TV, we weren't going to do very well. But we still couldn't get the money for the TV, so Peter Mc-Closkey ended up with 20 per cent.

BRODER. We'll come back and talk some more about that New Hampshire primary; but just for clarification, why did the announcement of Phase I dry up your money?

SCHMIDT. We had gone to liberal Republican contributors, primarily on the Los Angeles–New York axis, and were finding a real acceptance for what McCloskey was doing and credibility for his effort. We were really getting very good pledges and very good in-flow of money. With the announcement of Phase I, there suddenly was a wait-and-see attitude—at least with all the people we were in contact with. Then they started making money about three or four weeks after that, and the dissatisfaction with the President was not nearly so heavy.

BRODER. What considerations shaped the President's strategy for the primaries?

JEB S. MAGRUDER (Committee for the Re-election of the President). There were two things that we were primarily concerned with. We decided to enter basically every primary for a couple of reasons. One, we felt that the organizational needs were acute. Our strategy from the beginning was based on the belief that it would be a close race. We based our whole campaign strategy, our fund-raising, all of our efforts, on that assumption. If you go on that assumption, it's best to gear up your troops and get your organization set early. We felt the best way to do this would be to enter the primaries and create activity in the states. The party apparatus in many states is not strong in its ability to produce grass-roots workers, since in most states the individual candidates always have their own organizations. We felt we had to base our campaign on that fact and build an organization that could produce. Early on, we felt that there was an opportunity to build a new type of electorate for the President and the Republican Party, and this electorate would contain many people who had not identified directly with the Republican Party. We felt that it was important to get out early, to make our presence known in all states where there were no primaries but where there were important considerations. We started our work early in getting our organization built and entered all the primaries.

Secondly, the McCloskey candidacy in particular and John Ashbrook's to a lesser extent were built out of proportion by the media. I can remember in late '71 there were front-page articles in *Life* and *Time* and *Newsweek*. McCloskey made a major impression. Although we felt that he would not be able to garner the kind of votes he would need to have any impact, we wanted to be prepared to handle any activity in the primaries.

Pete Dailey joined us in October, and we started our advertising; the November Group started up in October; we started all of our work on the most extensive political direct-mail campaign ever run, as well as the financial direct mail; and we worked in conjunction with the Republican National Committee to put together an extensive data bank on voters to use in the general election for get-out-the-vote and voter-identification work. We started our state campaigns by bringing in our state chairmen very early.

BRODER. If I can stay with the Republicans for a moment, then we'll come back and pick up the Democratic scenario. I address this question both to Tom Houser and Pete Dailey: did you find that primaries actually did offer a laboratory for testing techniques, or are they very limited in their usefulness in that respect?

THOMAS J. HOUSER (Committee for the Re-election of the President, Illinois). In Illinois's case, the effect would be nil. We started out building an organization, getting people in place insofar as possible. We didn't receive the campaign design from Washington until, I think, April or May. So we really had no chance to experiment during that period of time.

MAGRUDER. We put campaign plans together only for those states where we were entered in primaries. So we concentrated, obviously, on New Hampshire, and then Florida, and so on, where we had opposition and we were entered. We did not concentrate in states like Illinois, where we were not basically on the ballot.

BRODER. From the viewpoint of the media campaign, did you learn things out of the primaries that were useful?

PETER H. DAILEY (The November Group—Nixon). We thought we would, but in the final analysis we didn't really feel that they were useful in that respect. They were a good training ground for the group that would be put together. The concept of having a task-force agency, which was brought together under the name of the November Group, was a basically unique process in which we started a fully staffed advertising agency from scratch for the sole purpose of working for the President. We planned to dissolve it after the election, which we did. It was an excellent way to bring all those people together and have them work together full time on special projects. We entered the primaries with a feeling that we should be overprepared and underspent. When we went into the New Hampshire primary, we were totally prepared for a contested effort with radio, television, and newspaper material, as well as direct mail. As it happened, a very, very limited effort in newspapers and radio was run in New Hampshire, and it was very distinctly pointed *away* from issues. We believed that it was too early to deal with issues. We were on a down side of everything at that point, and it could only get better. The whole media thrust was simply to reach Republicans and tell them that other Republicans were very satisfied with the performance of the President and were going to support him in the primary effort in New Hampshire.

RICHARD H. STEWART (press secretary for Muskie) [to Jeb Magruder]. In January of '72, was your strategy based on the prospect that Muskie would be your opponent in the election?

MAGRUDER. Yes. Until New Hampshire we felt that he was most likely to be the opponent. We had done the most extensive work preparing for an eventual Muskie-Nixon contest.

ALAN L. OTTEN (*Wall Street Journal*) [to Jeb Magruder]. I'm not clear on what you were saying earlier. Were you saying that you saw McCloskey as a greater threat in the Republican primaries, or just that the press had built him up as greater?

MAGRUDER. I think McCloskey was a minor candidate who was almost made into a major candidate. He was getting tremendous media exposure at that time; and just in case the media exposure that made him somewhat of a national figure overnight should turn into support, we wanted to be prepared in New Hampshire. I don't feel that the exposure actually had that kind of effect, maybe because he ran out of money. But he did campaign up there a huge number of days. We thought, "My God, if he's up there walking around that state, there are only 100,000 Republicans in the whole state, and in forty-five days of campaigning he could almost shake everybody's hand." And, of course, the President never appeared in New Hampshire during the campaign.

J. PHILIP REBERGER (Republican National Committee) [to David Broder]. You mentioned using primaries as a laboratory. I think the party did this to some extent. Jeb Magruder mentioned that, in some cases, he felt that the party organizations weren't capable of carrying on campaign activities to the necessary degree. I think that most Republican Party organizations didn't have the interest in carrying out their organizational activity almost a year prior to the election. We felt that it was important to capitalize on the interest in the primaries to try to test our party organizations. As one example, we watched the direct-mail efforts of the Committee to Re-elect quite closely, because we were testing the possibility of recruiting volunteers through direct mail. In the early primaries we didn't have the success that we were looking for there, and so we changed our organizational programs and tried to capitalize on the interest in the primaries to gear up the party organizations, as well as campaign organizations.

BRODER [to Robin Schmidt]. I think one of the reasons for the media attention that has been commented on is that reporters are like generals—we're always fighting the last war. Since we had missed, by underestimating so much, the McCarthy challenge in 1968, we tended to compensate by overestimating the McCloskey challenge in '72. You put great emphasis on McCloskey's running out of money. As you look back on it now, were there any strategic decisions that were made that limited his success and made the outcome so different from what it had been in the somewhat similar challenge in '68?

SCHMIDT. I think you're right, first of all, that because of McCarthy we got a lot more attention than we would have normally. Probably what was misread by the press was that it is much more difficult to "pull a McCarthy" in the Republican Party than the Democratic Party. I don't think any of the strategic decisions were wrong, but I don't think we ever had latitude to make very many. At the point where we would have made a decision on how to allocate the funds to media or to volunteers, then we would have come to a crossroads—but we were out of money before then.

BRODER. Why is it more difficult to "pull a McCarthy" in the Republican Party?

SCHMIDT. It's something that I think Jeb Magruder spoke about earlier—because Republicans tend to have that minority-party feeling. I think there's a much greater stress on party loyalty. You see them alienating a lot of their young stars because of it—John Lindsay is an example; and I think they may lose some more of their younger congressmen.

HOUSER. Did the issue in the primaries have something to do with it? When McCarthy took on Johnson, we were still escalating in Vietnam; and certainly the liberal wing of the Democratic Party was, I think, correctly, up in arms. There was a little different situation, at least in the Republican mind, with respect to Nixon's handling of the Vietnam situation. We were coming out of it. It was more difficult for McCloskey to generate the kind of heat that came easily to McCarthy.

DAILEY. In New Hampshire we [The November Group] ran a full-page newspaper ad that reprinted a chart from *Newsweek*—basically an upside-down U that showed the growth of troops in Vietnam prior to the election of President Nixon and then pointed out that with the election of President Nixon the number tailed off dramatically. We thought it was very effective among Republicans up there in pointing out that the President had been doing something about Vietnam.

SCHMIDT. I think you're right. The thing we knew early in the game was that McCloskey had to switch from the gut issue of losing American boys to the larger and more ephemeral one of morality, and that presented a great difficulty.

DAILEY. You deal with morality and you get down to the youth vote, which was probably more conscious of it. We took that ad with the *Newsweek* chart and tested among young people, and we found that they absolutely refused to believe it. The great majority of them said, "Well, those are facts and we don't want to deal with that." It gave us cause for concern later on.

SCHMIDT. That goes back to the basic mistrust of Nixon.

BRODER. Just one other question on the Republican side. After the mid-term election of 1970, there was great criticism of the President and the Administration from the liberal wing of the Republican Party. By mid-'71 there were resolutions of censure being passed by various conservative organizations. Why, when it came down to it, was the challenge to the President left to two men who have minimal stature in the national Republican Party? What happened? What did the President do to keep the heavyweights from the liberal and conservative wings of the party from breaking away? What did you do as a party to keep that from happening?

HOUSER. It seems to me that Barry Goldwater was a factor in this. Goldwater certainly remembered the help that Nixon gave at the end of '64. I think there was a personal relationship. Goldwater went to work on behalf of Nixon on the more conservative faction of the party.

REBERGER. Ronald Reagan didn't give the President much heat between '68 and '72. Nelson Rockefeller seemed to be on board. The party, prior to the Florida primary, was conducting some voter registration in the St. Petersburg area, and our questionnaire said, "Do you support President Nixon?" Obviously, the party was supposed to remain neutral in the primary—which we could do by saying that we were out registering Republicans—but the questionnaire had the President's name on it. We had very strong supporters of John Ashbrook that were recruited for this particular drive. They knew that most of the effort was directed for the President, and they were supporting Ashbrook quite strongly verbally during the canvass operation. But it was as if they didn't care that it was for Nixon, because they wanted their thoughts known about Ashbrook's candidacy. They wanted you to know that they supported Ashbrook and had some feelings against some of the President's policy, but they knew that Ashbrook was going to lose and that they were going to get on the Nixon bandwagon once the primaries were over. They just didn't seem to get that excited about Ashbrook's candidacy.

MAGRUDER. I think another factor is that you can't have a revolt against an incumbent President unless you have impending disaster. You can have resolutions now and then, and the liberal wing may get a little upset over one thing and the conservative wing over something else. But lacking circumstances like Lyndon Johnson's with the Vietnam war, I think it's very difficult for even legitimate dissent to occur in a political party when you have an incumbent President, simply because he does have the ability and the power to control party structure and the efforts made within the party. I'm sure Governor Reagan and Governor Rockefeller would have realized how difficult a revolt would have been unless there was an insurgence from the grass roots—which was not occurring. There was some dissatisfaction, but I think that President Nixon had taken his lumps early. He was coming up just when he would have had to be going down in order for any revolt of any substance to develop. So there was really no basis for any revolt of any substance; and I think that's why we ended up with McCloskey and Ashbrook as the opposition, rather than some of the heavy hitters who could have possibly been more difficult.

ROBERT J. KEEFE (consultant to the AFL-CIO). I get the impression from looking at the Republican Party that financially they drink from a smaller trough. They drink well, but from a smaller and more disciplined group of people. I have the feeling, watching the Republicans over the years, that there is some interaction among the people who have to pay the bills for various Republican candidates that imposes a greater discipline than Democrats have. We have a broader group of contributors.

MAGRUDER. That's just not true. The Republican Party has a much broader base of contributors, both of small and large contributors.

KEEFE. Ideologically broad based?

MAGRUDER. Oh, yes. In California—Taft Schreiber and Leonard Firestone on one end of the ideological base and Henry Salvatori and Holmes Tuttle on the other. They're both major factors in the party.

DAILEY. One interesting thing we [in the Nixon campaign] picked up in early testing was a great understanding among grass-roots Republicans that they are a minority party. They think that the President may not be doing well on this or well on that, but he is a Republican President and they basically agree with him and want to stick together to ensure his re-election.

KEEFE. A higher percentage of the money for individual congressional and senatorial campaigns comes from national sole-source funding: that is, on the Republican side, your campaign committees raise and finance a higher proportion of candidates' total budgets than on the Democratic side. It seems to me that your campaign chairmen and their major contributors have greater influence over people who might want to be candidates than is the case in the Democratic Party.

MAGRUDER. When figuring that, are you excluding from the Democratic contributions the labor contributions? The money from COPE [Committee on Political Education, AFL-CIO]?

KEEFE. Put it in, I don't care. In terms of dollars, the

COPE expenditure per candidate is reasonably small. The COPE expenditure for a major Senate candidate won't go over $10,000 from sole source.

OTTEN [to Jeb Magruder]. You keep saying, "We decided," and so forth. I have a fair idea of who were making the decisions in the Muskie campaign or maybe even the McGovern campaign, but I'm really curious about the "we" in the Nixon campaign. How was your decision-making done? How much was the President personally involved? What was John Mitchell's role? What was Bob Haldeman's role? What decisions were you yourself making? How was it all working?

MAGRUDER. There was basically a triad of senior decision-makers—the President, Bob Haldeman, and John Mitchell—until July of '72. They were in constant consultation with each other over major activities. The staff work for the campaign was done at the Committee to Re-elect primarily, with some additional staff work done by certain groups in the White House on certain specific subjects. We agreed that the Committee to Re-elect would not get involved to any degree in any substantive matters; we'd stay out of the policy decision-making process. We weren't going to send memos on the Vietnam war or on domestic issues because we knew that that would really cloud things up. Similarly, the White House stayed out of the political organizational process. We spent our time worrying about how to put on a direct-mail campaign, how to put together an advertising agency, how to set up effective relationships with the Republican National Committee. The White House worked on the substantive issues that would affect policy. We kept that definition right through the end of the campaign, and I think it worked very well.

We had very few of the internal friction problems that you normally have in a campaign, particularly in a large structure such as ours. We used the same staff system that is used in the White House. We broke up the campaign initially into sixteen groups and had deadlines as to when we had to have decisions made; we put the decision papers together and fired them off through John Mitchell into Bob Haldeman to the President. How many decisions the President actually made himself, I wouldn't know. How many were made by Bob Haldeman and John Mitchell directly were just a matter of percentages, I think. When Clark MacGregor [Counsel to the President] came over in '72, we remained exactly in the same posture; we added one deputy with myself—Fred Malek— and continued along in exactly the same process that we had started back in May of '71 when we actually formed the Committee to Re-elect. I don't think it was a mystery.

OTTEN. I realize I'm getting into a sensitive area. But take the decision of Maurice Stans [Nixon finance chairman] to go around the country and urge people to contribute before the April '72 deadline [before the new disclosure laws went into effect]. Is that the kind of decision that the President would have personally gotten into, or would Haldeman have gotten into that?

MAGRUDER. In that area, you know, we were quite separate—the finance committee was separate from the political committee. Ask me a question about the political committee.

ANNE WEXLER (Democratic voter-registration director). Tom Houser was mentioning that he didn't receive a state plan until April. Did you [in the Committee to Re-elect] devise a plan for each state and each campaign, for both primary and non-primary states?

MAGRUDER. Yes. In the general election we had basically eleven target states for which we had specific major plans, and then we had one plan for thirty-nine states. The eleven larger states got an inordinate amount of our resources in direct mail and in telephone activity. The other states had to, in effect, pay their own freight on those two programs. In the primaries we developed a state plan for New Hampshire, and we submitted the plan through John Mitchell. Whether the President actually saw all the details of that plan, I really don't know, but we got it back approved and went ahead.

WEXLER. What happened when it got to the state level? In other words, was the plan then accepted and implemented by the people at the state level exactly the way it was?

MAGRUDER. Well, maybe not exactly the way it was. I remember in New Hampshire, we and the Republican National Committee jointly sent up about ten people to help implement the planning on our telephone and direct-mail campaigns, which were lagging. We didn't feel that the people in New Hampshire understood the plan and how it should be implemented. We had that kind of problem, but that's not unusual. I think most national campaigns send out some of their people to each of the states. In the McGovern campaign they did that very effectively, and we did the same thing. We sent some of our key people out into each state; by the end of the general election, we had almost all of our people out of Washington in the states working with the state chairmen.

BRODER. Let's go on and talk about what happened in the Democratic primaries. Let me begin by asking the campaign people here to take themselves back to January of '72 and describe how they decided which primaries to run in, the view that they had of the opposition field, the scenario that they believed was going to lead through the primaries to an election victory, and the way in which the limitations of money and organization, or anything else, decided where the fights would come. Shall we begin with the Muskie campaign, which was on top at the start of the year?

STEWART. Actually, we weren't in bad shape in January of '72. Muskie made his formal announcement on January 4 after a year of playing the role of the unannounced candidate. I think it probably was his best press conference. He was relaxed; he was easygoing. It struck me that suddenly the weight of not officially being a candidate was off his shoulders. Being highly touted as the front-runner, he felt compelled to prove it; and the decision was made to run in as many primaries as were consistent with his capacity to do so. It was obvious that he had to run in New Hampshire. It was a symbolic primary in a state adjacent to his home state, and he had to do well there.

Financially, at that time, if I remember correctly, there was a cash-flow problem that was easy to blame a little bit on Hubert Humphrey. Hubert obviously was making phone calls. Hubert was tying up a lot of money, especially in California, by calling people who were able to give money and telling them, "Stay loose, I'm thinking it over; I may become a candidate; don't do anything." In so doing, he kept money away from other candidates, including Muskie. At that stage I think we were postured pretty well in terms of Nixon, and I still had a feeling that we were in pretty good shape. But we had, unfortunately, built from the top down rather than from the bottom up, and we were later to see how that worked against us. I've heard a lot of talk about the Muskie strategy. I never was quite sure, frankly, of what the Muskie strategy was. But I thought that Muskie was correct to conduct himself in the course of the primaries in a way consistent with winning the election. Whatever positions he would take were positions he could take both in the primaries and in the general election, so he never would have had to adjust or readjust after the nomination.

BRODER. What was McGovern's view of how the scenario was going to unfold between January and July of 1972? What shaped his view?

GARY W. HART (campaign director for McGovern). I will refer to 1970 because we did make some basic decisions back there that were fairly prophetic. Those decisions, together with the non-primary operation, are in my judgment the story of how McGovern got the nomination. In July of 1970 we decided to run in New Hampshire, Wisconsin, Nebraska, Massachusetts, Oregon, California, and probably New York. New York, at that time, seemed like light-years away, and it was just assumed that we would be in it, though it wasn't talked about much. We won every one of those states two years later. West Virginia was the only state that we had as a definite "go" state that we dropped. States which added primaries, or which already had primaries that we never really seriously discussed entering, were Indiana, Tennessee, and North Carolina, although the Senator flirted with North Carolina for a day or two. States that weren't discussed in '70 but that we subsequently entered and won were New Mexico, Rhode Island, and New Jersey. South Dakota was also a state that we always assumed but never talked about.

George McGovern had the same inclination that Muskie had for exactly the opposite reason: McGovern thought, in January of '72 and for months before that, because he was at 3 per cent in the polls, that he had to run in every primary. He had a theory that if he missed a primary, everybody would say he was a calculating politician like everybody else and was picking and choosing. One of the biggest hassles the staff had with the candidate during '71 and early '72 was to convince him that he could not enter every primary. There were too few of us, and we had too few dollars. He had, I must say, a very romantic notion about entering every primary, just submitting his name and letting the chips fall where they may. We pointed out to him that there were potential disasters involved.

We entered New Hampshire. It was debated several times at several staff and advisory meetings, but there was never really serious consideration given to pulling out of New Hampshire. We had to go head-on against Muskie in his own territory. This is one that the Senator always felt he could not duck. And—a key factor in the "co-opt the left" strategy—we felt that if we got in there early and dug in, we could co-opt the very limited constituency on the left and do a little bit of a McCarthy thing there. I would disagree with Bob Keefe on Birch Bayh or Harold Hughes or Fred Harris or anyone else getting into that. The next definite one was Wisconsin. There was never a real question about going in there, and going like gangbusters.

So that left two in between—Florida and Illinois. Those were both debated states. Serious arguments were raised that we should make an all-out effort in Florida and Illinois. I was against serious campaigning in both states, primarily on financial and candidate-time grounds. That is, if we entered seriously in Florida, McGovern couldn't run hard in New Hampshire for both those reasons. When Wallace got into Florida, that sealed it as far as I was concerned. Then, also, it was obvious that John Lindsay was going to try his media blitz in Florida. There was no way we could outspend him, and the only way to run in that state seemed to us to be to go heavily into the media. We just didn't have the money. We were strapped for money in January and February.

Illinois was a confused political situation. The Senator had attachments to that state, having gone to school there; he felt it was his kind of state—big campus communities, farmers, and so forth. We were hoping that the state legislature would put the primary off, as it toyed with doing until January or early February. When it decided to make the primary early, March 21, I argued strenuously against going in strongly. We essentially adopted a selective congressional-district strategy there to pick up as many delegates as we could by congressional district—to really rifle rather than shotgun that state. Everybody knows what happened.

After Wisconsin, which was obviously a very big turning point for our campaign, came Massachusetts and Pennsylvania. We were going to go all-out in Massachusetts, but what were we going to do about Pennsylvania? Pennsylvania fell into a kind of triumvirate with Michigan and Ohio—these were the middle primaries, and they were the three big industrial states. We had to do something in one of them. We couldn't duck them all. Yet they were states that many other candidates were entering. Wallace was definitely a factor in Michigan, and Michigan seemed very marginal because of the busing problem. In Pennsylvania we had difficulty just getting a campaign off the ground, and the vibrations weren't right. That led us, I would say within days after the Wisconsin victory, to look very hard at Ohio. We had Pat Caddell out there surveying, and what he found out was crucial. We took Humphrey on—head-on—in a state where he should have done very well, and we almost won it. There are still people who think we did win it. Then we got to the rest of the middle primaries—Nebraska, which we won, and later, at the end of May, Oregon and Rhode Island, which we won the same night. Rhode Island was originally a write-off state that we won as a result, I think, of our showings in Massachusetts, New Hampshire, Wisconsin, and Ohio. It was a definite plus that we never really counted on, and we had made an effort there in only the last seven or eight days.

And then, of course, came the four-primary night, June 6. My own feeling, which I think was shared by Rick Stearns and the Senator, was that California was the ball game—that whoever won it would get the nomination. The talk in January of '72 of Lindsay's staying out and then making a big rush in California was laughable. The battle would go through all the primaries, and two men would emerge; and there would be a battle, not only for the California primary and not only for the nomination, but for the Democratic Party. That battle came with the challenge to the California delegation, and it obviously became much greater than even any of us had anticipated. The theory always was that whoever wins California wins New York. And that was it.

So our strategy was to do as well as possible in New Hampshire, run against Muskie, get every vote we could, and hope to make it a race. I remember telling the Senator ten days before the New Hampshire primary that it looked as if we were going to be real lucky and get 25 per cent of the vote, and he almost went through the ceiling. He said, "We're going to win this primary." We always had the problem of the Senator predicting victory everywhere we went. We won Wisconsin; we won Massachusetts; we placed a very creditable third or close fourth in Pennsylvania—essentially a three-way tie for second; we almost won Ohio—maybe did; we won Nebraska; we won Oregon, Rhode Island, California, South Dakota, New Mexico, New Jersey, and New York.

RICK G. STEARNS (deputy campaign manager for McGovern). I think that Gary Hart's recollection is essentially correct. I did find one of the original memoranda we gave McGovern in December of 1970 outlining his travel plans for the year of 1971; and California, Oregon, Wisconsin, New Hampshire, Nebraska, and West Virginia (which was later dropped) were the states picked for concentration of McGovern's time.

I'll just add two observations that figured into our calculations when we were looking at the primaries that we were going to enter. One of them is a bias, unintentionally incorporated in the whole primary system, toward candidates in the liberal wing of the party. The Presidential primary was an invention of the Populists and Progressives and generally has been adopted, or at least has the longest history, in states that have had strong progressive movements, or movements that have had an impact on both the organization and the character of the Democratic parties—states like Wisconsin, California, and Nebraska.

Another is that most reporters had had their first real experience at reporting a Presidential nomination race in 1968; that was the first year that a nomination race attracted almost daily attention from the press. It was our assumption that, regardless of the changes that had taken place in a number of states and the fact that a number of new primaries had been adopted, the primaries that had been significant in 1968 would be the primaries that would be important to the press in 1972. That assumption proved to be true. Otherwise, there was no reason that Wisconsin should have been the watershed for the McGovern campaign that it was; the Wisconsin primary fundamentally was not that important. McGovern won the primary with 30 per cent of the vote, and I'm convinced that one-third of that was composed of Republican crossovers that came in to vote for McGovern. Yet the Wisconsin primary, much more than New Hampshire, established McGovern as the front-runner for the Democratic nomination.

I have a theory, which I'm sure is wrong, that another advantage that worked in our favor is the expense of moving television equipment across the country. The press prefers to start in the East and move slowly across the country to the West, and then fly it all back to New York from Los Angeles. So the natural progression of primaries would run from New Hampshire out to Wisconsin to Nebraska to Oregon and finally down to California and back to New York. And, basically, in terms of television coverage, that's essentially how it goes.

To summarize, there were two advantages working for McGovern. One was the bias that he inherited, which is not intentional or by design but merely has to do with the way the nomination system has grown up in this country. The second was the way the press covered the 1972 campaign. I don't think the press will tend to dismiss primaries in Tennessee, North Carolina, New Jersey, and so on to the extent that they did in this election.

BRODER. What was the Wallace campaign thinking about the primaries?

BILLY JOE CAMP (press secretary for Wallace). In January of '72, when the decision was made to go into
Florida, we knew that it had to be an all-out effort. I
think we all realized that the press would predict Governor
Wallace to win; we felt as if we were ahead; but if he
lost, the ball game was over with. As I said before, we
lacked money and organization, but with everything that
we could put together in a short period of time we moved
into Florida and did go all out. A poll we had taken at
that time recommended to us that we had the state won,
that we shouldn't take a chance on making any mistakes,
and that we should spend as little time as possible there
and concentrate elsewhere. I think if we had followed
that advice and moved into Wisconsin earlier, we would
have had a much better chance there.

Of course, all of you know the story of Florida. Governor Wallace campaigned extensively there, crisscrossing
the state several times. I think it became more obvious
from day to day that our primary opponent in Florida was
Senator Humphrey. We were a little amazed at the campaign that Senator Muskie was running. We appreciated
those full-page ads with Governor Wallace's picture—we
couldn't afford to buy them ourselves. We thought the
campaign was very successful, except that we expended
so much energy—personnelwise. I guess all the way
through the primaries, most of us had the same problems.
I don't think any of us on the Democratic side had an
abundance of money—maybe Muskie to begin with, but
he soon had his problems, too.

BRODER. Was the initial decision simply to go to Florida,
or was it to go to Florida and then on to someplace else?

CAMP. The initial decision was to go to Florida—we had
to win there. But assuming that we would, on to Wis-

consin, Indiana, West Virginia, North Carolina, Michigan, Maryland, and Tennessee, of course. We later dropped West Virginia. We entered the state, but we did not campaign there. We just simply found the support for Senator Humphrey too great to go in; we did not have the time or the money to get in and fight that support.

I would say the biggest mistake of the Wallace campaign was the delay in getting into Wisconsin after the Florida primary. We spent ten days to two weeks in Montgomery—I don't know what we were doing—when we should have been in Wisconsin. We did not have a single staff person in Wisconsin. When we went there eight or more days before the election, we realized almost immediately that the polls showing Governor Wallace running fifth were simply not true. Senator McGovern had been on the air, and he had a good organization—a well-oiled machine, you might say; his support was tremendous. But I think all of us realized from the beginning that if Governor Wallace worked hard and campaigned extensively, he could possibly move up to three and have an outside chance of beating Senator Humphrey for second place—which he did. We were a little surprised. It was our biggest mistake—not getting into Wisconsin immediately following the Florida primary, or, for that matter, having some staff people there before the end of the Florida primary.

BRODER. Why was no decision made to qualify for the California primary? Did that question ever come up?

CAMP. The question never really came up in our planning. I can just say that we erred—we erred grossly. The other states that we made a mistake on were Ohio, Illinois, and Pennsylvania. Although we made the decision to go into Pennsylvania, we did not have the knowledge of the rules and reforms of the party that we needed. We didn't have a slate of delegates. It would have been a simple process, in the two or three days that we had after we decided to enter, to get an uncommitted slate of delegates that we could have later promoted in our advertisements as a Wallace slate. I think we would have come out of Pennsylvania with a good number of delegates. But we didn't do that, and we realized soon that it was a mistake—certainly after we got some 20 per cent of the vote without more than two speeches there by the Governor. These were staff mistakes.

OTTEN. Why didn't Governor Wallace go more heavily into the non-primary states than he did?

CAMP. I think the reason that he did not go more heavily into the non-primary states was because of a lack of knowledge about the reform rules of the party on the part of people directing the campaign. There was a general feeling that if we got good votes out of the primaries, some of the non-primary states would fall in line. Maybe in the past they have, but it's just not going to happen with the new rules. Obviously, we realized that this was incorrect thinking later on, and we did get into Texas and we were going into some other states. At the time that the Governor was shot [May 15], we felt reasonably sure that we would win Michigan and win big, and we thought we had a good chance of winning in Maryland. From there, we were going to move into some non-primary states. I still think the pressure would have been enough for him to move into New Mexico and wage a campaign there, and probably into California for a few days for a write-in vote. All of this is projection, of course.

STEWART. When you decided in January to run on the

Democratic ticket, did you run, knowing that you would not get the nomination, to give George Wallace credibility in one of the two major parties for something that would happen four years or eight years hence?

CAMP. That was probably an underlying thought. It was never discussed. I don't know about the four years hence. We felt that it would help his political base at home if he could be successful in the primaries. The Governor has always viewed himself as a man who, regardless of whether he attains the Presidency or not, could go down in history as having had a tremendous influence on the direction of this country in his lifetime. By getting out in the primaries as a Democrat and putting forth his position on the issues, he felt that he could send a message to the party and to the voters throughout the nation, regardless of their party affiliations, for that matter, that would be helpful to the country.

STEWART. But it was to exert pressure, without any expectation of winning the nomination?

CAMP. Initially, I think that's a correct analysis of it. It was never expressed as that, though. There were some of us in the campaign who kept putting forth the idea, "Now we can win this thing if we do such and such." But it didn't happen. Obviously we didn't have the benefit that the McGovern campaign had of starting early. It was our fault.

DAILEY. Busing emerged in Florida as the major issue, but we [in the Nixon campaign] didn't isolate it as a major issue at all in our research prior to the election. I am curious whether you had research that showed it was an issue, or whether there was really a gut decision of the candidate himself to push it to the people.

CAMP. We had a good sampling of opinion from Florida that showed it to be an issue. Governor Wallace had had a number of communications with the President in regards to busing—a number of statements that got good press coverage. He was established as an opponent of forced busing, and we didn't feel that we had to go to Florida and make that a major part of his speech. He had to expand and be more than a one-issue candidate. So he went to Florida and Wisconsin and talked about tax reform, the remoteness of government from the people, and foreign aid giveaway. We realized from the outset the necessity of expanding Governor Wallace's appeal to the voters in the country beyond the type of people that the press projected him as appealing to. And I think this was done fairly effectively.

OTTEN. What was the origin of "send them a message"?

CAMP. The "send them a message" theme was not a product of any public relations agency or any one genius except George Wallace. And he didn't like the theme at the beginning. After three or four of his first speeches in Florida, staff members were listening to his tapes. We knew something was needed to use as an advertising gimmick, if you want to call it that. It was discovered that in each of his speeches, twenty times or better, the Governor used the phrase "send them a message." And that's what was pulled out.

DAILEY. We [the November Group] thought that was sheer genius, by the way. We were looking at research that showed that 60 per cent of the people were discontented with the direction that the country was going in. The slogan was open ended: whatever your beef was, if you voted for George, you got it off your mind.

BRODER. I want to get to the Humphrey and Jackson end of this thing.

JACK L. CHESTNUT (campaign manager for Humphrey). The Humphrey situation was a little different from that of some of the other candidates in January of 1972. He was now an announced candidate, but there was a substantial amount of thought in some political and journalistic circles that he was over the hill, that he was not really a viable candidate, that he needed to prove that he could win. Of course, one way of proving that he could win was to enter some primaries.

I think two areas have been overlooked in our discussion of the decision-making process involved in entering primaries. First, the laws of the particular state. In some instances, the decision-making process is not left to the candidate, or his campaign managers, but is pretty well determined by the particular state involved. In Florida, for example, I believe that the Secretary of State, on the basis of various news media sources, can make a determination with a three-member committee of who is and who is not a Presidential candidate, and accordingly put his name on the ballot. In Wisconsin, the Secretary of State, or his counterpart, has similar powers. So you were faced with the fact that your name was going to be on the ballot in at least two of the very early primaries, and you really didn't have anything to say about it at all. Somebody who had been around political circles as long as Hubert Humphrey had better be prepared to make a respectable showing.

The other thing that I think we're overlooking is that

in 1972 more delegates than ever before were going to be selected by the primary process—some 1,900 delegates, more than enough to nominate. The name of this whole game was to get delegates to get nominated, so you had to get into the primary process. The idea that you could sit back until California and all of a sudden come in and make a great big show was absolutely ridiculous. You'd flunk third-grade mathematics if you took that position. There was no way you could be nominated if you passed up all the primaries where the delegates elected were committed to particular candidates.

In January of 1972 Hubert Humphrey had to look down the gun barrel of Florida, so to speak. Florida is a state, by and large a Southern state, in which he had not had any great political activity. In 1968 he made only one appearance for a short period of time in Jacksonville, and outside of that, he did not campaign in the state and wasn't well known there. Floridians perceived him more in the 1948 image of Hubert Humphrey than in the 1972 image of Hubert Humphrey. So we felt that if he could make a respectable showing there, this would establish the fact that he did have viability, that he did relate to 1972, that he did relate to a broad spectrum of the party. As a consequence, one of our major tasks was to put together in approximately sixty days a campaign organization for Hubert Humphrey in Florida, where he did not have one in the past. I think that we had a very effective campaign organization in Florida, and I'm rather proud of our Florida team. I think the results were very good in view of the fact that a number of candidates had already been there for a length of time and had existing organizations. Part of the problem created by the lateness of the decision to open the Humphrey campaign was that a number of people who would have been for Humphrey were already in other camps, such as the Jackson camp. There were strong parallels between the Jackson and the Humphrey constituencies in Florida. So the lateness did hurt Humphrey there, as it did throughout the campaign. Nevertheless, he made a strong showing, and it was reported as a strong showing.

To give you another example of how the state laws had substantial bearing on campaign decision: even though the decision had been made to go as a Presidential candidate in December of 1971, our original strategy was to announce formally about the third or fourth week in January, in the form of a response to the President's State of the Union message that would come approximately at that time. We were prevented from using that strategy by Pennsylvania, a state in which we felt we wanted to run. It was the first state where we would have been somewhat on home ground—Florida was not Humphrey's state, and, I think, the crossover situation in Wisconsin practically voids that primary. But the Pennsylvania legislature during the last week in December decided that if you were going to run in the Presidential primary in Pennsylvania, you must declare yourself as a candidate for President by the tenth day of January of 1972. We decided on the first or second day of January that that's what we would do, and that dictated our announcement date of January 10 in Philadelphia.

BRODER [to Ben Wattenberg]. Is there anything you want to add to what you've already said about Jackson's thinking about Florida and other primaries?

BEN J. WATTENBERG (adviser to Jackson). We felt that Florida was a "must" primary and that Jackson's major problem was anonymity. We didn't expect that Governor Wallace and Senator Humphrey were going to be in that state. We had a steadily ascending poll there and were spending a lot of time and money in an effort to get the thing off the ground with a bang early on. Despite the fact that we suddenly got hit from the right and from the left by two people with great public identification—Governor Wallace and Senator Humphrey—we beat everyone else in that field. We beat Senator Muskie; we beat Senator McGovern; and we beat Mayor Lindsay. But the way the media reported it was enough to make a grown man cry. On its half-hour election special, CBS had on Governor Wallace, Muskie, Humphrey, Lindsay, and McGovern, but not Jackson; and NBC had all of those five, plus Mary Lindsay. The *Milwaukee Journal* carried a big headline that said, "Wallace wins, Humphrey second, Muskie fourth." And Wisconsin was a state where we had begun to spend some media money and were beginning to come up again before Governor Wallace's entry. We felt that, as Senator Jackson's first national primary, Florida wasn't devastating in itself. And we had some reason to think that things might look good in Wisconsin. At that time our Quayle polls were showing Governor Wallace running at 2 per cent in Wisconsin, and we were running at about 7 per cent and climbing because we were spending some media money.

STEARNS. I'd like to get back to the point that Jack Chestnut raised. The reform rules have been blamed for a lot of things during this past nomination year, a lot of things that, as far as the primaries go, would have been more appropriately blamed on state laws. But there was one reform rule, added almost as an afterthought, that required delegates running in state primaries to indicate their Presidential preference on the ballot. Humphrey in 1968 had entered only one primary, and that involuntarily—South Dakota's, which he lost. Yet he received almost 70 per cent of the votes from delegates from primary states in the 1968 convention. What the new rule of candidate identification did was pretty much move party organizations in large primary states out of the convention process. The uncommitted party delegation, which would be open to persuasion from any one of the candidates in the convention, pretty much disappeared. This made it much more difficult for the candiate in terms of the timing of his race, since he had to be determined to run early.

Then the reform rules further complicated things by adding a series of difficult and formal processes that you had to go through to put a slate together. I think the reason that Wallace didn't enter California was that the deadline for submitting petitions closed on March 7, the day of the New Hampshire primary; and prior to that, you had to have a series of slating caucuses organized in the state before you could begin collecting 15,000 signatures. In a state like California, 15,000 signatures does not sound like a lot—but if you've ever tried to collect signatures to get a candidate on the ballot, you know that it is an immense task. So the strategy that had worked in any prior Presidential years, that allowed you to come back at the delegates again a second time after the primaries, just didn't work this time. Most of the delegates went to the convention committed.

BRODER. Rick Stearns mentioned that this change took the party organization out of the convention process. Anne Wexler has a question that she wants to raise about the effect on labor from this change.

WEXLER. I am interested in whether or not it would have helped Muskie or Humphrey if organized labor had gotten in early in '71. Early in '72 after the reforms had more or less been accepted by the Democratic Party, organized labor made quite an effort, at least as reported by the press, to elect their own delegates. In fact, there were a lot of statements made at that time about electing as many as five hundred labor delegates to the national convention, not necessarily pledged to any candidate. That never materialized then and never materialized later, because labor was never in fact able to put together the kind of organization that could have done it. Bob Keefe said that had labor gotten behind a candidate, it probably would have helped him, and I wonder if in fact it would have at all.

KEEFE. What I suggest is that it might have given Muskie the kind of base organizationally that he needed, with everything else he had going at the time, to really get the job done for him. If labor had jumped behind Muskie in January [of '72], they would have really sealed it off for him, because they would have complicated things very badly for Humphrey and Jackson, who were counting eventually on labor support. If they had jumped behind Humphrey, they would have given him a real fighting chance at the nomination, which I don't think he had at that time because of his late start. They would have compensated, but as just another factor in the whole.

WEXLER. When they finally jumped, they jumped on the issue simply of trying to collect labor delegates, and that didn't work.

KEEFE. Labor took a position in late September or early October of 1971 that I was not privy to, but came in to help implement. They planned to go after uncommitted delegates as a first choice and then use whatever way possible to get more delegates. In fact, labor doubled the number of delegates they had at the Democratic convention between 1968 and 1972 but lessened the total impact they had on the electoral process. I think that what Rick Stearns pointed out about the requirement of candidate identification had a strong impact. I think one of the areas where Muskie messed himself up was that he took all of the favorite sons out of the race. Reform rules to the contrary notwithstanding, if Governor John Gilligan [of Ohio] says he's a candidate for President of the United States and "I'm going to run in the primary," I don't see how you can preclude that. Had he been a candidate in Ohio, for example, he would have won the primary; and I think that several other candidates wouldn't have run in it.

PATRICK H. CADDELL (Cambridge Survey Research—McGovern). I think he would have lost. Gilligan specifically, I think, would have gotten beaten.

KEEFE. You say he would have gotten beaten on the basis of polls, but what I'm saying is that I think that a lot of other guys wouldn't have gone in to alienate Governor Gilligan.

CADDELL. Well, that might be. But if Gilligan had had to run against a substantial candidate, he would have been in real trouble.

KEEFE. I allow that. But by the first of January there were no favorite sons left. As late as November, you had had potential favorite sons like Milton Shapp [of Pennsylvania] and John Gilligan in many of the big states.

STEWART. Reuben Askew [of Florida] was a possibility too.

KEEFE. Askew, sure. Muskie eventually got them all to support him and thereby cut off his second shot at the delegates—a traditional part of the process.

OTTEN. During the early primaries, some people started developing the theory that the Wallace vote and the McGovern vote were part of one big "alienation" pot. It seemed to me at the time that it was a rather questionable theory. What really gave the McGovern people the idea that the Wallace vote was potentially theirs?

CADDELL. I think you have to go back to distinguishing which voters you're talking about. In surveys we began very early [for McGovern], we didn't look for the people who said they were voting for George Wallace; you never get an approximation of his votes that way because of what we call the "closet Wallace vote"—people who won't say, but who are going to vote for him. But if you start picking out certain criteria, you can identify them pretty well. The Wallace vote in '72 was different from '68, but it was still partly a racial vote or ideological vote. Then you've got a lot of blue-collar workers, particularly young blue-collar workers, who are extremely alienated voters but who never voted for Wallace before.

When we went into Wisconsin and looked at it, it was clear that Wallace was starting off at about 8 per cent but really had potential anywhere up to 30. And so we made a concerted effort at that vote, on issues of tax reform and whether anybody cares about the voter. In a state like Massachusetts, our prospect was to win pretty handily. Wallace was showing at 6 per cent in surveys, but there was a potential Wallace vote of 18 per cent. Our whole campaign was devoted, in the blue-collar areas in the cities, to chipping away at that vote. People who were undecided going into most of the primaries were people who were very highly favorable to Wallace and most likely to vote for him. Three weeks before the Ohio primary, with Wallace not in the race, Humphrey was running at about 35; Muskie was running at about 22; McGovern was running at 15. But because of the undecideds and their attitudes about the other candidates, it was very clear that McGovern could pick up most of those votes and that's exactly what he did—particularly blue-collar workers under the age of forty.

JAMES M. PERRY (*National Observer*). Is there a point to be made here about the perception of McGovern earlier compared to what it was after California? I remember seeing in one of Ben Wattenberg's Quayle polls that Muskie was perceived in Florida as well to the left of McGovern.

CHARLES GUGGENHEIM (media adviser to McGovern). I think your point is right. We were very encouraged that the Wallace vote could be had until the perception of McGovern changed. What the Wallace voters began to understand later about McGovern they disliked more than the things they liked about him. I think that the turn began just after Ohio and Nebraska. McGovern felt that Jackson really started that trend—I don't know if that's fair. But we felt a start of that trend, and then Humphrey picked it up in California and put it to bed.

STEWART. I recall seeing a poll, just prior to the New Hampshire primary, which was related to Florida. I was fascinated by it because it showed that the second choice among Wallace voters was John Lindsay. As it was explained to me by people who are supposed to know something about these things, the reason Wallace voters had Lindsay as their second choice was that their only perception of him at that point was gleaned from the "To-night Show" with Johnny Carson. They saw this tall, handsome Mayor of New York, who looked good on the Johnny Carson show and said glib and funny things. But they also perceived him as a maverick of sorts outside the party structure, and the guy who liked Wallace was not part of the establishment.

BRODER. Some remarkable things happened immediately after [Wallace's victory in] the Florida primary [March 14]. Muskie denounced Wallace saying, "I'm going to spend every bit of my energy fighting this because it represents everything that I despise in American life." McGovern went up to Wisconsin and had a big staff meeting and came out in a speech at the University of Wisconsin saying, "Attention must be paid. There is much more despair in this country than I had ever realized until I saw what happened in Florida." Hubert Humphrey came up to Wisconsin, and in his first major speech up there said, "I have now read the fine print on the President's busing proposal, and I find that I am diametrically opposed to what he is trying to do here." Jackson came up to Wisconsin and appealed overtly for Republican crossover votes. George Wallace went back to Montgomery and sat there. Now what was going on in these five campaigns at that point?

WEXLER. You really should go back to the conflict in New Hampshire [March 7], because it had great effect, I think, on the Florida primary.

STEWART. For Muskie, the problem in New Hampshire was that he had to run in it. Muskie kept playing a game with the press, or the press kept playing a game with Muskie. The question was constantly, "How much do you feel you have to win by here, since it's a neighboring state, to be a viable candidate going out of New Hampshire?" Muskie always said, "I've been in politics all my life, and I've always felt that the guy who got one vote more than anybody else won the primary." Unfortunately, however, one of our coordinators in New Hampshire was asked how well Muskie should do, and I think her comment was, "If he doesn't get 50 per cent, I'll blow my brains out," or words to that effect. From that moment on, 50 per cent stuck. Despite whatever Muskie said, that comment by that woman stuck and 50 per cent became the target which he was held accountable for.

Another thing was the issue of disclosure, which McGovern used very successfully against Muskie. Muskie was constantly being asked by the press, "Why don't you say where your money's coming from?" Muskie said, "Under the law I will disclose when the time is appropriate." But still, McGovern had disclosed, and Muskie was put in the position of being suspect as to what kind of money he was getting. Guys were writing columns about it—the story was constantly harassing him. The chief reason for Muskie's not disclosing was the fact that we had so damn much Republican money at that stage that to disclose the sources of that money would have been disastrous to many Republicans who gave the money with the specific understanding that they would not be revealed. Some of them were fairly close to the President of the United States, or were related to people fairly close to the President of the United States.

MAGRUDER. We [in the Nixon campaign] had some of your best people, too.

STEWART. Then there was the harassment for debate. McGovern kept insisting, as he rightfully should have from his position, that Muskie and he should debate. The right position, of course, from Muskie's point of view would be to have no debate at all, because it would only give McGovern exposure; but eventually the pressure became so great that he had to accept. We all remember the fiasco that was the debate—all anybody can recall of the debate was the gentleman from Connecticut [Edward Coll] with the rubber rat. Then, of course, there was the famous Loeb incident in which Muskie stood on that platform in front of the *Union Leader* and sobbed.

JAMES M. NAUGHTON (*New York Times*). How was the decision reached to go to the *Manchester Union Leader* building that morning [February 26]?

STEWART. As I recall, the decision was made in New Hampshire by our coordinator there, in consultation with the Washington office. Muskie at that time was ill in California. He had an infection and was laid to bed in Palm Springs for two or three days. And he was fatigued. A phone call came from George Mitchell asking Muskie to make a decision on the proposal that he go to the *Union Leader* to confront William Loeb [the publisher] on the alleged "canuck" letter. It often happens in campaigns that the people who might have some impact or input just don't happen to be in the right place at the right time to give counsel. I'm not sure what my counsel would have been. I think I would not have said, "Don't do it."

Another ingredient was added at the very last minute before Muskie was to go to the *Union Leader*. A day or two before Loeb had picked up a segment of *Women's Wear Daily* attacking Jane Muskie and had run it on the front page of the *Manchester Union Leader*. Muskie had been unaware of that while deciding whether or not to go before Loeb. I believe it was late the night before he was to go to the *Union Leader* that somebody showed him that clipping. Thus, a factor that had never entered into any of the discussion at that point suddenly became, at least to his mind, very important—it was a slur against his wife. I think if he had never been shown the clipping, the "crying incident" would probably have never taken place.

Another ingredient might have been a very emotional encounter that Muskie had with a group of kids in Fort Lauderdale, Florida, in a place known as The Seed, a rehabilitation center for young kids who have been on drugs. The kids sat around, and Muskie and the guy who ran the place sat in the middle with a microphone. To these kids the most important thing is a demonstration of love and affection for one another. And each time one of the kids who was there for rehabilitation would stand up and give an explanation of how he or she got hooked on drugs, the kids in unison would say, "Love you, John," or "Love you, Mary." After a while, this became very overwhelming and, when Muskie spoke, they said, "Love you, Senator," after every pause. As Muskie was leaving to get into a car, there was a black girl reporter with a microphone who said, "What did you learn from your experience here today, Senator?" And Muskie said, "That love is a very powerful weapon." My own feeling about this is that the emotional experience in New Hampshire was directly related to that summer day in Fort Lauderdale. It's important to know that the fellow who ran The Seed stood beside Muskie on that platform in front of the *Manchester Union Leader*. It's my own theory that the emotion of the encounter with the kids suddenly flooded back in on Muskie and contributed fully as much as the Jane Muskie thing to the emotionalism of the confrontation at the *Union Leader*.

BRODER. I'm very much tempted to go on from that point and talk about changing images in the campaign, but I think we need to make a stab here at the immediate post-Florida primary decision-making.

HART. What I'm specifically interested in is the response of the respective candidates to the Wallace victory in Florida, because I think it was some kind of turning point. The decision that Senator McGovern made there, like most of the good decisions in our campaign, was almost solely his own. He did check it with me, Frank Mankiewicz [national political coordinator], and Ted Van Dyk [press secretary]. He said, "I can go out and call Wallace a racist and say that people who vote for him are wrong and so forth. But it's obviously not the case; he has too many votes down here—half a million votes or something like that—and all those people aren't racists. I just don't believe it. This is a much bigger phenomenon or different phenomenon. That's going to be more or less my response. The job of the Democratic Party and the other candidates is to try to identify that phenomenon." We had been smashed [in Florida]. I think we got 5 or 6 per cent of the vote there, and it was one of the lightest weeks of campaigning that we ever had. Senator McGovern watched Muskie give his statement and then went downstairs and gave his own. Senator Muskie's was, as I recall, a fairly harsh analysis of what happened in Florida. It was a temptation to react that way. I am interested in whether Muskie reached his decision instinctively, or whether he was advised to do what he did.

STEWART. When Muskie left the room to go downstairs to make his statement, George Mitchell had a look of terror on his face because there had just been a rather heated discussion about Muskie's pulling out. I'm not sure whether he was testing us or whether he meant it. I remember George Mitchell saying, "What are you going to say when you get downstairs?" Muskie turned to Mitchell and said, "I can hardly wait to hear it myself, George." At that point, none of us knew what he was going to say. He could have announced his withdrawal as a candidate, or he could have said he was going on. As Muskie began to speak, I stood in the background and kept my eye on Mitchell. Mitchell was rather frantic about what Muskie was going to do; he thought he was going to announce a pull-out. I wasn't convinced that he was, but Mitchell had known him a lot longer than I had. Then when Muskie started to speak and attacked Wallace, Mitchell was smiling.

BRODER. What was happening in the Humphrey campaign? Humphrey went into Florida, it was the first real primary that he ever ran, and he lost to George Wallace. What was going on in your heads at that point?

CHESTNUT. We were pleased with the vote that Humphrey received. I don't think anybody expected us to win the Florida primary once George Wallace had entered it; I think it was generally conceded that Wallace would win the primary. Maybe the size of the Wallace vote was not quite anticipated. But we thought that in terms of what happened to Muskie, who was looked on as Humphrey's principal opposition, it had been a substantial victory for us.

We picked up our campaign organization and moved to Wisconsin as rapidly as we could, with what money we had. As for the issues, the themes that we spoke about in the Wisconsin primary [April 4] were pretty much the same as the ones in Florida. The thing that was so difficult about Wisconsin was that it has a crossover primary.

It is not a true Democratic primary. Somewhere I read that the winner of the Wisconsin primary has never won a Presidential election—I'm not sure whether that's accurate or not. In any event, I don't want to take away from the McGovern campaign in Wisconsin. I think they had an excellent campaign both from the standpoint of their organization and from the standpoint of the media used there. However, I think that even the McGovern and Wallace people recognized that the number of votes they received were greatly enhanced by the crossover. I think it was the Yankelovich study that indicated afterwards that had it not been for the crossover, Humphrey would have won the Wisconsin primary. Pennsylvania was really the area that we were pointing to, and we did substantially win the Pennsylvania primary [April 25].

However, from a practical standpoint, these primaries were all very difficult; they were all very complicated; and they were all very confusing to the voter. Very seldom was it a head-on-head vote between Hubert Humphrey and George McGovern and Ed Muskie and George Wallace. In some instances, the race was simply a beauty contest, and the real vote was for slates of delegates. In some states, the slates of delegates were identified as to the candidate they were going to be for, and in other states they were not. In New York, not only wasn't the name of the candidate on the ballot, but who the elector was for was also not on the ballot. We had a tremendous job to educate the small segment of the public that did vote in these primaries as to who it was that they were really casting their votes for when they went to the polls. The whole primary machinery was very complicated. The McGovern campaign must have had this problem in the primaries as well.

STEARNS. I think the McGovern campaign had the problem. We were talking before about the advantage of early planning. I had begun studying state laws just after 1968 in the primary states, but we began to do it systematically, in terms of the McGovern campaign, in the summer of 1970. I think that was probably an advantage. I think our campaign probably had a better sense of the operation of the primary machine than any other campaign. We have already touched on the weakness that hurt Governor Wallace's campaign, not just in Pennsylvania but in Maryland, where the local organization clearly did not know that there was something besides the preferential vote in the primary.

KEEFE. Do you agree that the press still hasn't studied it?

STEARNS. Really very few people have. There's no real incentive to learn very much about it because it's a boring subject.

KEEFE. I kept seeing a lot of articles about it written by renowned reporters. Alsop, for example, had a column in *Newsweek* late in December [of '71] suggesting a late primary strategy for Humphrey and others that, clearly, under the rules you couldn't do. If you wanted to go to California, which was the late primary [June 6] that he was suggesting people enter, you had to make overt moves to declare yourself as a Presidential candidate on January 24; and if you did that, you got hooked with Wisconsin [April 4] because you couldn't say you were a candidate in California without the Wisconsin people putting you on the ballot. There were a lot of things like that, and the press, to my knowledge, never got a handle on what the ground rules were and confused the general population quite badly.

BRODER. I think it's evident we cannot take the primaries state by state and analyze the decisions in each. Perhaps a useful thing would be to raise the question of what you tried to do in terms of shaping the images of the candidates in the primaries and what people found out about the candidates that you hadn't planned. First, though, let me slip in one quick question to Morris Dees. A question that's raised often about the primaries is whether the field is really limited by financing. Is there a serious problem in terms of financing a candidate, or is that something that we know how to do if we just use the kind of techniques that you did?

MORRIS S. DEES, JR. (direct-mail chairman for McGovern). That's a serious question. In McGovern's campaign each primary financed the next primary. We had serious problems in New Hampshire, scraping nickels and dimes from everywhere. Florida helped us in no way; we got no money there. In Wisconsin we still had serious problems because we hadn't won anything. We had to really be a winner first. We had the ideologically committed group of about 40,000 or 50,000 people who had helped us from the very beginning, and we flooded the people who had already donated with letters and telegrams to try to push us through each primary. We didn't get any money from big donors ever in the campaign, except a very little at the end, but in the primary period virtually none. All the money we got was from going back to the people who had given to us in anticipation of winning the next primary.

STEWART. You can't discuss financing without discussing the effect of Gallup and Harris polls. It's just huge in my experience.

DEES. It's difficult to measure the effect on the small donor, but it's definitely important with the big donor.

HART. Very definitely with the big donor.

MAX M. KAMPELMAN (adviser to Humphrey). In connection with what Morris Dees was saying, I had the experience of talking to some of the McGovern people and getting the very distinct impression that if McGovern had not done well in New Hampshire, he probably would have pulled out of the race. That's my very definite impression. This could have been a function of mood, but the financial problem in New Hampshire obviously hit the candidate very hard.

Humphrey had this problem very seriously in the primaries. Jack Chestnut mentioned that we looked upon Florida as a kind of victory, which did help us a little bit. We had proved we could win. But we got into Wisconsin too late. I was with Humphrey in the western part of the state, and I went to a number of Farmers Union meetings with him at that time. These fellows were saying, "Hubert, if only we'd known that you were going to run. We're committed to McGovern. We'll try to do what we can, but it's late." And, of course, in the industrial areas of Milwaukee, we were concerned about the ethnic vote, the Polish vote with Muskie. The fact that we came out number one among the Democratic voters in Wisconsin encouraged us. We then won in Pennsylvania. But for some reason, the money didn't come as it should have. Jack Chestnut, for example, whose responsibility it was to manage the campaign, found that he was spending most of his time worrying about the finances rather than the management of the campaign. However, you do end up, somehow, in California, and you do end up with two candidates, and California is going to decide it. In California the finances hit us very hard; at a crucial point we had to shift several hundred thousand dollars to Washington out of the California primary. We had to do it. I think we made the only decision we could make, but it cost us California.

The financial part of the primaries is something that has to be paid attention to, and also the impact of the press and the polls. I want to say for the McGovern people that they picked up after Wisconsin miraculously. Money kept coming in; their organization moved in. Every place we turned there would be a cover of McGovern. We kept saying, "Why doesn't *Newsweek* have a cover of Humphrey sometime?" or "Why doesn't *Life* have a cover of Humphrey?" But we couldn't get it.

DEES. That coverage didn't translate into any money for McGovern.

KAMPELMAN. Didn't your money begin coming in after Wisconsin?

DEES. No, absolutely not. McGovern's big asset was that we had, starting from zero donors, about 50,000 donors at the time of Wisconsin; and none of our money came in from big donors. We picked up $5,000 there, or $10,000, but really not that much money; 80 per cent of all our money in the primaries came from small donors.

KEEFE. Could you have gotten that money from the small donor if you'd gotten 15 per cent in Wisconsin and finished fourth?

DEES. Oh, no. As I said, one primary led to the other.

CHESTNUT. Hubert Humphrey ran in Pennsylvania, Ohio, West Virginia, Nebraska, and Indiana—those primaries all coming practically in a row. He won the Pennsylvania, Ohio, West Virginia, and Indiana primaries; and as Gary Hart disputes Ohio, we have doubts about Nebraska yet. The total expenditure in all five of those states for electronic media, the total, was $75,000—almost incredible in terms of running an election in states with the population they have.

KAMPELMAN. That figure was only because we didn't have it, not because we didn't want to spend it.

NAUGHTON. Did these problems dictate the change in the Humphrey strategy in California—the attack on McGovern and what that led to in the whole process?

KAMPELMAN. There was a combination of circumstances that led to that. First of all, McGovern turned out to be a great deal more serious a threat to Humphrey than we had anticipated. We were also finding that McGovern was not well known. Humphrey had, of course, the experience, and everybody knew who he was. Many of the staff were pressing Humphrey to begin debating the issues and exposing some of McGovern's positions. Little things happen—you don't know why decisions are made. The strategy change, of course, was Humphrey's final decision to make. I think the bulk of the recommendations favored his making a change. I think he was reluctant to do it.

OTTEN. Just because of being a good fellow?

KAMPELMAN. A number of reasons. One, Humphrey

perceived himself throughout the campaign as a healer. When we entered the race, he expected that all the other factions would be killing each other off and that he would be able to heal the wounds. But I think really what pushed him over personally were the attacks from the McGovern camp—not from the Senator himself, but from the staff—that were getting into the press. Attacks were made against him on Vietnam and for being part of the "old politics," as though somehow he was over the hill. I can't now recall the exact quotes, but we had them. Humphrey decided at that point that this was going to be a fight—and that he was going to fight. He rationalized it by saying, "Look, if I don't raise these issues, Nixon will. Somebody will. And these are legitimate issues." So off we went.

CHESTNUT. The decision to go for debates in California was made to a large degree on the basis of the fact that we did not have any money at that time to purchase television. So if Humphrey was going to have television exposure in California, it was going to have to come through the debate process. By and large, I think that ended up being almost all of our television time. We did obtain a little money in the final week of the campaign and we were able to put on some of our television material, but it was very slight.

DAILEY. I'd like to make a point, if I may, just to bring the forgotten [Republican] side up to date here. It's an interesting fact that our research showed that we were running well behind in Wisconsin; and while the campaign organization was being worked very heavily at the grass-roots level, we had kept a low profile in the media. Because of the situation in Wisconsin, we decided that we probably should get going and try to make some progress against our bad showing in the primaries and maybe build some groundwork for the general election. We had quite an extensive campaign mapped out. We started it, got a week into it, looked around and saw the blood flowing all around, and decided this was no place for the President, regardless of the issues. We got out quickly because it was quite hot and heavy at that time.

BRODER [to Jeb Magruder]. It was alleged at that time that you got out in hopes of encouraging a crossover vote for Wallace. Was that at all a factor in your decision?

MAGRUDER. Actually not.

DAILEY. That recommendation did come from different areas within the [Nixon] campaign organization. Then after looking at the commercials—we used to get competitive commercials as soon as they were on the air—and seeing what was going on there, we just decided that it was not a good environment for the President.

BRODER. Why wasn't money an enormous problem for the Wallace campaign?

CAMP. It was. I think we had about the same approach to it that Morris Dees mentioned. First of all, we had no money to begin with in Florida. So we went to people who had contributed to Governor Wallace before, by direct mail and other means, and asked them for assistance. Of course, having been involved in 1968, we did have a pretty good mailing list compiled by primary time. I can say our percentage figure would be 80 per cent or better of small donations. That gave us the money for Florida. From that point on, it was matter of what you do in this primary determining how much money you have in the next primary, or, at least, the ease or the difficulty of getting it. We did have a serious financial problem at times —actually throughout—it just fluctuated as to degree. It's very expensive when you're campaigning in about five states at the same time and trying to fly staff people back and forth to all of them; and obviously the candidate cannot spend a lot of time in each place, so you feel you've got to be on television two or three times a week or more with a good substantive political program.

BRODER. Looking at the change in McGovern's image during the course of the campaign, what happened and what caused it to change?

GUGGENHEIM. First of all, there are what I call real events, and there's what we call paid media. I think it was the real events that began to change the perception of McGovern. I think that Wallace votes are votes, in a sense, of discontent—sometimes translated racially because obviously race touches the lives of those people more than any other American group. What happened was that McGovern came on as sort of the political virgin, and that's always attractive to a group that wants to make a change. Somehow there's a man who can solve problems that really basically people don't feel can be solved —many of the racial and economic problems. McGovern came on as a new person talking on populist issues, and populist issues attracted that group very much. But then, I think, when Jackson began to go on the three A's—acid, abortion, and amnesty . . .

WATTENBERG. It was Senator Hugh Scott [of Pennsylvania] that coined that phrase.

GUGGENHEIM. Whether accurately or not, McGovern

felt that Nebraska was where it began. After the Wisconsin primary, some people thought that McGovern was really going to be a threat—he was moving ahead—he was the front-runner—and that they should expose his underside, so to speak. The underside was more abhorrent to the blue-collar vote than to any other group in the American electorate. Originally, McGovern was attractive to these people because he was new, because he was talking about tax reform, because he was going against the establishment. And then the underside began to be exposed, and that was really abhorrent to that group. In the early primaries, we really felt that we could get the populist vote, and we could get the blue-collar vote, and we could get the Wallace vote. I think the discussion that took place when Pad Caddell brought in the material from the Ohio primary [May 2] was that the Cuyahoga County vote—I use that as a symbolic place—could be had; it was a blue-collar vote, a Wallace vote in many respects. And it was had, and I think we came out of Ohio feeling that that really gave us another step upward, that we were not just a primary candidacy, that we were a general candidacy. But then in Nebraska [May 9] the dream began to crack.

WATTENBERG. I think that we're going to have to discuss why the other Democrats decided to attack Senator McGovern—particularly Senator Jackson and Senator Humphrey. It's very interesting that Charles Guggenheim says that Jackson attacked Senator McGovern in Nebraska. Jackson had already dropped out after Ohio; he wasn't even in Nebraska.

GUGGENHEIM. I'm saying that McGovern felt that Jackson was in Nebraska, which he had campaigned in, as I recall. Or am I wrong?

WATTENBERG. I think Jackson was in there one afternoon. I would go along essentially with what Max Kampelman said earlier about Humphrey's decision to attack
McGovern, adding perhaps that there were legitimate
issues which by their own weight were going to fall upon
McGovern's head. It was just a question of time and tactics as to when it was going to happen. In viewing that
decision, both from Senator Jackson's point of view and
later from Hubert Humphrey's point of view, you've really
got to view it both tactically and substantively.

Tactics dictate that no matter what kind of a candidacy
you're running within primaries, you don't start attacking another Democrat until you see you're behind. This
is what happened to Senator Jackson in Ohio. All along
during the early parts of the primaries he resisted attacking anybody; there were many on his staff who suggested
that he ought to, but he didn't want to. The same thing,
I would suggest, happened with Senator Humphrey's campaign in California, though I was not involved in that.
There was a point where polls were showing Senator
Humphrey fifteen to twenty points behind.

Then you get into the substance of this issue. I know
Senator Jackson felt, and I think Senator Humphrey felt,
that George McGovern stood for a lot of things that neither
of these two Senators stood for and that a vast majority
of the American people didn't stand for, and that an election, after all, ultimately decides issues. In Ohio, Jackson
said very simply, "This is where I stand on these issues,
this is where Senator McGovern stands on them; this is
where Senator Humphrey stands on them; this is where
Senator Muskie stands on them." Those were the only
four candidates in that race. Jackson didn't misrepresent
the McGovern position. He said that McGovern was for
amnesty, and that he, Jackson, was against it; he said
that McGovern took one position on busing and that he,

Jackson, took another position on it. These were very substantive points of view. It seems to me that the basic nature of the McGovern candidacy, what it stood for, was going to be revealed; it certainly would have been revealed by Spiro Agnew and Richard Nixon [in the general election]. Jackson and Humphrey both did attack it, but what really pulled the mask off was Miami. The McGovern people did it on national television. The whole troupe was going around—the people who were pro-busing and pro-abortion and pro-amnesty and stop-bombing-the-dikes—and 50 million people watched it on color television. Speaking in terms of perception rather than necessarily in terms of accuracy, that view told the American people exactly what the substantive nature of the McGovern candidacy was. I would agree only with one thing that President Nixon has said—it was then that the election was decided.

HART. A lot of points made there were fairly preposterous. Our surveys showed us all along that what Ben Wattenberg says comprised the substantive nature of the McGovern campaign were considered very, very minor issues by most people.

WATTENBERG. Busing was a minor issue?

HART. No. We're talking about the three A's.

CADDELL. One thing that I am consistently thunderstruck by in American politics is the difference between what people like us here make out of events and what the public makes out of events. For instance, take the issue of amnesty. The major place that McGovern faced the issue of amnesty was New Hampshire, and that's the place where he got it the most; but it was not costing him votes. Amnesty never really appeared as an issue ever again, in terms of moving numbers of people.

STEWART. I don't recall it as a big issue in New Hampshire.

CADDELL. It was the one negative that we got on McGovern. When it came to "What do you dislike?" or "What are you suspicious of?" it was amnesty. That was the thing that we kept getting hit with.

OTTEN. What was the importance of the Vietnam war issue in terms of determining the outcome of the Democratic primaries?

STEWART. In any poll we ever took from the time I joined Muskie's campaign in April of '71, the Vietnam war was either number one or two in importance.

OTTEN. But what was the effect of the issue on the Muskie candidacy? Did it strengthen or weaken him? It obviously strengthened McGovern. How did it react on each of the other candidates? Who did it help? Who did it hurt?

WEXLER. The best week that we had in the Muskie campaign in the early days was the week after he made the speech to the United Church Women on Vietnam. That was the only time that I can recall that the White House ever responded to a candidate during the entire campaign. I guess it was Mr. Haldeman who accused Muskie of having questionable patriotic motives.

CADDELL. I think that the issue was critical for the McGovern campaign in the sense that there were people for whom it was the major reason for voting, and McGovern had them pretty well locked up very early on. The issue was important in underlining his consistency and the strength of his stand. He had been there for so long and been so persistent.

CHESTNUT. Once we were able to establish that Hubert Humphrey wasn't personally responsible for the war in Vietnam, I don't think it was a significant issue for him as far as outcome was concerned in any of the particular primaries. I think the war was primarily McGovern's issue, at least in the early primaries. It was a major concern of the public, but in terms of being a voting issue, I don't think it cut one way or the other particularly. It was McGovern's issue in the primaries, but I think the President effectively took it away from him in the general election.

STEWART. I think that's true.

KEEFE. I think the issue hurt McGovern in the early going. I think that most of the activists on the peace side were frustrated by the lack of pragmatism in '68, and McGovern lost an awful lot of people early on who should have been for him and wanted to be for him because they thought he couldn't win and they didn't want to go through another McCarthy-type exercise and lose. Many of them ended up with Senator Muskie, when they really should have been McGovern's ideologically and emotionally.

CADDELL. On that same point: before we started surveying [for McGovern] in New Hampshire, the assumption was, on the basis of the '68 returns, that McGovern's strength should come out of Rockingham County, which is in southeastern New Hampshire and is sort of a suburb of Massachusetts. It was assumed that McGovern would not do well in Manchester. But we went in there and found out that he was doing particularly well in Manchester and getting beaten in Rockingham County. People there were saying, "I really agree with George McGovern; I'd rather vote for him, but we've got to vote for a winner this time."

WATTENBERG. We visualized a point at which, had Jackson started moving up, the war issue would have been a major problem for him. I think Scoop's position on the war was always very misunderstood. He was portrayed in the press as a hawk, but I never viewed him as a hawk; for a long time he was one of the few realists about this whole thing. It seems to me that what has been said is quite correct, that the war was a major concern but not necessarily a major voting issue. I think the issue eventually did go to Nixon because McGovern overdid it rhetorically. The correct political stance for McGovern, it seems to me, would have been to say, "We ought to get out of there; it's not our war, period." But what came out was that we're immoral and genocidal, and that we ought to go beg to Hanoi, and a whole lot of other things that Americans don't want to hear. They don't want to think that their sons or their Presidents are genocidal barbarians. And comparing Nixon to Hitler, that sort of thing, was catastrophic.

STEARNS. Although I agree the war issue hurt McGovern, I don't think you can underestimate the extent to which the war linked together and associated a faction in the party. Even though McGovern may have lost some of the more pragmatic members of the '68 peace movement to Muskie or whatever, the real basis of the Mc-

Govern campaign initially—until the point where the first primary successes scored and we began to attract people who were motivated by issues other than the war itself—was to bring together this faction and provide a network. That gave us the fifty-state campaign.

KEEFE. It gave you Morris Dees's list, for one thing.

DEES. I'd say that without the war issue, McGovern could not have raised his seed money from small donors. We mailed to lists like SANE [National Committee for a Sane Nuclear Policy], and we'd pull 25 per cent; it's a small list, but still that's a lot of dough. That's where we got our seed money. Also, all of our ideological money that we didn't get from the traditional Democratic fat cats came from antiwar people who had given up on all the peace groups doing anything and were looking for a candidate. We ran a lot of half-hour television programs and put a fund-raising pitch at the end of them. The one in which McGovern came out against the war brought in nearly $1 million at the end of it. And there was just a mere mention at the end to send money. The one he gave on the economy brought in about $50,000—this was in the last two weeks of the campaign.

HART. It would be a tragedy if we try to analyze '72 without serious discussion of the California primary. Maybe I'm just hung up on it, but I think it's an historic phenomenon. It was not just McGovern against Humphrey, it was a changing of orders. It was control of the party. That's what the fight was about, and that's why it didn't end June 6, why it went right down to the convention. So we ought to go into some depth about the California primary.

STEWART. Could we mention Illinois—because Muskie won Illinois?

NAUGHTON. Why, having gone through the attacks in Ohio and Nebraska, was McGovern not better prepared to take them on in California?

HART. I think he was. The issue that was raised in California that was not raised before was the $1,000 welfare thing. As I recall, that came out in force with the first debate [May 28]. The thing that surprised Senator McGovern in California was not any particular issue being raised; what surprised Senator McGovern—and I can remember the very second when it first occurred—was the vehemence and the depth of the Humphrey attack. It was about three minutes into the first debate. It was the first time, and the only time, that Senator McGovern's jaw almost literally dropped, because he could not believe what was happening. I know he felt that way for some time afterwards. He'd been through many campaigns and he'd been through a long series of primaries where a lot of these issues had been aired. We went into those primaries at 3 per cent and won our way up, and it wasn't without gloves being laid on us. But for the first time he really realized the depth of the feeling of some people in the Democratic Party, as represented by Hubert Humphrey, against his candidacy. Frankly, I don't think it had that much to do with the issues. It's an age-old struggle for control and power, and that's what the California primary and the California challenge were all about.

BRODER. But that should not have surprised you in terms of your original analysis that there is no middle in the

Democratic Party, that there are two warring camps, one of which has to be dominant.

HART. That's why I thought McGovern had the nomination as of June 6. Not only did we win California, we won three others that night, and that was it.

WATTENBERG. Are you maintaining that there are no substantive differences between these two warring camps?

HART. No, I think there are substantive differences.

WATTENBERG. Would you describe the nature of those substantive differences?

HART. Change versus stagnation.

WATTENBERG. Which candidate represents change?

HART. That's a rhetorical question. I'm not sure what Hubert Humphrey's program was. He was against cuts in defense spending.

WATTENBERG. That's a very important program, if one would accept that the most important issue in the 1970's is America's role in the world and what the nature of the world balance of power is going to be. That is a very positive and important program.

HART. Keeping the status quo.

WATTENBERG. Keeping a strong defense.

KAMPELMAN. Are we going to have a repetition of the

McGovern-Humphrey debate? I'd be delighted to have it right now.

BRODER. No, because Tom Houser has a question and then I have one final sort of half comment, half question.

HOUSER. I have a question of Gary Hart. As I recall, about four days before the California primary, McGovern had a lead of 15, 18, or 20 per cent, and he won the primary by 4 or 5 per cent. McGovern clearly had the superior organization, and one of the assets of a superior organization is the ability to get out the vote. What happened in those four days?

HART. First of all, your statement is premised on the accuracy of the 20 per cent gap, and I don't think we ever accepted that.

CADDELL. Going into the first debate, Quayle had a survey for NBC which showed McGovern leading by 8 per cent, and our surveys showed a 10 per cent lead. Coming out of the first debate, we had a 15 per cent lead. We were holding at 15 per cent, but the undecideds did not look very friendly, which was unusual for us. We were at 46 per cent total, which was basically where we thought we were going to stay, and did. So the 20 per cent figure, which would have been a landslide, was seriously misleading. Predictable erosion among undecideds closed the gap, although our basic vote percentage remained stable at 46 per cent.

MAGRUDER. I think this is probably the most critical point in the campaign. We [in the Nixon campaign] were looking at it as interested outsiders, of course. [To Gary Hart] I think you're overplaying your part. Earlier you said, quite correctly, and your strategy was brilliant in its conception, that you were going to co-opt the left, and you did co-opt the left. We were polling the same time that you were polling in California and before that in Ohio. I don't happen to think that amnesty was a critical issue myself, but I think the $1,000 welfare giveaway was, and I think your defense posture was a critical problem. I think that the American public, when it first perceived Senator McGovern, saw him as a candidate representing a very extreme view. I'm sure to many people it was the correct view, but to the majority of the public the first lock they had on McGovern was as a candidate of a relatively extreme left position in the American political spectrum. It was just as Barry Goldwater became perceived as a candidate of the extreme right in '64. Our surveys showed you starting to erode as soon as that perception set in, and you went downhill from that day on and never recovered. I don't think you can brush it off as being just rhetoric. It was issues.

HART. Let me correct the record. I did overstate our case. We had, in fact, to continue with the labels, what could be called a left-centrist strategy. We knew that, first of all, McGovern had to become the liberal candidate of the party, but it didn't end there. I want to make it clear that we did not think that that was all that had to be done. Our schedules will show, and every use of the candidate's time, the staff time, and everything else will demonstrate, that from the minute the McGovern campaign was conceived, we made every reasonable effort not to alienate the so-called center or the so-called regulars. The Senator talked to labor leaders, to farm leaders, to county chairmen, to state chairmen, to party leadership, and to practically everyone else. We knew we had to get the nomination without alienating the regular party, the rank-and-file, the mass of people who would, in fact, elect a President. We didn't have a kamikaze kind of mentality about it. We knew what the ball game was. On the substantive issues, all I'm saying is that, for one reason or another, the success of Senator McGovern's candidacy so threatened enough people that the issues that he had raised and raised successfully with a large number of voters—millions of them—became the rationale for personal attack, which later hurt us.

STEWART. Could I make one observation as a guy who is now a member of the press who was during the campaign observing it as a non-member of the press? I'm going to talk about the press because you can't have these discussions without talking about the press. The bulk of the press was so busy with the personalities of Frank Mankiewicz and Gary Hart and the nuances of the politics of the campaigns that it was not until California that the press actually concentrated on the issues—and only then because Hubert Humphrey made the issues important. The public should not have had to wait until California to develop a perception of McGovern's positions because McGovern had been a candidate for two years at that stage. It struck me that the press was so busy with the feature stories on the campaign that it was not doing its job in terms of reporting what the candidates were saying.

STEARNS. Part of the reason was the press's difficulty in coming to terms with the candidate [McGovern] who by every traditional measure of political success was going to fail. They never could quite square the guy at 3 per cent in the Gallup poll with the guy who was winning in Wisconsin and Massachusetts. So a myth began that around McGovern there was a Machiavellian group that managed to translate the most unpromising Presidential material in the nation's history into the successful candidate that he really wasn't. What I detected was an immense curiosity in the press.

OTTEN. When can we get equal time?

KEEFE. Somebody said it was the "Ted White syndrome." His books, made up of all those little things, sold so well that every reporter went out to cover those little things so he could sell a book like that.

DAILEY. When you're running for the nomination of the opposition party in order to run against an incumbent President, maybe you are led to take an extreme side in order to get the nomination. Goldwater took the right in '64. You all took the left in '72. Then by the time you get the nomination, you can't get back to the center fast enough.

BRODER. I have a final question, which I'm going to give to Jim O'Hara. After listening to the discussion here, I want to state a premise, which is that if the resources and knowledge of the rules of the game had been equal, and no chance events had intruded, the winner of the Democratic primaries this year would have been George Wallace.

JAMES G. O'HARA (chairman of the rules committee, Democratic convention). That is a difficult one for me because I have a particular local situation involved in Michigan, and it's hard, sometimes, for me to see the rest of the country when I see my own situation so strongly. But I would say that, if all those things had been equal, George Wallace would have done very considerably better than he did. He wouldn't have done so well everywhere as he did in Michigan, where there was a crossover primary. As in Wisconsin, there were very substantial numbers of Republicans crossing over to vote for Wallace in the Democratic primary in Michigan. And then we had the busing thing in Michigan. But I think that a lot of the resentments that expressed themselves in Michigan, Wisconsin, and elsewhere where Wallace did make a showing are common to the country generally. I think if Wallace had had equal financing and equal knowledge of the rules, and had been able to foresee how well he might have done in some of these places, he would have been a more substantial factor at the convention, certainly.

3
The
Conventions

ALAN L. OTTEN (*Wall Street Journal*). We are now moving into what is probably the most familiar part of the campaign because it was certainly the most closely watched—the period of the two conventions. I'd like to ask the representatives of each Democratic candidate about their perception of the make-up of that convention, how it differed from previous conventions, whether they believed that the nomination really was pretty well locked up before they went to Miami, and what strategy they started off with at the convention. What was the stop-McGovern strategy—was it a strategy to take the nomination from him, or just a strategy to preserve bargaining positions for after November? What were the realistic chances of stopping him? Let's start with the McGovern people.

GARY W. HART (campaign director for McGovern). We went into the convention [July 10] with only one real question—whether or not we would get our California delegates back. We believed that if we got them back, we would have the nomination. That question occupied almost all of our time after the credentials committee meeting in Washington [in June]. A great deal of time and effort went into the factoring out of the possibilities. Rick

Stearns and a lot of other people spent time counting noses, talking to delegates around the country. Then there was the parliamentary side. We spent a great deal of time on that, particularly in the few days immediately preceding the convention and then in discussion with the convention chairman [Larry O'Brien], Congressman Jim O'Hara, and others. What had started out as a very broad issue involving the future of the Democratic Party finally narrowed itself down in the hours immediately prior to the convening of the delegates to some intricate and fine procedural questions. Almost everyone here was involved in those—certainly Congressman O'Hara and representatives of all the campaigns. The reason the debate was so intense on those obscure parliamentary questions was that everybody knew that they were the ball game. That's why we spent time in endless meetings trying to come up with all kinds of possibilities. I think that Senator McGovern made himself very clear on his view of the attempt to steal those delegates from us. We saw it as a struggle to the death.

OTTEN. One of the things that did come up in the period just before the convention was some rather inflammatory talk by Senator McGovern of a party bolt. Was that a calculated tool, or was that just something he wanted to get off his chest?

HART. I can't really say. I expect there was a combination of several motives. I know McGovern was genuinely incensed. He used stronger language on that particular issue than I ever heard him use prior to the heat of the fall campaign. I know he felt very, very strongly about it. I don't think it was an intemperate outburst; I think it was a temperate outburst, if you will.

OTTEN. Several people here have suggested that we slighted the California primary earlier due to the pressure of time. So I wonder if we could just drop back for a minute before we move on to the other campaigns. How did McGovern people see California? Was it just the struggle for the California delegation and the ['72 Democratic] nomination, or had you come to see it as a broader, longer range struggle?

HART. By the time we got to California, we thought that McGovern was going to win that primary and win it much more easily than any of us had ever anticipated. What was really the shock to us was the intensity of the feeling that developed against McGovern out there. The reason that that is important is that it laid the groundwork for the hatching of the stop-McGovern movement. Bob Keefe and others, of course, know the background of that much better than I do.

ROBERT J. KEEFE (consultant to the AFL-CIO). You're giving me greater power than . . .

OTTEN. Why don't you take it? That's one of our privileges here. How was the stop-McGovern movement and the California challenge put together?

KEEFE. First, McGovern won the California primary. I think he would have been prepared to challenge the California delegation had he lost; if he didn't, it would've been the only one he hadn't challenged. The Democratic Party nominates by the convention system, and we all try to win the convention. The convention system gives you certain alternatives in the way you conduct your convention campaign. When you control the credentials committee, you can control the people and thereby control the convention. It was as simple as that. We thought that somebody other than George McGovern should be nominated.

OTTEN. How did you establish the liaison among the Jackson, Wallace, and Humphrey people?

KEEFE. It's hard to believe, but it evolved during the credentials committee meetings before the convention. There was no planned program for a stop-McGovern movement. In the credentials committee a caucus developed and evolved; it included people who were not principals in the campaigns. Stanley Bregman, for example, became the unofficial leader of the group, and his role in the Humphrey campaign prior to that time had been not minor, but not major.

JACK L. CHESTNUT (campaign manager for Humphrey). He was a regional coordinator.

KEEFE. Yes. [To Billy Joe Camp] And who represented Wallace up there?

BILLY JOE CAMP (press secretary for Wallace). Drayton Pruitt.

KEEFE. Had he been a principal in your campaign?

CAMP. No, he was elected as a Wallace delegate in Alabama.

KEEFE. It was generally so. In the course of working together in the credentials committee, this second layer of campaign people developed a cohesion that was not supplanted by top-level coordination until everybody got to [the convention in] Miami.

OTTEN. Did you all perceive this as the only way of stopping McGovern?

KEEFE. I thought that in order for someone other than George McGovern to be nominated, you had to bring him into the first ballot under 1,200 votes. The only way you could do this was to keep him from having 271 delegates from California.

HART. Did the second-level people bear portfolios from their principals?

KEEFE. They did on the questions of credentials. The cohesion just developed—it really happened that way.

HART. Whose idea was the challenge?

MAX M. KAMPELMAN (adviser to Humphrey). The labor man from California, Sig Arywitz. It was his idea originally. He's the one that turned up the California polls, got all the Humphrey people, got everybody. He talked to me and said, "You know, in this state now, the majority of the Democratic voters don't want McGovern, and they don't even have one delegate."

OTTEN. Hadn't Senator Humphrey been fairly firm in saying he would not bring that challenge? What did you have to do to persuade him to retreat from that position?

CHESTNUT. As a matter of fact, at the time, I think Senator Humphrey wasn't even aware of it.

KEEFE. Well, Sig Arywitz got it started, and then it was developed by Stanley Bregman and Mark Siegel.

CHESTNUT. They brought it to me, and I approved it.

OTTEN [to Ben Wattenberg]. Do you have anything to add to this?

BEN J. WATTENBERG (adviser to Jackson). I was not involved in it. I was Jackson's representative on the platform committee, and during its hearings the same sort of anti-McGovern coalition developed organically. We sat down in a room for two full days—about twenty people —and splits developed. Bob Nathan was representing Humphrey, and I was representing Jackson, and we started agreeing on a lot of things. On certain things the Wallace people came with us; on certain things the Muskie people came with us; and we just disagreed substantively with many of the things that the McGovern delegates—Toni Chayes, Bella Abzug, and a number of other people—were saying. I would stress that organically these things do grow up, and they stay pretty rigid for a while.

KAMPELMAN. By the time of the convention there was indeed a strong feeling on the part of the other candidates that it was in the best interests of the Democratic Party to stop McGovern from getting the nomination.

OTTEN. There was a period when Muskie was on the point of endorsing McGovern, and then he didn't. Every day in Miami there was a new rumor, but Muskie stayed in as part of the coalition. What pressures were working on him?

RICHARD H. STEWART (press secretary for Muskie). From everything that was going on around us, everything we had heard, everything we had heard him say, some of us were convinced that Ed Muskie would endorse George McGovern during his speech at the National Press Club [June 9]. He asked me for a point of view, and I gave it to him. He listened to me for about ten minutes, and then he said, "Thank you very much." He never indicated to me one way or the other what he was going to do; but I just believed, and it was a consensus among my associates in the campaign, that Ed Muskie that day would endorse McGovern.

KEEFE. Had Muskie pulled out on that day, it would have been all over.

HART. That was it.

STEWART. To understand the decision Muskie made about the Press Club speech, you have to understand the man. He honestly believed that by endorsing McGovern at that point, he would shut off the process; he was not unaware of the fact that his endorsement at that stage would lock it up for McGovern and preclude any other candidate, including himself, from having any opportunity to get the nomination. Apparently it was a responsibility he did not wish to assume at that point. It was just that Muskie felt the convention should go its way and work its will and be done. He felt that he could not become God. He said that in public, and he also said it in private.

OTTEN. Why did Wallace stay in?

CAMP. Let me add one thing here in historical retrospect. The first word of a stop-McGovern movement came to us at the time that Governor Wallace was hospitalized in Maryland prior to the California primary. It was not directed towards delegates, but called for all of us to get together in California and help Senator Humphrey there so that the thing would still be open.

OTTEN. Who did that come from?

CAMP. I can't recall. To my knowledge, though, it did not come from any of the particular campaign staffs. I think it was more of a movement on the part of some governors. We decided not to go along with it, but to think about it for a while. That must have been the attitude that many of the other candidates took also, because the movement did not materialize. When the movement to challenge the California delegates came up in the credentials committee, the Wallace people there were without portfolio as to what their action should be. I guess I was the first staff member to talk to Drayton Pruitt at the credentials committee. He asked me what I thought about it, and, like Mr. Chestnut here, I said to go ahead. I got to Governor Wallace with it and found out that he agreed, also Charlie Snider, our national director, and others. So from that point on, we were in the ball game to stay.

RICK G. STEARNS (deputy campaign manager for McGovern). I would like to speak to the point about the large number of challenges brought at this convention and their relationship to the McGovern campaign. Prior to the credentials committee meeting, I was charged with approving or disapproving challenges on behalf of the McGovern campaign. We supported four challenges officially. One was in Washington, where the state credentials committee, which Jackson forces controlled, threw all of our delegates out of the state convention. We also supported local challenges in Oklahoma and Missouri, as well as a challenge in two congressional districts in

Illinois. This challenge, largely in retaliation for the California challenge, was later expanded to include the Daley delegation as well. Thus there were only four challenges at the convention that were officially backed by the McGovern campaign, and, with the exception of Illinois, they were not brought to the floor. We were accused, for example, of inspiring a particularly brutal challenge in Alaska. In fact, we did not have a campaign representative in Alaska before August. The Young Alaska movement, which did bring a challenge, was created by Alaskans who were incidentally drawn to the McGovern campaign because it was the insurgent campaign going. But they weren't about to listen to us insofar as bringing or not bringing a challenge was concerned. We had no real contact with them, other than mailing bumper stickers occasionally.

OTTEN. A lot of people believed that if you managed to stop McGovern, the Democratic nomination would not then be worth anything—that the McGovern people would walk out into a third or fourth party, or they would sit on their hands. It was thought that what the anti-McGovern forces were really doing was opening the battle to control the party after the November defeat.

CHESTNUT. I don't believe that. First off, I think that everyone who had gone through the campaign recognized that the convention process would ultimately determine who the candidate would be. This period was merely one part of the convention process, just as the primaries and precinct caucuses were part of it. Of course there were going to be acrimony and some speeches and some harsh words; but I think that the ultimate goal of obtaining the Presidency of the United States is certainly far more important, and I think that all of the candidates recognized that and would have pulled together after the convention was over. There was no more reason for the McGovern people to have pulled out of the campaign than for labor to have pulled out of the campaign, or for Humphrey forces or Wallace forces to have pulled out. I think this is the type of thing that can be said about any convention at any time when the position that you particularly favor doesn't prevail. The important thing is that the organization has to stay together, and I think, ultimately, the people who were involved recognized that and by and large did that. I think that Gary Hart will agree that Hubert Humphrey lined up strongly behind George McGovern during the general election and did a number of things to assist that candidacy, and to ensure that his campaign people and a number of his supporters did as well.

KAMPELMAN. I think that the idea that the nomination would not be worth having if McGovern did not get it motivated Larry O'Brien's parliamentary decisions [as convention chairman]. I so told him, as you know. I was quite indignant about these decisions, and I openly attacked Larry and said that he was responding to intimidation. In my opinion he feared that if McGovern was not able to seat the California delegates, he would not win the convention; and if he didn't win the convention, there'd be a walkout and the McGovern people would not support the nominee and the party would be split. Larry did not want to have this kind of a split, and I accused him of making decisions based on that consideration. I fully agree with Jack Chestnut that there shouldn't have been that kind of feeling, but I think there was.

WATTENBERG. As I recall it, the only candidate at the convention who indicated that he would walk out in the event that somebody else won was Senator McGovern. Some of his staff people—I think Rick Stearns, but I'm not sure—went so far as to say that Senator McGovern would head a third-party ticket if he didn't get the nomination. If there was splitting going on, as I recall that whole crazy week, it was not on the part of the non-McGovern forces.

HART. I'll report some hearsay in the absence of Frank Mankiewicz, since he attended the session on Sunday night [July 9] and I didn't. I do believe there were statements made by representatives of one or more candidates that they would sink the party rather than see McGovern get the nomination.

KAMPELMAN. I was present. It was on that occasion that I accused Larry O'Brien of selling out his principles. But I didn't hear anybody at that meeting say they would walk out—Wallace's representatives or anybody else's.

ANNE WEXLER (Democratic voter-registration director). I have to disagree strongly with Max Kampelman that Larry O'Brien was responding to any intimidation of any kind. Given the situation that he was in and given the choices that he had to make, he had no alternative except to do what he did.

KAMPELMAN. I think his so-called legal opinions were horrendous.

OTTEN. I don't think we want to refight that battle.

KEEFE. Let me go back to what Alan Otten said about the nomination being worthless if it did not go to McGovern. The people who were trying to get somebody else nominated thought that the nomination would be worthless in the hands of McGovern, which proved to be the case.

WEXLER. There were ways and ways of taking care of that problem, but we never took care of it.

STEWART. This was not all going on in a vacuum. One might get the impression that McGovern was off in a corner someplace, and that all the other candidates were together in one room, and that there was no communication. As a matter of fact, I know at least in the case of three of the principals—McGovern, Humphrey, and Muskie—there were telephone conversations of some duration on three or four occasions during this period.

OTTEN. To what end? Trying to work out a compromise, or what?

STEWART. It was an attempt to avoid the floor fight, to try to work out some sort of a compromise. My point was that it wasn't angry conversation.

OTTEN [to James O'Hara]. Do you want to go through very briefly what the pressures were on Larry O'Brien and yourself in connection with the question of what constituted a majority in voting on the California challenge or any other credentials challenge?

JAMES G. O'HARA (chairman of the rules committee, Democratic convention). There were numerous efforts to impose pressure. It's perfectly true that Larry O'Brien and I talked to representatives of all camps. I recall talking to Frank Mankiewicz and Gary Hart and their suggesting that McGovern delegates would be very unhappy if the parliamentary ruling was such that it resulted in the loss of the 151 California delegates, and that some of them might ill-advisedly wish to bolt the convention. There was no threat, but the possibilities were frankly outlined and discussed, and I suppose you could say that was a pressure. We talked to others as well—Humphrey and Jackson people, representatives of the AFL-CIO, and Wallace people. They represented the bulk of the regular Democrats—the kinds of organization Democrats that O'Brien and I were used to dealing with—and it was clear that our positions with them would be considerably weakened if we ruled in a way that permitted the McGovern people to get the 151 delegates in California.

But I think the biggest pressure on O'Brien, and I know the biggest pressure on me, had to do not with those who made an effort to bring some pressure, but with the pressure of doing a job. I'd worked on the convention rules for three or four years at that time, and I was determined that the convention rules would be fair and would work. If they weren't fair and didn't work well, that would be an indictment of my efforts over that period of time. I know that Larry O'Brien felt that the Democratic convention was sort of his swan song, and he wanted it to be a good convention. He wanted to be able to walk away from that convention and say to himself that he had done a good job and that he had put on a good convention. I think those were the biggest pressures on us. Frankly, most of the other pressures that were brought to bear were brought to bear too late. The decision on California was made sometime Friday night before the convention, and it was announced on Sunday. Most of the talking that went on, went on after the decision had been made; and it didn't change what had been decided Friday night and nailed down over breakfast on Saturday morning.

KEEFE [to James O'Hara]. Let me ask you just one question. Was your committee involved in the drafting of the temporary rules that were included in the call?

O'HARA. Yes. We drafted the temporary rules.

OTTEN. So we had the ruling on what constituted the majority.

O'HARA. The question of what constitutes a majority never became an issue, because on the California challenge, the minority report—the McGovern viewpoint—received in excess of a majority of the entire delegate body.

STEARNS. The important decision was not the decision about a constitutional majority. We [McGovern people] had more than enough votes for a constitutional majority at that point. The important decision was to honor past precedent in the convention and allow the unchallenged portion of the delegation to vote on a credentials challenge brought against their state. What was important to us was that the 120 California delegates which the Humphrey campaign conceded that we had won were voting.

O'HARA. That's exactly the point. The important decision was not what constituted a constitutional majority of the convention, but who should be permitted to vote. There were 120 California delegates going to be seated, in any event, whether the minority report—the McGovern position—prevailed, or the majority report—the anti-McGovern position—prevailed. The important decision, in terms of how it came out, was whether or not those 120 ought to be permitted to vote. In that respect, the temporary rules, under which we were operating, were identical to the rules that had been followed by every Democratic convention since 1832. And the 1832 convention rules were copied from the rules of the House of Representatives, with which I am fully familiar. There was never any doubt in my mind about the right of those 120 to vote. An effort was made to create a question, but there wasn't one, and among those that I was in consultation with on this matter was the parliamentarian of the House. The rules provided that we use the precedents of the past conventions and the House as an aid to interpreting these rules. There just wasn't any question about it. And that turned it.

OTTEN. I don't want to refight the battle of parliamentary rulings. We understood in Miami that you didn't agree with each other. We got the ruling, we got to the floor, and the first test came on this very peculiar and widely misunderstood South Carolina vote. The McGovern people had obviously done their homework very well, but I'm not clear whether anybody but the McGovern people had.

HART. We [McGovern people] had endless meetings, and the agreement was that we would try to support the South Carolina challenge for a lot of political and other kinds of reasons. Rick Stearns and I, having pretty good communication with the convention floor, thought that, at a point roughly ten states into the count, he could project whether or not we had enough.

WEXLER. The thing that really got into the craw of the people who were not supporting McGovern and wanted the rulings to come down on the other side was the one definitive ruling which Larry O'Brien made—that in the event of a dispute, someone could challenge the chair on his rulings. So, on the issue of the constitutional majority, if the vote ever fell between what was an actual majority of those present and voting or permitted to vote and a constitutional majority, there would be an opportunity to challenge the chair. This is what the whole South Carolina challenge was about.

HART. We felt that we had done the counting back and forth on this issue, and we felt we had a pretty good idea of where the cutoff point was. I was on the phone to Rick Stearns, who was on the phone to our boiler room, which was, in turn, on the phone to all the delegations. Rick's judgment at the cutoff point was that we had a problem, and that we were in possible jeopardy. We couldn't take the chance, and so, at that point, I just said, "Let's drop it." That's when the order went out to specific states to start dumping votes toward the end of the count.

STEARNS. The important part of our strategy at that point was to avoid a test vote on anything before we got to the California challenge. I knew it was going to be a relatively close vote, and so there was a chance of a test vote arising. Also, unlike Gary Hart, I felt that the South Carolina challenge was utterly without merit.

HART. The difficulty was that there were an awful lot of women delegates on the floor who didn't agree with you.

STEARNS. Exactly.

OTTEN. Was McGovern a party to the decision?

HART. We told him what we were going to do.

OTTEN [to Max Kampelman]. Was there nothing you could do?

KAMPELMAN. It seemed to us [Humphrey people] that if there were to be a vote taken of all delegates but California, we'd win the California vote. At least, this was our count. As Anne Wexler points out, Larry O'Brien's ruling made it impossible for us to challenge him because he said he wouldn't accept the challenge unless he had a real question before him. Then he said that if the real question were to come up on California, the 120 McGovern votes could vote but the non-McGovern people could not vote, even though they had been seated by the credentials committee. We felt that the cards were stacked against us, and I think it is very clear why we would feel this way. So we looked for a chance to challenge Larry O'Brien some other way. We were keeping very close track by phone of how the votes were going on the South Carolina question, hoping that that would give us the chance to challenge Larry because we felt we could overrule him on the floor. Obviously, the McGovern people saw the count just as we did and switched their votes.

OTTEN. When they started switching, there was nothing that you could do?

KAMPELMAN. Oh, we knew that.

KEEFE. We had a political question that we were dealing with—the question of a governor who was a favorite of other governors and who didn't want games played with his challenge. We [Humphrey people] had pressure on us not to screw around with the South Carolina challenge, just as you [McGovern people] had pressure from the women delegates about it.

WEXLER. The thing that we [McGovern people] were really most concerned about in the South Carolina vote was the one possibility of challenging a ruling of the chair after that vote was taken and before the vote was announced, which is the one place you [Humphrey] guys dropped the ball. If you had done it then, and we had to take a vote on it, you might have turned around a great deal of that convention. You did not have to challenge Larry O'Brien on the ruling of what is a constitutional majority; after the vote you could have challenged him on who votes.

O'HARA. On who votes, exactly. We just finished agreeing that the crucial ruling was on who has a right to vote. That could have been challenged at the end of the South Carolina balloting. Frank King had indicated that he might have such a challenge. Larry O'Brien and I were standing up at the podium, with the result in hand, waiting to announce it, expecting King to make his point of order. But he never made it. We sat there waiting for the point of order to come, and it never came. And so finally I said to Larry, "We might as well announce the results."

WEXLER. We were ready for it [the challenge], but we couldn't figure out why people didn't do it.

DAVID S. BRODER (*Washington Post*). Was there a plan for King to challenge?

KEEFE. Mr. Kampelman was our parliamentarian, and he was in touch with Mr. King.

WEXLER. And what happened?

KAMPELMAN. He didn't challenge.

KEEFE. The leadership of the South Carolina delegation, Governor John West and [former Governor] Bob McNair, were principal supporters of both Hubert Humphrey and whatever the coalition effort was. During the voting, Minnesota reported about eight votes for the position of the Governor, and fifty-six or so votes against his position. I understand from Anne Wexler that the McGovern camp thought we [Humphrey people] were throwing votes. That wasn't the case. It was an honest vote, but the problem was that we thought certain people were doing a better job on the Minnesota delegation than they actually had been doing. When the Minnesota vote was announced by the chairman, the phones lit up everywhere from the South Carolina delegation. Governor West and Bob McNair personally got Senator Humphrey on the wire and gave him "what for" in no uncertain terms. They were as irate as they can get, and they can get very irate. The report coming back from Senator Humphrey was to try to get those guys settled down and see if we couldn't get this worked out some way.

At the conclusion of the voting, the position of the Governor had been sustained by the convention. We then had opportunities to make certain parliamentary maneuvers. But the fact of the matter was that Frank King, the man who was supposed to make those maneuvers, was seated directly behind Governor West and Governor McNair, who were still bouncing off the ceiling. It was, to understate it, politically inopportune for us to do anything that might jeopardize Governor West's position. To do what we really needed to do, we had to question Governor West's ability to vote on his own challenge. So it was just one of those things: we lost complete control of our ability to act in our own best interests, because we had not done our homework very well in Senator Humphrey's home state.

CHESTNUT. A little defense for the people who had the responsibility for the Minnesota delegation. The prime responsibility for what happened was with a national committeewoman, Koryne Horbal, who was very emotionally involved with the South Carolina challenge and failed to see the Presidential ramifications in that particular challenge. As a matter of fact, she totally misunderstood what was happening on the floor and accused me of manipulating the vote. I did go to the Minnesota delegation to try to change some votes so that Governor West would be somewhat reassured that we still loved him, but she refused.

JAMES M. NAUGHTON (*New York Times*) [to Gary Hart]. At what point in that day did you decide that you would dump votes, if necessary, to lose the South Carolina challenge?

HART. That afternoon, when we were meeting—Rick Stearns and myself and Anne Wexler and Frank Mankiewicz, and maybe one other person.

NAUGHTON. And when did you consult with Senator McGovern?

HART. That night.

CHESTNUT. I wish you'd explain that to that angry committeewoman from Minnesota, because she is still mad at me. She thinks it was a Humphrey plot that changed all those votes.

HART. That was part of the plan! [To James Naughton] Why did you ask the question about McGovern?

NAUGHTON. My recollection is that it became a question after the vote when some of the supporters of the South Carolina challenge contended that McGovern must have known well in advance of the time the issue arose that it was going to be handled in that way.

HART. We were a little exuberant afterwards, and word went out that we had calculated this for weeks. In fact, the intention of the leadership of the McGovern campaign was to support that challenge if we could carry it.

KEEFE. Without jeopardizing your position.

HART. Yes. We carried that policy into the vote.

OTTEN. Given what happened, given what was at stake, was there any way that this convention could have been less divisive than it was? Were there potential compromises that somebody missed?

KAMPELMAN. Yes, there was one—a Humphrey-McGovern ticket.

OTTEN. Were there realistic compromises?

CHESTNUT. I think there was a compromise missed on the Illinois challenge. Frank Mankiewicz and myself and several others had agreed to forego our other challenges and agreed to forego a challenge on the final count for the seating of the Illinois delegation. After a period of deliberation, Frank determined that their delegation would not go along with that. Had they gone along with it, it would have certainly helped the situation.

OTTEN [to Gary Hart]. Do you agree with that account?

HART. Only in that Illinois was the state in which, in the fall campaign, we had the least trouble with the organization.

STEARNS. My impression, from watching the convention on television from a trailer outside the floor, was that things did appear divisive and somewhat strained during the procedure that surrounded the unseating of the Daley delegation and the seating of the delegation that took its place. I don't think anyone now would defend that delegation as a proper or representative delegation from Illinois. But Frank Mankiewicz had given his word of honor to the leaders of the insurgent delegation in Illinois that, in exchange for their support on California, we would not pull the rug out from under them after the California vote. We did not control the insurgent delegation—it was a group more interested in seeing itself seated than seeing McGovern nominated or McGovern's California delegates restored, and it could always retaliate against us on passage of the final report of the credentials committee. At one point Frank got Bill Singer and Jesse Jackson to agree to a compromise whereby each of the delegations would be seated with a half vote each. That, naturally, was unacceptable to Mayor Daley but we tried to go ahead with it anyway. But it was a compromise that was essentially unacceptable to everyone, and it failed to get the two-thirds required to suspend the rules.

HART. The reason the Illinois challenge delegation was seated was that the California delegates were taken away from McGovern.

WEXLER. Throughout the whole credentials committee deliberations, there was every effort made for a compromise on Illinois. But the vote on Illinois came right

after the vote on California, and the McGovern representatives on the credentials committee were in no mood,
at that point, to compromise on anything. There was
absolutely no hope that there could be any compromise
on Illinois in the credentials committee then. It was a
totally runaway situation where nobody was doing anything but seeking revenge.

OTTEN. What was Governor Wallace trying to accom-
plish with his platform effort, and why did he fail to ask
for a roll call or to force a roll call on it?

CAMP. To begin with, the Governor felt that he could
send the Democratic Party a message. All of the issues
that were presented at the convention—his platform—
were brought out in his opening statement in the Florida
primary, and he wrote that statement himself. He felt
that if he was going to get anything out of the Democratic
convention at that time, after the California question was
settled, it would be to project to the American people that
the platform issues reflected what his fight was all about.
And he felt quite sincerely that if the party adopted these
issues, it could win. Also, he wanted to see the party
realign itself again with what he called "Middle America."
Sometimes we forget that in 1948 he was the Southern
delegate at the Democratic convention that was urging
those other Southern delegates to stay in and support
Harry Truman, the nominee of the Democratic Party.
He's just more of a Democrat than people gave him credit
for. So he was trying to sell his platform to the Democratic Party. I think the election results would have been
different if the party had adopted that platform.

OTTEN. Why didn't Wallace really force a roll call?

CAMP. First of all, I don't think that there was any question that the platform planks were defeated. Had we called for a roll call, I think many of the viewers would have thought it was just a delaying tactic. This would have served to further confuse the convention, and many of us felt it was confused enough at that point.

KEEFE. I think you're understating Governor Wallace's desire for a harmonious convention. We had some discussions on the platform with several of the candidates. Clearly the Governor wanted his message to be heard, but he didn't think there was a hope of carrying it, and to push it would only create greater confusion. The Governor sincerely seemed to want to promote harmony within the party at that time.

OTTEN. One of the traditional devices for mobilizing and making psychological warfare at the convention is the platform, as well as credentials challenges. Why didn't the anti-McGovern forces coalesce on a platform fight as well as on the credentials fight? And then another question: didn't the make-up of the convention require a platform so liberal that it was completely out of touch with the electorate at large?

WATTENBERG. The reason there were no major floor fights on the platform was because of the way the rules were constructed. There were very short amounts of time to debate the planks. Opposition planks had to be filed three weeks in advance, and you couldn't bring up any new opposition planks. The McGovern people on the more extreme planks were undercutting some of their own supporters, and there wasn't very much to fight about. Everybody, I think, realized that fights wouldn't influence anybody's vote on the candidacy.

STEWART. There was no fight because every candidate at the convention had coalesced with the McGovern forces to help them keep the so-called far out planks from being adopted. There was no need for a battle because they were all on the same side.

STEARNS. I think the voters who made their decision in the November election on the basis of the platform of either party could probably be assembled in this room. Party platforms are generally not read, unless possibly when a plank jars people's expectations of the platform. Aside from its tactical significance in the convention itself, I think the platform is adopted and forgotten. All in all, the Democratic platform was a pretty non-controversial document. There was something in it for everybody—each of the special-interest groups of the party got its moment of recognition, and that was that, and everyone was happy.

WATTENBERG. I would disagree with that very strongly. There are time bombs ticking in that platform that people haven't really realized. I don't know why the Republicans didn't ever go after it more specifically. But there are issues and positions promulgated there that, if this election had been close, would have been very, very difficult. There's a massive increase in welfare spending suggested in the language there. In a close election, the busing plank could have been highly injurious. A candidate could have been forced either to renounce his own platform or to stick with its unpopular positions.

KAMPELMAN. I, for one, was impressed with the activities of the Wallace representatives in the period from the California primary through the convention. I got the message that this force was looking ahead to working within the Democratic Party. I was impressed with the number of questions from Wallace people about the rules, as though to say, "Hell, if these are going to be the rules, we're going to master them for the future and understand them and see what they can do to help our objectives in the future." There were meetings that took place during the week prior to the convention dealing with the California credentials; and during the convention week, meetings took place with a view toward action at the convention, and for the future. I don't think a meeting took place at which Wallace's representatives were not present. I thought that the clear message of the no-roll-call vote on platform was that they didn't want to embarrass or hurt the Democratic Party by requiring people to stand up and be counted on issues that might hurt them in the general election or might hurt them somehow within the Democratic Party.

OTTEN. There are a lot of things at the Democratic convention that we're going to have to skip over, as we want to move on to the Republicans. One of the things I hope we're going to skip over, on the grounds that no single episode has been so widely hashed and rehashed, is the choice of Thomas Eagleton [as the Democratic Vice Presidential nominee]. But I want to ask a concluding question on the Democrats. Once McGovern was nominated and the ticket was chosen, were there steps that he intended to take at Miami, or actually did take, to bring the party back together again for the general election? And what were the other candidates doing at this point—walking out, falling in line, or getting ready for the battle for the national committee in December? Were there things that you feel McGovern did that were a large step toward healing the party, and were there other things that he had planned to do that he never got around to doing?

HART. The business surrounding the national committee occupied us [McGovern people] immediately after the unity breakfast. And then people began packing up. In retrospect, I think what we could have done and probably should have done was to ask key people to stay. The feeling was one, first of all, of exhaustion, and that we had time to reconvene leadership in South Dakota or Chicago or some other place. I don't think it was a failure of intention—it was a failure of opportunity.

KEEFE. You probably would have [done that] had other things not happened.

HART. I'm not sure. First of all, a lot of this may have been done by Senator McGovern himself at that unity breakfast, which I did not attend. What the Senator said at the unity breakfast, I don't know—whether it provided enough of an opportunity to make a sincere effort. Without question, he felt that he was not going to win the election without the party behind him; regardless of what others considered him, he considered himself a regular Democrat, a centrist. He had come up through the party; he had created the party in South Dakota. He was not antiparty and he never intended to be antiparty, and he never thought he could win the election against Richard Nixon without Humphrey's support and Kennedy's support and Muskie's support and everybody's support. Any thought that the McGovernites were going to end-run the party is just preposterous.

OTTEN. Does anybody else want to talk about what he should have done that he didn't do before we leave the Democratic convention?

WATTENBERG [to Alan Otten]. You asked earlier

whether, given the situation at this convention, there was any possibility of a compromise that would have left the party in a healthier condition going into the election. On one level, the answer is no. There were two definite camps that had polarized; and whichever side won, the other side was going to go away mad. But in terms of the perception of the potential voters watching us on television, if somebody other than McGovern had won this terribly brutal fight, the results, in terms of November, would have been far, far less damaging. The perception that the American voters had of who and what McGovern was representing at that convention was nothing short of catastrophic; and once they felt that the McGovern element had taken over the party, it was all over. Had that element lost, you would have still had all the minuses of a split and a fight, but not the minuses of substance.

STEWART. I'd like to ask a question, just because it's always intrigued me. Why did George McGovern in Miami not ask Ed Muskie to be his Vice Presidential candidate? Why was Muskie vetoed?

HART. I don't think he was ever vetoed. He just did not have that much support from people inside the campaign. There were no champions for Ed Muskie, as there were for some other people. I suppose there may have been some residual resentments.

STEWART. It's my theory that there was some residual resentment from the fact that Muskie did not meet expectations in his Press Club speech [in June].

BRODER [to Robert Keefe]. Was there a meeting before the Democratic convention ended to set the stage for a separate campaign focused on the re-election of a Democratic Congress?

KEEFE. I think that people put two things together that weren't together. One thing was the effort by Robert Strauss [Democratic Party treasurer] to form and carry out a fund-raising effort to re-elect a Democratic Congress; the other thing was a meeting of people who had lost at the convention to establish some liaison to try to regain control of the party in the event that George McGovern was not elected. These were two separate things. I think the Strauss effort happened before the convention. I think he and Senator Mike Mansfield [of Montana] and so forth had come together on that plan before the convention, but I'm not sure of that. It's my recollection that he told me in Miami, before other events transpired, that that's what he was going to do after the convention.

CHESTNUT. I don't think that the meeting after the convention really had much stature. We planned to try to keep lines of communication open in the event that McGovern didn't win the election. We had lost the convention, but in the process of doing so, had found out that we had some community of interests. Suffering from exhaustion and acute lack of adrenalin at that moment, we tried to find some way of keeping in communication for the next few months to see where we might be going. I don't recall any discussion about regaining control of the party.

KEEFE. That meeting was not the genesis of Strauss's efforts?

CHESTNUT. No, not at all.

OTTEN. I want to move on to the Republicans, but I hope the Democrats don't all leave because we will come back to them. Although it actually took place before the

Republican convention, the first major decision of the Republican convention was taken by the President in late July—the decision that he wanted Mr. Agnew kept on the ticket. Had he decided this before the Democratic convention, or did the Democratic convention have some input into his decision?

JEB S. MAGRUDER (Committee for the Re-election of the President). I think the only important decision of the whole convention happened long before that. Though they've said the re-election committee and the Republican National Committee didn't get along, I think we did get along well; and we cooperated on the convention and on what was really the critical decision—the decision to move the convention from San Diego to Miami. If we had had the convention in San Diego, I think we would have had an absolute disaster on our hands. Not only did we have all sorts of problems with the building and the hotels and everything else, but we were going to face a demonstration situation that we would not have been able to handle in that city. We jointly decided with the Republican National Committee—with Dick Herman, who was their arrangements chairman—that we had to move that convention in April. It was an almost impossible change that we made—and we barely made it. We had a Democratic city council in Miami that wasn't always too cooperative, and we had to get out of California in a reasonable way. That move really laid the groundwork, I think, for a successful convention in the sense that we didn't have the problems that we would have had in San Diego. That, to me, was the critical decision of the whole convention from the standpoint of how our campaign was handled. If we had had a Chicago [like the '68 Democratic convention], I think we would have had considerable problems, notwithstanding the problems I am finding out that you all had.

STEWART. Was it Richard Nixon himself who decided to go to San Diego?

MAGRUDER. I think you could say that it was decided at the highest levels.

OTTEN. How about the Agnew choice?

MAGRUDER. That was built up in the media as a major decision point, but I don't think it was. I was not privy to the decision personally, but I do not know of any point when it was not considered that the Vice President would be the candidate for the Vice Presidency. The other person that was always talked about was John Connally, but I don't think that he felt or anyone else felt that it was the appropriate situation for him, or that it was an appropriate time for a change. I think that the President felt very comfortable with the Vice President. I guess if things had been different—let's say we were still in the trough of '70–'71 and it looked as if other problems might arise—maybe it would have become a major decision. But I don't think it was a critical decision. There was no time since January of '71, when I started working on the campaign as the primary staff person, that there was any question about the Vice President being the candidate on our ticket.

OTTEN. What was the overall image that the White House was trying to project with the convention? Were you trying to present an image of order versus disorder, or to bore the audience to death, or to show ethnics instead of blacks? What were the kinds of things that you were trying to do?

MAGRUDER. We tend to do our business a little more quietly than I'm finding our friends here do their business. We had major changes in our convention. We think we had a very representative convention. The changes might seem minor in comparison to the Democratic convention, but we had more women than we had ever had before, and we had made major changes in our rules. I don't blame everybody for chuckling, because it was a closed deal; but on the other hand, the Democratic convention would have been a closed deal if a Democratic President had had four successful years. I think any incumbent President who is successful has a pretty good set-up for the next four years. We felt very good about our convention. We had excellent ratings from the networks, and I think we put on a viable expression of our party's position for the electorate.

OTTEN. Who was picking the keynoters? Who was making the decisions on what went into the platform?

MAGRUDER. We had a joint group that consisted of approximately twenty people—White House aides, re-election committee aides, and Republican National Committee aides—who basically programmed and decided the whole convention—with the approval of the President, of course. It was a joint effort, with about five people from the RNC, five or six from the re-election committee, five or six from the White House.

OTTEN [to Peter Dailey]. Do you want to talk about the convention television show?

PETER H. DAILEY (The November Group—Nixon). I think the dramatic impression only turned out by accident. There was a definite effort on the part of the campaign organization to get a viable young voter group together out in the field. As a by-product of the interest that was generated early by this, a number of them came down to Miami. Of course, once they were down there, we used them in every way possible. We wanted to get them involved and integrated. As it turned out, the voter that we were interested in talking to was able to look at the youth that we had, who were vocal and energetic and articulate when interviewed on television, and then compare them to the demonstrators who appeared on the last night of the Democratic convention. I must say that I think that comparison really worked to the disadvantage of the opposition. Insofar as the media served to push the image of McGovern as a radical, the tendency was to identify him more with that group of demonstrators than I'm sure he wanted to be identified.

OTTEN. You used the phrase "the voter we were interested in talking to." Who did you see out there watching TV that you were trying to talk to?

DAILEY. I think it would be the average TV viewer—the Middle American.

MAGRUDER. The ticket-splitter. We [in the Nixon campaign] were trying to build up a new majority, in effect, which we did successfully do by attracting a group of people who historically had voted Democratic for most of their lives. You can chuckle about our programming, but we had a very effective program at that convention. Of course it was stacked; there was no opposition. We had to put on three days of television to show the country our point of view. And the fact is that we came out of our convention and moved up in the polls, and McGovern came out of his convention and went down in the polls. We were in the campaign to win, and we were going to do everything we could to hold our situation through that convention. This could have been very difficult considering the problems you have when you don't have the excitement of a contest.

DAILEY. It was also very important that the Republican convention was run with a degree of precision and organization that added to the impression that the President was a man who was able to control his own destiny and therefore to control the destiny of the country.

OTTEN. The one unprogrammed thing that seemed to come along was the fight over apportionment. Did you not see that coming, or did you decide that one fight added a little excitement, or did you try to head it off?

MAGRUDER. We did see it coming, but we really weren't interested in it. It was a fight that had historical significance, possibly, for the next convention, but it did not involve the Nixon campaign and we stayed out of it. As it turned out, though the liberals lost in the convention, they gained from the outcome of the election in that the major states will have broader representation in the next convention because President Nixon won states like New York and California. The apportionment fight in the convention was a legitimate fight essentially between big states and small states. Our convention is somewhat loaded to the small-state side.

DAILEY. One other point. If you go down the viewing quintiles of television viewers, you find that the heavy viewers are basically the voters that the Nixon campaign was trying to appeal to. We were not trying to get to readers of *Harper's,* for example. Such an effort would have been of no value to us.

BRODER. It seemed to me as a reporter that, while it was called the Republican national convention, it was actually the Nixon national convention. Was there any consideration given to using the convention as a device for building the Republican Party or Republican candidates?

MAGRUDER. Our thesis has been all along that, as a minority party with 25 per cent of the registration, we could best build the party by building a Nixon majority first. Voting habits were broken in '68, even further broken in '70, and then even more in '72. In '74 and '76, if we do the right job as a party—put up the right candidates, fund them correctly, and do the necessary planning—we will benefit from the fact that people broke habits to vote for Nixon. They will not feel so reluctant to vote for another Republican. We have felt that, by building a Nixon majority, we would eventually build a Republican majority. Of course, that did not work out in this election. In no way can we claim a Republican majority from the '72 election, but I think the changes in voting habits will have a residual effect and will assist the party in future elections.

O'HARA. What's good for Nixon is good for the party?

MAGRUDER. That's right.

J. PHILIP REBERGER (Republican National Committee). Prior to the convention, I think that some of the key state chairmen resented the fact that decisions about the convention were being made in "high places." But when the convention was over, when it was all said and done, the party leaders and the delegates—county chairmen and other lower echelon party leaders—were extremely pleased with the way the convention went and left Miami with an amount of enthusiasm that we really didn't anticipate. Those of us concerned about the purely organizational aspect of the campaign had viewed the convention as an interruption of our efforts in the field. That is, all of a sudden the state chairmen and half the county chairmen were traipsing off to Miami when they should have been doing things in the precinct. But they came back from Miami truly enthusiastic. I think even some of the reporters on the convention floor commented on the fact that they felt that some of the demonstrations were from the heart, surprisingly enough, even though the thing was obviously well scripted. We had some good benefits.

WATTENBERG. Did your plans for the convention change substantively when you saw who the Democratic nominee was going to be? I'm thinking specifically of some of those pro-labor planks. Eight months earlier, Richard Nixon was telling George Meany where he could go, and George Meany was telling Richard Nixon where he could go, and all of a sudden there was this lovefest. Did that represent conscious change, or just an organic change?

MAGRUDER. In the White House over the last four years, there was some division among the staff as to whether we should go the labor route or not. Obviously, in the end, we went the labor route. But from when we started the planning for the campaign until the end of the campaign, we literally did not have to change our basic approach.

WATTENBERG. If Humphrey had been the Democratic nominee, mightn't the stance of the Republicans have been to beat up on the unions?

MAGRUDER. I don't think so, because we were starting to see a movement that we probably would have had even if Humphrey had been the nominee. Of course, it would not have been so great a movement with Humphrey the nominee. But with Governor Wallace out of the race, the Nixon campaign was working to get that 51 per cent, and we were seeing enough movement there that I don't think we would have changed our program. As events unfolded, they just accentuated our planning. The 1970 Labor Day lovefest we had at the White House with all the labor leaders was the result of a year or two of effort. Then there was a decrease in this good feeling because of the wage-price controls. And then, with the beginning of the McGovern movement, there was an improvement again. I think that improvement was actually occurring long before McGovern was the candidate. Muskie was not in a strong position with many of the kinds of labor leaders that we were going after—not the AFL-CIO on the whole, but mainly the independents and the craft unions.

MORRIS S. DEES, JR. (direct-mail chairman for McGovern). I believe that President Nixon announced that he would keep Vice President Agnew after Eagleton was selected, but prior to the announcement about Eagleton's emotional problems. Did your security people have information about Eagleton? And knowing that this information was going to be made public, was it thought to strengthen Nixon's hand by announcing his candidate first?

MAGRUDER. I can say, without qualification, that we were aware of rumors, as everyone else in Washington was, of problems that did not relate to mental problems. We were aware of them, not from any investigative sources of our own, but mainly through our friends in the press, who knew about those problems and had discussed them at length. Then there were people in the press who suddenly realized that McGovern had put up a guy who —you know, and that was the first we really heard of it. We did not know anything about Eagleton's situation until the story broke.

OTTEN. Between the two conventions, we had the Eagleton fiasco and finally the choice of Sargent Shriver [as the Democratic nominee for Vice President], and obviously these have to be weighted into the answer to the question that I'm about to ask. But trying as much as you can to focus on the events at the two conventions—the fights that took place there, the choices, the overall image —what effect did these have on the public's perception of the two tickets—the two parties—as we come to Labor Day and the start of the campaign? [To Jeb Magruder] Do you want to start off?

MAGRUDER. I believe that the McGovern slide started before California but began to accentuate with the California primary. We were pleased with the California debates because we thought they effectively exposed the McGovern record. We were, of course, going to do that if it hadn't been done by the Democrats. Our polls showed the slide starting there, and that continued. McGovern went down after the Democratic convention, which has to say that the convention was unsuccessful and did not achieve what a convention should achieve. President Nixon went up after our convention, which said we had a successful convention. That's the way you play the game. We were very pleased by both of these events. Of course, the Eagleton problem eroded his position, but I don't think you can say that any one thing was the downfall of George McGovern. It was a series of events that occurred for all sorts of reasons early in the campaign and just continued. Our position, on the other hand, continued to get stronger. We had our China trip [in February] and our Russian trip [in May].

OTTEN. Is it your feeling that the campaign was really over at the time of the convention?

MAGRUDER. No, we never thought the campaign was over; we never let up; we went right through the campaign going at absolutely 100 per cent capacity. But I think we all realized that only a miracle could change the results, and we felt comfortable that we were going to win the election. The question was, by how much.

OTTEN [to Patrick Caddell]. Do you want to start off for the McGovernites?

PATRICK H. CADDELL (Cambridge Survey Research—McGovern). In May, in both Gallup and Harris, McGovern was trailing by eight points, and the other Democratic candidates were also trailing by eight and nine points in May. But McGovern's position relative to Nixon in July was better than the other candidates being measured at that time.

MAGRUDER. But that is not a good comparison because by July McGovern had become the front-runner of the Democratic party and was getting all the benefits of being the front-runner.

CADDELL. As of July, you have a candidate—McGovern —leaving the convention, and somewhere between one-third and 40 per cent of the people don't have any hard, tough perception of him. In May, that was a much higher figure. In the primaries, he was not a well-known candidate. There are surveys that indicate that McGovern went up in the period after the debates in California.

KEEFE. Did you have any tracking going on day by day during that period?

CADDELL. Yes.

KEEFE. When did it appear to you that Humphrey was coming back up at you?

CADDELL. When people say the California debates, they mean the first California debate [May 28]. What we had been doing all through the primaries was looking at the undecideds and figuring out where they were going. The undecideds that we were looking at in California, unlike the other primaries, did not to be disposed toward going for McGovern. There was no tremendous hostility toward him, but their leanings tended to be toward Humphrey.

KEEFE. I couldn't figure out why there was a delayed reaction. If, in fact, the debate was critical to the perceptions of the candidates in the voters' minds, why did it take them six days to react, which is about what we saw? The debate was on a Sunday, and the following weekend—the last weekend before the primary—Humphrey's strength firmed up. I can't explain it.

DAILEY. Didn't the Humphrey organization put a very

strong media effort into the Southern California media market?

CHESTNUT. No, absolutely not.

CHARLES GUGGENHEIM (media adviser to McGovern). I think Humphrey had some media, and I think it helped a little bit. It was the first time he had any, I think. But I think the McGovern media was becoming too strong. I think we began to over-kill ourselves, and our own media began to hurt us.

CADDELL. We started surveying [for McGovern] after the first debate, and we found that not very many people had seen it. But the people who had seen it did not like the nature of the debate itself; it seemed to be shifting no voters. The people who tended to watch it were the people who tended to be the strongest in their support of the two candidates.

KEEFE. Yes, I understand. [To Charles Guggenheim] You say you think possibly your media was over-killing?

GUGGENHEIM. I think everything was over-killing.

HART. But we pulled McGovern out of there for a full day.

OTTEN. What image did the public have as it entered the month of August?

HART. We all tend to talk to people that think the way we do. Strangely enough, all the people I've talked to thought that the Democratic convention was extremely well behaved, was a model of democratic procedure, even with several weeks of speculation by some columnists that there would be bloodletting on the floor, and people stripped naked, and all kinds of bizarre behavior.

WATTENBERG. You think the convention was truly representative of the Democratic party.

HART. I think when you reform an institution and open it up, you let people in who have some interests of their own—whether they be women, blacks, tax reformers, or chicanos. And then it's a little unfair and unrealistic to say, for example, that George Wiley [of National Welfare Rights Organization] was a McGovernite.

WATTENBERG. But I'm talking about perceptions— that's my whole point.

HART. What are you going to do, keep Gloria Steinem [of National Women's Political Caucus] off the floor of the convention?

WATTENBERG. I'm not telling you what you should do, but I'm telling you what happened. If that was such a wonderful convention and worked out so well, how come it was the only convention since the advent of public-opinion polling in the United States where the nominee of the party lost ground? That is an absolute fact, and I really want an explanation of it. I really don't understand it.

HART. The Eagleton business came within days after the Democratic convention.

WATTENBERG. There was a Gallup poll immediately after the convention, before Eagleton, that indicates that the gap between McGovern and Nixon rose at the time of the convention. Even after the Chicago convention in '68, with blood in the streets, Hubert Humphrey gained five points.

CAMP. I'd like to ask Gary Hart one question. Did you have any way of controlling Senator McGovern's acceptance speech at the convention?

HART. Absolutely not.

CAMP. That was the one thing I could never understand about our convention.

HART. We did not control that convention; the agenda was set by Chairman O'Brien. But Senator McGovern, in retrospect, wishes now he had called Mr. O'Brien that night and said, "Let's put it off until tomorrow night; hold everybody until Friday."

CAMP. I don't understand why he didn't.

HART. But we did not control that convention in that respect.

GUGGENHEIM [to Gary Hart]. May I correct you here? I take as much responsibility as anybody for this, but McGovern could have gotten prime time. The convention was ours as soon as he was nominated. I happened to be in Mr. O'Brien's office, just by accident, to see if I could get some tickets to put some cameras someplace. I had no authority—perhaps I should have been given it, but I didn't ask for it—to have said, "We want McGovern on at a certain time." There was nothing in that office that was in our way in having that happen—nothing. We could have had it. The representatives of McGovern at that time were one man on McGovern's staff, myself, and [California fund-raiser] Warren Beatty. It seems that I'm critical of Gary Hart and Frank Mankiewicz and the Senator and so forth, but they were involved in the selection of the Vice President—which was a terribly important thing.

OTTEN. It might have been better if they had been with Warren Beatty.

GUGGENHEIM. There was some business coming up— but why it was put on the agenda at that point of the convention seemed sort of idiotic to an amateur. The most important thing was to get the acceptance speech on, but there was this other business. No one knew how long it would take because we had this very democratic convention and the voting could go on for hours, which it did, and the discussion could go on for hours, which it did. I asked, "How long will this thing last?" They said they guaranteed that it would not last beyond 11 o'clock.

OTTEN. After the two conventions, did the Wallace people think it was all over?

CAMP. As far as Governor Wallace's involvement in the Presidential race was concerned, yes. Shortly after returning to Alabama we found that Governor Wallace would need additional surgery, which, of course, removed him from practically any activity in the race. We further found out that in Alabama the vast majority of people were just plain mad about the Democratic convention. And I don't mean just the Wallace supporters. I had many people tell me personally, "I know what I'm going to do—I'm going in and pull the ear of the elephant and to hell with all of them." At that point the Governor was, of course, concerned with his health, but the staff members realized that we had an in-house, in-state Democratic problem. Our first thought was about how we were going to save Senator John Sparkman. As to the Presidential race, the people of Alabama seemed to have made their decision; and our efforts turned to support of state Democrats.

O'HARA. To go back to the Democratic convention: the timing problem came from a couple of things. One of them was a flaw in the rules—it was much too easy to put somebody in nomination for the Vice Presidency. If I'd had my way [as rules committee chairman], it would've been harder, but I was out-voted on that subject. I think we ought to make it harder next time. I think we ought to abolish the Vice Presidency to start off with, but, failing that, we should make it harder to get nominated. The remainder of the delay was caused by the fact that the McGovern people couldn't control their own delegations. They weren't their delegations, in effect. They happened to be for McGovern, but they weren't in a position to be disciplined. It was the New York delegation, the Colorado delegation, and the Massachusetts delegation that hung that thing up until 3 o'clock in the morning. People were working to get them straightened around and couldn't do it.

GUGGENHEIM. Could you have put the acceptance speech before that?

O'HARA. None of us anticipated that we would be so late. We anticipated possible difficulty on the Vice Presidency, which we had; but if that had been all, we still would have gotten through in time to get most of America while they were still awake. It was the additional problem that we didn't anticipate—getting hung up by obduracy in several delegations that were McGovern delegations. I think we lost the election at Miami. It was not any specific issue, not anything Senator McGovern did. But the American people made an association between McGovern and gay lib, and welfare rights, and pot-smoking, and black militants, and women's lib, and wise college kids, and everything else that they saw as threatening their value systems. I think it was all over right then and there. I don't think there was anything, really, that could have been done afterwards either.

HART. The irony is that we [McGovern people] were fighting as hard as anyone else to beat those planks down.

O'HARA. That's right, but that's the way it worked out.

OTTEN. Let's finish with Humphrey.

CHESTNUT. Obviously, we went into the Democratic convention fully intending to win it for Senator Humphrey. We felt that we had a chance, and we had put together a pretty hard-working team to run the necessary delegate checks. When it became apparent that it wasn't going to happen, we lost a certain amount of adrenalin. We were tired from running in eight or nine primaries over a period of some six seven months. But Senator Humphrey made it very clear that he intended to support Senator McGovern—that this was not a situation where he expected us to take our marbles and go home. Senator McGovern assisted him in 1968, and he expected to assist Senator McGovern in 1972. We recognized that it was going to be a very difficult fight. I think the one criticism that I would register is that we did not really receive overtures from McGovern's staff. I had a campaign staff at my disposal and was never asked about who might be willing to work in the McGovern campaign—who in a particular state would be good, this type of thing. Perhaps I should have volunteered this information, but when you lose, you like to be approached.

OTTEN [to Richard Stewart]. Do you want to add anything?

STEWART. I remember Muskie marveling after the convention that the cynics had been wrong. He was impressed with the fact that the convention had been controlled enough to prevent the ugly demonstration on the floor that had been predicted by the press. He thought that was a major plus in terms of the outcome of the convention.

However, I think one important thing happened that nobody has alluded to. McGovern made a statement before the nomination about retaining a residual force in Thailand. This came as a shock to me, and I know it came as a shock to many others. It seemed that McGovern, with the nomination in his grasp, was suddenly reversing his position and trying to capture the element of the party that had eluded him. He was trying, in effect, to become a Muskie, while still being perceived as a McGovern. As I recall it, the kids were so upset with that statement that they came in great numbers to the hotel, and McGovern was forced to come downstairs to confront them on that position.

It's my theory that the manner in which McGovern won the nomination made it impossible for him to win the election, because he suddenly had to shift from being a so-called radical and try to win back labor, the Hubert Humphrey supporters, the Muskie supporters, and others. I will always believe that if he had just maintained the position of being a maverick and being hard on the positions he took, he would at least have had the respect of the public—which I think would then have been more apt to vote for him. Also, of course, the contrast of the two conventions worked against McGovern. The Republican convention was a masterpiece of promotion and public relations.

4
The
General
Election

JAMES M. NAUGHTON (*New York Times*). We move on now to the general election—although there seems to be some question why. The suggestion was made by someone earlier that the election was determined in May. Someone else said it happened in July. Someone chose August, and someone even suggested that it had been predetermined by the strategy McGovern adopted in 1970. In any event, the election did occur, and we would like to discuss some of the decisions that were made in the general election and their ramifications. Was there any way that McGovern on Labor Day of 1972 might have resurrected this campaign that we apparently have all decided was dead?

GARY W. HART (campaign director for McGovern). I don't think at that time or at any subsequent time, contrary to what some people have written, we felt it was a losing cause. Until the moment that one of the networks gave Ohio to the President, I personally felt that we were going to win that election. Certainly no one ever thought that if we did lose it we would lose it by the margin that we did. So it would be wrong to make any attempt to look back and say that the McGovern campaign organization at some particular point felt that the campaign was lost. However, it became apparent to us sometime during the fall that there was a strong possibility that this might be the first election in history where the popular majority was lost and the election was won by an electoral majority. We talked a lot about that, and about what states might constitute an electoral majority, because we knew there were a number of states we were going to lose very badly. We had pretty well written them off in the sense of allocating statewide media or the candidate's time to those states.

We had campaign organizations in all fifty states, and we encouraged those organizations. August was a very bad month for the campaign, first Eagleton and then one thing after another. It was like trying to get started, and every time you stood up, somebody knocked you down. By the first of September, we had state organizations in all fifty states, and we had state coordinators out of Washington or somewhere else assigned to those states. About thirty or more states had, in effect, national staff members in them running the campaign. We had campaign committees set up.

The absolute rule of the campaign adopted by the Senator and myself and everyone else was that the campaign was to be a part of the Democratic Party. That is to say, nobody who was a Democrat was to be shut out of participating in the fall campaign. We did not consider it a McGovern campaign; we considered it a Democratic campaign. If we did make mistakes, they were errors of not taking enough time to contact people like Jack Chestnut to get names, and so forth. We did finally meet sometime in September—the second or third week in September—with about thirty or thirty-five key Humphrey organizers and gave them all job assignments; and some of them performed very well. But if we'd had more time and if we'd had more manpower in the McGovern campaign, we could have done that outreach, bridge-building effort a lot better. It was primarily Larry O'Brien's task to build bridges between the original McGovern campaign and the regular party, mainly through its elected officials, its party officials, labor leaders, and others. It was a difficult task, but I think we were trying to carry it out.

What sticks in my mind about that fall campaign was its brevity. In one respect, it seemed to go on forever and never end. In another respect, compared to the nomination race, it was a very, very brief campaign of ninety days. We had done rather extensive planning beginning in May, when it looked as if we would probably get the nomination. Although almost all of our efforts through May and June and early July were directed towards locking the nomination up, there was still extensive planning, particularly on political organizations and budgeting and so forth. So it wasn't as if we got the nomination and only then had to start thinking about winning the election. A lot of thinking had gone on in the mechanical, functional areas of budgets, allocation of staff members, and so forth; and we had done political analysis as well. We knew which states we would do well in and which states we would do poorly in. In states where we had run strong primary campaigns, we felt that we had a chance to crack what would normally be considered Republican states, such as Wisconsin, Oregon, perhaps even Ohio. There was discouragement over the troubles we'd had in August, and we were still trying to recover from the Eagleton matter. But there was a great deal of hope and everybody was working.

NAUGHTON. How, specifically, did the Eagleton affair change your strategy as you had conceived of it in May? And what impact did that have in your decisions about which states to go into?

HART. The one obvious change was Missouri; it was a marginal state for McGovern anyway, but we had thought we could win it with an all-out effort. In terms of the other states, I don't think the Eagleton matter changed our political strategy at all. The biggest impact it had, in terms of just getting the campaign off the ground, was financial. There was no question that it set back our financing of the fall campaign by three or four weeks, and that proved to be a very difficult problem for us.

NAUGHTON [to Jeb Magruder]. How did you folks perceive the campaign in September, and how did the Eagleton affair change your strategy?

JEB S. MAGRUDER (Committee for the Re-election of the President). No matter which side you're on in a campaign, whether you're looking very good or not looking so good, I don't think you ever give up; nor do you ever think you have it made. We didn't think we had it made. We thought we were certainly ahead, and we thought we were going to win; but we had to think that something could happen and events could change, or we could make a gaffe, or McGovern could somehow turn things around. But by September 1, most of us felt that we were going to win, and the question was how we could build a bigger win than was forecast in the polls. We were surprised with the size of the win. I don't think at any time, even up to the last week, we had any indication of anything more than 56 or 57 per cent, which we thought would be a very good win. So we never gave up trying to do better, right up until the last week of the campaign. We made Gary Hart an important figure in our campaign when he was quoted as saying, "If the Nixon people underestimate us as the Democrats did, we'll kill them."

We took that and put it on a big two-by-four sheet and passed out over 4,000 copies to every headquarters we had. I had it on the door of my office from the day he said it.

Another thing: Bob Teeter [of Market Opinion Research] has a theory that once a negative impression of a candidate is fixed in the mind, it is almost impossible to reverse it; and, similarly, if it's a positive impression, even if it's incorrect, it's difficult to reverse it. What we feared most about Muskie was that the positive impression that he had made on election night in '70 was possibly irreversible, but, fortunately from our standpoint, he reversed it himself. We thought that in May and June, and then later because of things like the Eagleton affair, McGovern was locked into a public impression that was very negative; and it would have been very difficult for him to revise the public impression that he had made.

Basically, our strategy, which we really did not change to any great extent from the beginning in '71 when we started contemplating the campaign, called for a heavy use of surrogates in place of the President. We found this was very effective. We cooperated with the Democrats for Nixon in their emphasis on what we thought were McGovern's deficiencies. We made moderate use of advertising and a very heavy use of direct mail, and used telephoning only for identification and get-out-the-vote purposes. We did absolutely no persuasive work because we felt that it was not necessary; we saw our problem as simply getting our vote identified and getting it out. So our people did not go in and try to pitch the President's record or anything of that kind; they mainly tried to identify all pro-Nixon voters, and then we tried to get them to the polls.

MORRIS S. DEES, JR. (direct-mail chairman for Mc-

Govern). Would you explain your use of direct mail in a get-out-the-vote effort?

MAGRUDER. We took the ten or eleven states that we had targeted early as going to be important under any circumstances with any candidate, and we computerized the voter-registration lists for both parties, if there was party registration, or for the total electorate, and then we cut it demographically and by past voting behavior.

DEES. How did you cut in past voting behavior with the voting lists?

MAGRUDER. For example, we took an area that according to the Census Bureau had income levels over $10,000, and then went back to the past voting behavior and found out where, say, the Reagan vote came in California. If the Reagan vote came in areas with incomes over $10,000, they were targeted as areas we were interested in. Or if our polls showed that we were going to do well with blue-collar, labor union workers, with certain demographic characteristics, we computerized the relevant information so we could pull it out by area. Obviously, we got overlap, but we were able to target our mail and our telephone activities into those areas where we felt we had the highest potential opportunity. These included areas of the basic Republican constituency plus what we have called our emerging new majority, primarily the blue-collar, urban, ethnic-type people. So in eleven states we had this computerized activity and mail and telephone; we had 250 telephone centers in those ten or eleven states. In the other thirty-nine states, we asked the state organizations to try to produce similar programs, but we knew full well they couldn't do it because the lead time was just too short. It was to our great advantage that we did have lead time, because this program was expensive and very

complicated and took us a good six months to put together.

DEES. How would you compare the expenditures of telephone and direct mail with expenditures of television and
radio media?

MAGRUDER. Pete Dailey and I always disagreed about
this subject—Pete thought we were spending too much
money.

PETER H. DAILEY (The November Group—Nixon). The
resources went into direct mail and various voter-identification things, but our media group in the general campaign was counseling that we hold off on our media expenditures. We held off two weeks in starting, or a week
and a half in starting, and spent substantially less than
we had originally budgeted. We thought we should plan
to spend the maximum and then move off of it, rather
than plan at the beginning to spend less.

NAUGHTON. Could you go into your general strategy for
use of the media and how you made the decision on what
it was you were attempting to convey, in terms of both
the President and McGovern, and how you went about
that?

DAILEY. Maybe I should, first, go into the structure of
our operation. Jeb Magruder and his group decided very
early in their planning to move toward a "house agency."
But when I was brought in, we agreed that a house agency
would be the wrong thing to have. If we had a house
agency, all of the people in the media function and the
advertising function would have to be on the payroll of
the Committee to Re-elect; and if that was so, our group

really couldn't operate as an outside council, with independence. So the November Group was established and organized as a separate company with a separate budget, which was only approved in total, not in its individual units.

Very early on, we tried to set up a positioning statement for the President. The President likes football analogies, and the relationships of field position and ball control really were the essential elements of what the campaign organization tried to do. I think we all felt very early that the most important thing we could do was to find a position for the President that we could move from. The research that we looked at in January, when we really began to put this together, showed us that on the issues we were in a relatively bad position; and it also showed a general dissatisfaction among the electorate with the direction of the country. While the people agreed with the President on some things and disagreed with him on others, this overriding dissatisfaction was going to work to our disadvantage if we weren't able to find a way around it.

But the more that we looked at the research, the more we found that the President really had the beginnings of a unique position, and that was that while people were dissatisfied with the direction of the country, their feeling seemed directed more at intangibles of government, and bureaucracy, than at the President. So, very early, we felt that the most important single thing we could do was to have the President take a position on the side of change. He had to be somebody who was identified as being for change, who was operating for change; and even though his performance in certain areas was not necessarily what people were satisfied with, he would be identified as a person who was moving for change. Everything that we developed from then on in the positive advertising that we did under the banner of the Committee for the Re-election of the President embodied in it the concept that the President is working for responsible change. A week before the election, there was a Harris study that came out showing that the President was perceived to be more on the side of responsible change than George McGovern; we were quite pleased with that because it was quite a dramatic change from what had appeared in January.

Looking at the research, we found that the President had, in terms of his personal characteristics, a number of strengths and a number of very obvious weaknesses. He was perceived as being rather cold and as having a lack of frankness. We felt that we could not try to change the negatives—that if we began to position our media against those negatives, we would really be working against impressions that had been built up over his entire life as a professional in politics. So we believed that we had to move from the positions of strength—the professionalism, the toughness, the competence in office. As for the areas of weakness, we would either ignore them or try to create a better understanding of them.

In the area of frankness, we felt that deep down the voters were willing to accept a President who was less than frank with them. There's a difference—and a very fine line—between being honest and being frank, and we felt that the American electorate was willing to accept the fact that a man as President sometimes had to do things, in relation to his international stance and other things, about which he couldn't always be candid with the electorate or with the country. Honest, yes. So we just simply didn't move against that at all.

As for the area of lack of warmth, we thought this was a problem only if we were going to face a candidate who could turn the campaign from issues to personality, and we didn't see any such candidate on the other side. We also felt that we could deal with this area of lack of warmth in a modest way by trying to create an understanding of the man as being shy rather than cold. Interwoven into the documentaries and into some of the commercials were little touches of lightness to try to show this shyness. In one, for example, there was a thing with Tricia Nixon talking about the fact that on the night before her wedding, the President wrote her a note and slipped it under the door. It was a very warm, personal note from father to daughter, but he just couldn't tell her his thoughts personally and he felt that he could express them better in a note. Our testing showed that by using things like this we were beginning to create an understanding of the President as a shy man rather than a cold man.

One of the most effective things that we did during the campaign, of course, was the negative material for the Democrats for Nixon. Looking at the vote, there was a core of 43 per cent which was basically Republican. To get from 43 to 50 per cent and beyond, we used positive work—to provide people with reasons why they should vote for the President—and, as we got deeper into the hard core of the Democratic vote above 50 per cent, we used negative work—to show them why they shouldn't vote for the other man. We wanted them to "consider the alternatives." Some of this negative material was already developed before the Democrats for Nixon organization was established, and we tested with the signature of the Committee for the Re-election of the President. Then later, when Democrats for Nixon was formed, we changed the signature to Democrats for Nixon and found in testing that the same commercials were far more effective with that signature than they were with the signature of the Committee for the Re-election of the President. What the material did was to reinforce the attitudes of Democrats who were defecting. These Democrats had made their decision to vote for Richard Nixon, maybe for some of the reasons we were exploiting in the commercials, but the fact that people like John Connally, who were highly credible Democrats, were doing the same thing served to reinforce their decision.

There was a recent study by a Syracuse University political group comparing 1968 and 1972. In '68 in the last three weeks of the campaign, the Democrats who had shown a preference for Richard Nixon earlier went back to their regular party affiliation for the election; but in 1972, the Republican candidate was able to hold on to those disaffected Democrats. The study felt that one of the strongest factors in this change was the series of commercials run by Democrats for Nixon. According to the study, the most effective commercial showed a picture of George McGovern looking south on one side and north on the other; there would be a quote from McGovern facing this way, and then the picture would flip to him looking the other way and there would be an opposite quote. That one, more than any other, was effective in reinforcing attitudes as to why you shouldn't vote for George McGovern.

We had prepared for an all-out campaign. We were, in our early planning, really preparing for the worst. We were looking at a strong Democratic Party candidate and at an even stronger George Wallace as a third-party candidate. We were also looking at a whole new stricture on the campaign that had never existed before—the new federal election law. What this law did was to restrict the total spending for each candidate to 10.43 cents per voter, which is about $15 million in the general election. In 1968 the Republicans spent about $26 million on media, and the Democrats spent somewhere around $18 to $20 million. And Richard Nixon only won by a very slim margin. If you have a minority party and you have outspent your competition by maybe 40 to 50 per cent and barely won previously, and then somebody tells you that you have to play under new rules the next time whereby each party has the same amount of money to spend, you have to say that you really have troubles.

In 1968 in the latter stages of the campaign, when we found that we were in trouble in a state like California or Illinois, we would run around and find people with money and say, "We've got to get some more money to put another three weeks of television in here." We would raise another $500,000 for California, another $200,000 for Illinois, and we would scrape by. But coming into 1972 in the planning stages, this was no longer possible. You had one bag of chips and that was it. You had to be able to move your funds around in the latter stages of the campaign without violating the law, so you had to have absolute and total control every day of every dollar that you had committed. You didn't want to be in a situation in the last two weeks where you badly needed more media effort in California, which is a very costly state to advertise in, and find that the only place to get the money was from New York or Illinois or Ohio, other states that also have high media costs. So absolute and total control of the financial situation was a major concern for us, and up until the first week in October, we had a daily report on each dollar spent and each media authorization that was provided.

THOMAS J. HOUSER (Committee for the Re-election of the President, Illinois). Coming back to Jim Naughton's original question, those of us who were working for Nixon in the heartland certainly didn't feel that the election was over in August. We really didn't have our total game plan in place until July, and we were not rolling until August. There was every opportunity to fail to do the basic job of identifying the Nixon vote, getting it registered, and getting it out to vote. We were very much impressed with the organizational ability of the McGovern campaign, and at that point in time we were certainly capable of being out-gunned at the precinct level. That fact, combined with the three months that McGovern had left to establish himself as a competent candidate who was qualified to be President of the United States, coupled with the opportunity for a substantial turnaround in international developments, still left the campaign to be won or lost.

MAX M. KAMPELMAN (adviser to Humphrey). Over the years we've learned so much about politics. In '68, for example, despite the effect of the convention, through accident, work, or whatever, Democrats started coming back home and we nearly won the election. You could conceivably have had that same thing happen this time. No group that captures the nomination can act on any assumption other than that the other fellow can make mistakes. I say this even though I personally felt, both before and after the Democratic convention, that McGovern could not win. My surprise in the election was the Massachusetts vote. But in politics, you can't do anything but what Gary Hart was trying to do. You never know.

NAUGHTON [to Charles Guggenheim]. Would you go into some detail about what the McGovern media strategy was, particularly in light of the events of the summer that you had to overcome? And how did you manage to win Massachusetts?

CHARLES GUGGENHEIM (media adviser to McGovern). I'd like to tell you how we won in Massachusetts. First of all, I think that you're only capable of carrying out grand strategies when you have money in hand. I think there's a fundamental difference between the problems that the Nixon campaign had and the problems that the McGovern campaign had. I think it's fair to say that the Nixon campaign had a budget and money in hand, or at least it was predictable if they didn't. But for us the problem in the general election was sometimes even more difficult than in the primaries, because our money was coming in literally on a day-to-day basis. The man who financed the McGovern campaign was Morris Dees, using the process of direct mail. I think we raised about $19 million, and $17 million of it was raised by Morris's direct mail. I would call Morris and say, "How much money do we have?" And he would say, "Well, we haven't opened the mail yet." So though you could project what you would like to do in a campaign in terms of production and strategy, it was fairly unreal to say you would go out and produce the material when you didn't have the money to go out and produce it. As an example, we came out of the convention with pledges of about $3 million, and then the Eagleton affair took place and none of that money came in. People reneged on their pledges, or they wanted to wait to see how that problem was resolved. So we had that kind of thing, but I don't want to use that as an excuse for what we did.

I think the way that Jeb Magruder and Pete Dailey have described what they did is extremely accurate, and I have nothing but praise for how they took the material they had and implemented it. I think it was absolutely impeccable, and, obviously, the results showed that. Our problem was more difficult, not only in the money sense, but insofar as we were faced with a series of what I call real events, as opposed to unreal events. I think what Pete Dailey and I do is unreal in a sense. We try to do a thing and put it on paid television and hope people will accept it as being the truth. I think that oftentimes they do, and oftentimes it gives information. But people see hours of television each day, they hear the radio news broadcasts, they look at the newspapers, they hear things by word-of-mouth, and this is also information. Paid television is a supporter to real events. If people are inclined negatively, television can help them go negatively. If they're inclined positively, it can help them go positively. I've seen that in all the elections that I've been in. But media really has a dramatic effect when people do not know either of the candidates very well and do not feel one way or the other; or if they have a small dislike for one, a man whom they know nothing about can often do very dramatic things on television. The McGovern-Nixon election was a case where people began to feel very, very strongly—both candidates were very strongly defined. As George McGovern said, "People will have a choice in this election. Never has there been an election where the choice has been so clear." I think all our data showed that people were inclined to make that choice long before the election.

In a strategy for the mass media, you must decide whether to exploit the negative or to exploit the positive, and I think that's the only choice you really have. That's where I think people have serious disagreement with the strategy that we implemented. The polls showed that Richard Nixon, as has already been discussed by the Republican side, was negative in many, many areas. There was a feeling that he wasn't quite frank and that they didn't particularly like him as a human being; but also there was the feeling that he was extremely competent. George McGovern was not considered as a viable alternative in the minds of many people. Richard Nixon wasn't particularly liked, but he was considered a viable President. You can choose to use the media to accentuate the negative—to go after Richard Nixon and make people know in more vivid terms why they dislike the man; or you can take George McGovern and make him a viable alternative. We chose to make George McGovern a viable alternative. I think you could have a long discussion of whether that was the right choice. I was under great pressure to go negative against Richard Nixon. But I thought that the only chance for George McGovern was to make people go to the polls at the end and say, "You know, I think this man has been so consistently decent and forthright that I'm going to vote for him." I thought it was a very small chance, but I thought it was our only chance. I thought to go negative against Richard Nixon would have been destructive.

In the last ten days of the campaign it prevailed that we went negative. I did not produce the material because I did not want to produce the material. Gary Hart called me up and said he was under pressure to do negative material against Richard Nixon. I said, "Gary, I have not been successful. The polls show that I've not been successful, if indeed paid television can be successful, and, therefore, I can't stand in your way." Gary said, "Look, if you say no, we'll say no." I thought that was a very decent thing to do, but I said, "No, I can't stand in the way." I said, "I think you should do it. I've obviously had no effect on these polls." And they went ahead and did roughly ten days of negative material. There were maybe two weeks of mildly negative material previous to the election. I could easily say that that was the reason why McGovern lost as badly as he did. Lou Harris [public-opinion analyst] has indicated to me that the negative material was destructive to us, as little as it was and as mild as it was. I think that needs looking into. But the grand strategy was to build George McGovern into a viable alternative.

If you want to have a man run a city, who do you select to run a city? If you want a man to run a baseball team, who do you get to run a baseball team? If I was going to pick a man to run a city, I'd pick Dick Daley, because I think Dick Daley probably runs the best city in the United States, though I'm not particularly fond of Dick Daley in many aspects of his life. With George McGovern, it was a question in people's minds as to whether or not he could really take the most sensitive job in the world and be responsible for it.

I'm convinced that the Presidency is looked upon by the American people in total awe. They don't mind slapping the hand of a senator and throwing him out, or a governor, or a congressman; they'll play with that because they're not playing with really crucial aspects of humanity. But you don't fool around with the Presidency. And with George McGovern, there were—fair and unfair —many things that made people say, "He scares the hell out of me." Whether you were a Democrat or a Republican, whether you were a radical or a conservative—this was crucial. And there was nothing that paid television could do to overcome it.

HOUSER. McGovern media was positive until the last ten days; on the other hand, McGovern on the platform was quite negative personally against the President throughout the course of the entire campaign. Why the dichotomy?

HART. There's no question about there being two schools of thought inside the McGovern campaign. Even with Jeb Magruder and others here, we have to be frank. An awful lot of Democrats don't like Richard Nixon, and when you bring Nixon up in a Democratic campaign, you get some very strong opinions strongly expressed. The two schools of thought did not just apply to paid media, but to the entire posture of the campaign. Senator McGovern's instincts were not to run a negative campaign, whether on television or in his own personal conduct. When you saw a harsher, more strident George McGovern on the stump, that was not the real George McGovern. I don't think he enjoyed some of the things he did and said, but he felt, both instinctively and on the basis of advice, that he had no choice. There were a number of key people telling him this is what he had to do. A lot of people felt very strongly about the implications of this election for the future of the country, and they felt that it was McGovern's duty to point out what kind of country this could become if certain practices prevailed. There was a positive wing of the campaign and a somewhat negative wing of the campaign, and different wings tended to prevail at different times.

DEES. I was right in the middle of the whole media thing. Senator McGovern is a lot easier to convince than Charlie Guggenheim is. I was on Charlie's side. In the last ten days, we only ran about three of those negative commercials. I sabotaged two or three of them by not funding them. Charlie is the most stubborn man I ever met.

DAVID S. BRODER (*Washington Post*). Pete Dailey pointed out that the Nixon people carried on their negative campaign through the vehicle of the Democrats for Nixon. On the other side, it always struck me as odd that the negative things were being done by Senator McGovern himself, who seemed to need some enhancement of his own prestige in Presidential terms. Was there nobody else in the Democratic Party who was willing to take on the job of hatchet man?

HART. We had our own surrogates [for McGovern]. Senator Humphrey did come out and speak a lot—also Senator Kennedy and Senator Muskie towards the end. Muskie went out on the stump, and we started scheduling him, and he traveled with Senator McGovern for three or four days a couple of times. And towards the end, he told people that he had gotten to know Senator McGovern and felt strongly about him. It was to be expected that Democrats would support the Democratic candidate, but we didn't have a Connally counterpart.

ROBERT J. KEEFE (consultant to the AFL-CIO). Also, the target group for Democrats was not Republicans.

GUGGENHEIM. There was a phenomenon that took place that I hope doesn't take place again, though I don't know how it can be avoided. Let's say that television news has more influence on the electorate than anything we do. We recorded all of the network broadcasts every night, as I'm sure the Republicans did. And I looked at them the other day—it's a dreadful experience. If McGovern would say something, the obligation of the networks was for equal time. Do they go to the White House and knock on the door and demand that the President respond? They couldn't do that—so there was McGovern against the surrogates. This was the strategy of the Committee to Re-elect the President, but who allowed it to happen? I tried to persuade Larry O'Brien to write the networks and say that we would not accept the surrogates as constituting equal time. I think that would have been a very strong issue. The process was against us.

MAGRUDER. We looked at the same news broadcasts you did, and we kept saying to ourselves that the only place the Nixon campaign could get coverage was in local markets. We found that we did well with the local newspaper and the local TV show, but we were very disappointed, to be honest with you, with network coverage of our surrogates. We didn't feel we were getting proper equal time. It was clearly our strategy from the beginning to use the surrogates. And I do not think it was improper, personally. We had the thirty-five surrogates selected and briefed a year and a half before the campaign.

ALAN L. OTTEN (*Wall Street Journal*). Can you tell us a bit about the make-up and theory of what was called the attack group?

MAGRUDER. The attack group was a joint group of some Republican National Committee people, some White House people, and some Committee to Re-elect people who met daily at the White House during the campaign. Basically, the attack group and the surrogate activity represented a coordinated effort to develop what the response would be to what George McGovern was saying, and then to get the word out to the people who were speaking. We had direct contact with our thirty-five surrogates and others who were speaking for us, and each morning we'd agree as to what our approach would be. We felt welfare and defense and credibility were the three weaknesses that we could zero in on. Those were the three commercials we used from Democrats for Nixon. We tried to schedule a week on welfare, a week on defense, a week on credibility, but that didn't always hold because what the opposition was doing really determined what we did. It was simply a process of communicating on a daily basis what we thought were the most current and choice things that should be said.

DAILEY. I think the Nixon campaign people were under

a great deal of pressure here. The people in the Administration who had to sit and take their lumps for three and a half years saw the campaign as a chance to go out and give it back to them. It took a tremendous amount of restraint to maintain a calm and clear posture throughout this.

NAUGHTON [to Gary Hart]. There were some who felt that the most effective surrogate that McGovern might have had in the general election was Tom Eagleton. Could you give some background on why Eagleton was never, for example, used in the media campaign?

HART. First of all, Senator Eagleton did campaign with Senator McGovern in Missouri—there were two or three major appearances—and I think he went out once or twice on his own. The judgment was that he was too symbolic and too much of a raw nerve. You could send Eagleton out on his own or bring him with the Senator on the theory you would allay fears or put down bad feelings. But it might have just the opposite effect and remind people of the so-called Eagleton incident.

To me, there were two tragedies in our campaign: one was, of course, that Senator McGovern lost; the second was that there were so many things that we did well, and they all got buried in the defeat. I guess all of us are great respecters of professionalism and expertise. Charles Guggenheim's media program was just superb, one of the best media programs that anybody's ever had. Morris Dees's direct-mail operation was just spectacular—there's been nothing like it in the history of American politics, and there may never be anything like it again. It is, in fact, the reason why there was a McGovern campaign. Pat Caddell's polling operation was also spectacular. We had a superb grass-roots organization in terms of direct contact with voters through canvassing and phoning and leafleting and so forth. The voter-registration operation that Anne Wexler was involved in was equally remarkable. There were all these elements that were phenomenal, but for one reason or another—the issues or the problems at the convention or divisions in the party or Eagleton or whatever—a lot of very, very good work just got buried.

RICHARD H. STEWART (press secretary to Muskie). Do you think, in retrospect, that McGovern would have been better off if Eagleton had remained on the ticket?

GUGGENHEIM. My guess is as good as any, but I don't have any insight into it at all. People were criticizing the McGovern campaign for, in a sense, not being Presidential in its thoroughness in selecting the Vice President. That was really what was hurting McGovern. That's what the staff was being pressed with all the time. I was very, very defensive about why Mr. Eagleton hadn't leveled with us. You couldn't help when you talked to the press, and you couldn't help when you talked to friends, and you couldn't help when you talked to anybody, but say, "Well, Tom Eagleton wasn't honest. He wasn't forthright." That information got through the political family very, very quickly, and Tom Eagleton was hearing it. If I were Tom Eagleton, I would have been very, very sensitive to the fact that the staff was saying this about me. But what else could the staff do when they were being pounded by this problem? I think that Tom Eagleton was not an asset to us on the stump. With all due respect to him, and I like him personally as a friend, I just think he was not —because in a sense he had to defend his own being all the time. To answer your question, I think, in retrospect, that it would have been better if we had kept him, but I certainly would not have made that decision at the time.

BRODER [to Patrick Caddell]. Do you have anything in your polling data on that?

PATRICK H. CADDELL (Cambridge Survey Research—McGovern). By the fall campaign, the most popular person in the country was not the President, or Senator Kennedy, or Senator Humphrey, or Senator McGovern—but Senator Eagleton. And his popularity was derived from the fact that people felt that he had gotten a raw deal. From what we could see, sending Eagleton out to campaign would only hurt. It brought the questions out again, especially when McGovern and Eagleton campaigned together. Since we were suffering so many defections because of Eagleton, I think his campaigning would have only accentuated our problems.

KAMPELMAN [to Charles Guggenheim]. Were you suggesting that for George McGovern a negative campaign against Richard Nixon could not work, or were you suggesting that in any Presidential campaign a negative approach could not work? I ask the question because, obviously, I keep thinking of Humphrey, and it's inconceivable to me that Humphrey would not have run both a positive and a strongly negative campaign against Nixon as a way to unite the Democrats. He did it in '68. Maybe it wasn't natural for McGovern to have run that kind of a campaign because he had a different set of problems; I wondered whether this was what you were saying.

GUGGENHEIM. Are you speaking of being negative on paid television, or on the stump?

KAMPELMAN. I'm certainly thinking in terms of the

candidate on the stump. It may be that you would have said, "Well, you do it on the stump, but you don't do it on paid TV." Is that a distinction that you're making?

GUGGENHEIM. It's a question that I've thought about a lot, and I think it's a good one, but I'm not sure I can give you a good answer to it. I personally feel—and no one can ever prove that I'm right or wrong, which may be fortunate for my profession—that Hubert Humphrey could have been President of the United States in '68 if he had not used the negative television he did. In '68 you could scare people about Richard Nixon, with all the suspicions that had accumulated about his personality— and he was not President yet. Once he became President and had run the shop for four years, the negative thing became a different kind of problem. But getting back to '68, when neither man was an incumbent, I think that the difference between Hubert Humphrey and Richard Nixon, which was really the most exploitable thing in terms of Humphrey's favor, was that Humphrey's record showed a thoroughly decent human being. Richard Nixon, on the other hand, had, rightly or wrongly, suspicions about him. Once the Humphrey campaign went on the air and was as tricky as Mr. Nixon, Hubert Humphrey was in the same boat with Richard Nixon.

KAMPELMAN. But I was thinking about '72. I thought that one of the most effective acts for McGovern at the convention was Ted Kennedy's speech. He united the Democratic Party that night with his magnificent performance. He had a positive program, but he was uniting them against the Republican Party.

OTTEN. Do you really think that it was what Kennedy

said? It struck me that the drama of the moment was as important as the content of the speech.

DAILEY. Following up on Charlie Guggenheim's remarks about negative advertising—I completely agree with him. In 1972 a negative campaign against the President, which would probably have had to get very personal, would have been very offensive.

MAGRUDER. We [at the Committee to Re-elect] felt very strongly that a negative campaign could work only if it was credible. I think that's why we were successful with our Democrats for Nixon advertising. You might disagree with the facts behind it, but the public agreed with our position. To be honest with you, we couldn't believe it when McGovern started on the personal attacks. It struck us as being really out of context, and, not only that, it was so blatant against a man who was President. It wasn't credible. There were things that were said that maybe 20 per cent of the public agreed with, but certainly the majority of the public could not agree with those statements. We were just delighted, but really appalled in a sense, because we couldn't believe that McGovern would go off on that tack after having run a campaign up to then on the issues of trust, honesty, openness, and so on.

HART. I think it was a serious mistake, myself.

BEN J. WATTENBERG (adviser to Jackson). I would like to ask a question using Charlie Guggenheim's distinction between real events and unreal events. As I understand it, unreal events are all the organizational and tactical and media sorts of things that we professionals do, and the real events are what actually happens. Given the real events up through Labor Day, say, has there been any calculation about what effect the unreal activities had in terms of changing votes? [To Jeb Magruder] Suppose, for example, on Labor Day the Nixon campaign suddenly found out that it didn't have any money to do anything. How much difference do you think that would have made in the election? And I'd ask the same question of the McGovern people. You've talked about the media time you got on the network shows—what McGovern got as compared to what the surrogates got. In my judgment, McGovern was losing votes when he got on media television for free. He was getting free television worth millions of dollars, and he was losing votes every time he was seen. Those were real events, as opposed to what we professionals do.

MAGRUDER. I think we technicians felt that the campaign was worth 2 to 4 per cent maybe. If we had stopped in September and not gone into our voter-identification and get-out-the-vote direct-mail campaign, I think it would have made a difference of 2, 4, 5 per cent, no more and no less.

HART. I agree with that exactly; an organization is worth no more than 5 per cent.

DEES [to Jeb Magruder]. You had the Republican National Committee and the special campaign organization. Could the RNC have run the campaign as effectively as the Committee to Re-elect did? Why did you separate the two?

MAGRUDER. It's very simple, I think. The problem is that the Republican National Committee is a body placed on top of fifty state chairmen, who are independent and autonomous. And I think every Presidential candidate feels that he has to control his state organizations. What we did, and I think it worked well, was to put together a coordinated effort between state committees and our state organizations.

HOUSER. There's an additional basic fact that you didn't mention. In most of the major states, the Republican Party is a very substantial minority party, and no Republican candidate can win unless he is successful in attracting a very substantial amount of the independent vote and even some dissident Democrats. No Republican can win in Illinois unless he does that. And if you're going to get volunteers—independent volunteers and Democrats—they will not walk into a Republican headquarters. It's a basic fact of life—you have to organize this way.

NAUGHTON [to Jeb Magruder]. How did you decide to handle the Watergate affair and all that it represented? And, incidentally, what really happened?

MAGRUDER. First, let me say that there is a trial that is beginning next week, and all of us at the Committee to Re-elect are under court order not to comment on the Watergate case. So I honestly cannot comment on the case. I don't mean to dodge the issue: I'll clearly comment sometime.

STEWART. Let me ask you another question then. We all kept hearing about, and some of us experienced, some harassment of Democratic candidates. I would cite the "canuck" letter [attributed to Muskie] in New Hampshire, which was obviously a bogus letter.

MAGRUDER. I can honestly say that I do not know of any harassment that we engaged in on a planned basis.

OTTEN. I realize that you can't discuss whether you were wiretapping, or if you got the memos and all that, but can you discuss how much of a danger you perceived the Watergate issue to be and whether you had a contingency plan for how you would cope with the issue? Why didn't the issue catch on? Am I right that it didn't catch on? How were you prepared to handle it if it did seem to be catching on?

STEWART. Let me just say, for a moment, that I'm not convinced that some of the harassment with which the Republicans have been credited did not come from Democratic candidates.

MAGRUDER. To my knowledge, there was no harassment of any kind. But with individuals operating basically independently in a campaign with hundreds of thousands of people involved, I think some probably does happen. I think John Ehrlichman [Assistant to the President] once remarked that it's endemic to a volunteer-type activity. I don't say that there wasn't some, but I think there was much less than was reported, and that much of that came from other than our side. As for the Watergate issue, we saw it as a bothersome problem. We felt very comfortable with our position on it, but it continually harassed us. We felt that it was not an important matter in a Presidential election, and I don't think the public felt it was an important matter in the election.

DAILEY. I think there were a few things that kept it from being a major issue. For one, there was no villain in it—

there were some guys named Joe—and it was stretched out over a long period of time.

KAMPELMAN. I listened to what I presumed to be a major McGovern speech on ethics, on bought television. He started on this Watergate affair, but I was really incredulous when I suddenly heard him bringing in the Berrigan case. It seemed to me that he suddenly began to becloud the Watergate issue with something controversial that could only be negative as far as he was concerned. What was the reason for that?

HART. I don't know. I think it was a mistake.

OTTEN [to Patrick Caddell]. What did your polls find on the Watergate affair?

CADDELL. In the beginning it was having very little overall effect. When we were interviewing people in September that we had interviewed in July, we found some who had moved from the President to undecided, and these tended to be upper-income Republicans who were concerned about Watergate. The sabotage stuff in October began to have a much greater impact than did the Watergate thing in terms of shaking people's commitment to the President, but it was not moving votes. People got to the point where they were not pleased and were very concerned; but when they were faced with voting for McGovern, they found themselves unable to do it. Some of them didn't vote.

HOUSER. I heard the comment from time to time that the Watergate issue was actually helping the President's campaign because it was throwing up a smoke screen that prevented the public from focusing on the real issues.

People were really not taking this issue seriously, but there was a lot of attention given to it. This blotted out an opportunity for discussion of other issues.

BRODER. How was the Watergate incident viewed by the Democrats? What was the thinking in the McGovern campaign about the potential of the incident and how it could best be exploited?

HART. We thought that the potential was vast. We were convinced at the time, and are convinced to this day, that there was an intricate and vast Republican, Nixon-sponsored effort to sabotage the Democratic campaign, and that the financing for it involved money transferred through foreign banks, and so forth. We believed it was a very high-level operation, and we sought to get the implications of that across to the American people, in terms of the integrity of the political system.

OTTEN. Did you make any effort at hiring investigators or anything like that, or did you just rely on the press to dig it out?

MAGRUDER. Come on, guys, 'fess up.

STEWART. We will if you will.

HART. We did assign only one person to try to find out what was going on.

RICK G. STEARNS (deputy campaign manager for McGovern). Like everyone else, we were initially astounded at the target that had been chosen; and we considered it a comic episode until some of the ramifications of the original incident became clear. I think the McGovern campaign was divided over the value of Watergate. We were anxious to exploit it to the extent that we could politically. I frankly think that we made more political mileage out of the wheat-sale scandal than we did out of Watergate. I think most people took the view that there was nothing exceptional about the Watergate incident except that the perpetrators were caught. Most Americans seem to believe that political parties engage in this kind of activity as a matter of course. Political parties as institutions are in such disrepute that sabotage directed at a party fails to arouse the average American. The case never translated itself from a question of pure partisan politics into a case involving civil liberties, an aspect that we tried to introduce somewhat later into the issue— perhaps too late to make very much of it.

KEEFE [to Jeb Magruder]. As I understand what you were doing [in the Nixon campaign], you were identifying and trying to get people to the polls and so forth. Yet the total turnout tailed off—it went down again. Do you think your efforts really did the job of getting your vote out?

MAGRUDER. Absolutely. It wasn't our turnout that went down—it was Gary Hart's. We had a very high vote for a Republican candidate for President. We had tremendous results from that program.

NAUGHTON [to Anne Wexler]. Could you speak to the same point, and also tell us where the youth vote went?

ANNE WEXLER (Democratic voter-registration director). I think a lot of them stayed home. A substantial number of college students registered, but less than 50 per cent of non-college students did. We were counting very heavily on college students voting for McGovern, and less than we had counted on actually voted at all. If you look at the figures the Census Bureau put out the other day, you will see that around 48 per cent of the eighteen to twenty-one-year-olds voted, which was much lower than we expected.

NAUGHTON. Would the effort made by Senator McGovern after the convention to establish contacts with the Democratic regulars have affected that whole situation?

CADDELL. I think that when we looked at the people who defected from McGovern, just a little less than half of them were under the age of thirty, and they tended to be people who had been very strong supporters. That group tended to be moved particularly by Eagleton, much more than by the other things. Enthusiasm for McGovern certainly declined on a lot of campuses as a result of his dropping Eagleton for what looked like a political reason. They had thought he was different from other politicians.

KEEFE. Whereas in other groups of the electorate the McGovern campaign was hurting on the other aspect of the affair, on the question of McGovern not having done his homework?

CADDELL. We were hurting to some extent on that competence problem, but we were also hurting because a lot of the public viewed McGovern's dropping Eagleton as a political move. But about the turnout: normally in a Presidential race, the vote for President runs anywhere from 7 or 8 to 15 per cent higher than the vote for state races. In twenty of the thirty-nine states this year where there were statewide races for senator or governor, the votes cast in the statewide races were actually higher than the votes cast for President. Insofar as I can discover, this is a phenomenon unmatched in American history. In another eight of those states, the vote was almost even, or less than 1 per cent different; and in another five, it was less than 2 per cent. In fact, although the total number of people who voted this year was higher than the number of people who voted in '68, in twenty-five states—including Pennsylvania, Ohio, New Jersey, and some other really large states—the number of votes cast was actually less than in the '68 Presidential race. In Texas, where about a million and a half new people were registered, the actual increase in votes was only about 50,000.

J. PHILIP REBERGER (Republican National Committee). The inner-city black vote fell off considerably from '68.

OTTEN [to Jeb Magruder]. In turning out the Nixon voters so efficiently, mightn't you have been doing in a lot of the Republican gubernatorial and senatorial candidates, in that you were turning out Democrats who voted for the President and then went back over on the Democratic side?

MAGRUDER. We've done some work since the election on that subject, and we come down on two points. First, we do not think that the President could have affected anything but what I would call the statewide offices— gubernatorial races possibly, but particularly senatorial. When you get down to a state legislative race, to say that a candidate for state assembly lost when the President won because the President turned out Democrats is just ridiculous on the face of it, because local issues are much more important in any state race. If you take the case of each Republican candidate for the Senate who was an incumbent and who lost, you will find that not only did the candidate not ask for any help from us, but the candidate will now admit that he just didn't run a campaign. In Maine, Senator Margaret Chase Smith spent $10,000, and William Hathaway spent $150,000; she did not campaign once, she ran no advertising, she did absolutely nothing. To say, therefore, that her defeat was brought on by the fact that Richard Nixon turned out some Democrats in Maine to vote for him is just absurd. I think many Republican candidates thought that because the President was doing so well, they could just sit there and come in on his coattails. But when you've got a minority party and when the electorate is now turning to ticket-splitting in increasing numbers, I don't think any candidate can run on that basis any more.

JAMES M. PERRY (*National Observer*). According to some Republicans, you had a computer print-out that you refused to make available to them.

MAGRUDER. That's absolutely incorrect. We put a tremendous amount of money and effort into that computer print-out in the eleven states we did it in. Early on, we asked each Republican state chairman and each candidate for statewide office if he wanted to join us in this effort. Across the board, they said, "No, you do it." We did it, and then we said to them, "Okay, if you want to use it, it's yours, but of course you're going to have to pay the cost of doing your computer runs and so on." In some cases they did use it. In other cases, they said, "We don't need it." As examples, Senator Robert Griffin in Michigan and Senator John Tower in Texas said, "Look, these guys have got something, and we'll use it." Senator Tower and Senator Griffin ran excellent campaigns and won big, though they were supposed to have been in very tight races. In every state for which we had that print-out, we made it available on a cost basis, which I think was absolutely fair. We had put a tremendous amount of money into it.

DAILEY. There's another point on this too. The Committee for the Re-election of the President had the responsibility to get the President re-elected; the Republican National Committee had the responsibility for the other candidates. We very definitely did not want Nixon to be perceived as the Republican candidate for President, but as Richard Nixon running for re-election, or the President running for re-election. We had to move away from that party affiliation in view of the low registration that we had.

REBERGER. That's not entirely accurate. Early in '71, John Mitchell and Jeb Magruder met with my boss at the Republican National Committee and the technicians there. They said, "Let's start getting the party organizations ready to do as much as they can do for the '72 election." We asked for a role in the Presidential campaign, and we got a role in the organizational work—registration, get-out-the-vote, and voter identification. In '71 and early '72, we were testing and developing techniques that later on we jointly worked out with the Committee for the Re-election of the President—to go out into the precincts and use the computer print-outs in the states where they were available and where the party wanted them. In many cases, this happened, and otherwise, we just used the regular old Target '72 techniques in joint efforts throughout the country.

We talked earlier about there being separate campaign organizations set up in the states because we couldn't get Democrats and independents to walk into Republican headquarters to do the work. Along these lines, I think you would have to agree that getting a Democrat to vote for Richard Nixon and getting a Democrat to knock on doors for Richard Nixon are two different things. So we were still going to the same well, basically. The Republican National Committee and the Committee for the Re-election of the President jointly sponsored a national canvass kick-off in September and jointly sponsored a national get-out-the-vote kick-off in late October. We had a lot of problems with party chairmen talking about allocation of resources—the Republican National Committee had less than 10 per cent of the Presidential campaign budget; but still the Republican National Committee did have a role in the Presidential campaign—probably for the first time in recent history, a significant role.

HOUSER. I think it should be stated, though, that the level of cooperation at the Washington level was a lot more intimate than it was out in the states. If we had depended on the regular Republican organization to start a registration drive in Illinois, we'd still be waiting. I think that's true throughout most of the country.

REBERGER. That's right.

MAGRUDER. I think our problem was more with the candidates for statewide office than it was with the Republican Party. In fact, we used everything that Phil Reberger and his people came up with. We used their programs jointly.

OTTEN [to Gary Hart]. In view of all the publicity given to the crucial role of the "on the plane" staff in the McGovern campaign, how important were all the strategy decisions that we've been talking about that were made in

Washington by you and Charles Guggenheim, Rick Stearns, and Anne Wexler?

HART. There are all kinds of decisions made in a campaign. There's a school of thought that says that the most important decisions made in a campaign are those that determine how the money is spent—how you allocate the budget. In the McGovern campaign, those decisions were made in Washington. Organizational decisions were made in Washington, financial decisions, staff decisions, and so on. Obviously, it's much more difficult to make decisions in Washington on what the candidate should be saying when he's off in Portland on his way to Albuquerque and after that to Butte.

I'd say the area where the traveling staff and the Washington staff had to cooperate most thoroughly was on the question of the content of the media. We would hold meetings in Washington, and a lot of us representing different points of view would narrow down the recommendations for what kind of speech the Senator ought to give on the half-hour that we had bought the following week. That advice would be forwarded to him, and there would be further debate among the advisers and staff with him on the plane. Sometimes the Washington view prevailed, and sometimes it didn't; sometimes it was a mix of both. But a candidate tends to rely for advice on the people closest to him, and not call Washington and say, "Let's get a conference call here and talk about what I ought to say in Chicago tonight."

JACK L. CHESTNUT (campaign manager for Humphrey). Who had the ultimate decision-making responsibility on any major question involving the McGovern campaign, you or a committee?

HART. There are different kinds of major questions. Senator McGovern made it clear to the people in the campaign that on budgetary questions, on organizational questions, and on, to some degree, media questions, he considered me the campaign manager and that my decision would be final. On questions of what positions he was taking, we did have an issues and research operation that prepared papers and proposed speeches and so forth; but the candidate himself, with the consultation of those around him on the plane, tended to make his own decisions about what he would be saying. In other words, he did not say, "Gary, is it all right if I take such and such a position on tax reform?" He just did it. Sometimes he consulted, and sometimes he didn't.

NAUGHTON. That leaves us without a description of Larry O'Brien's role in the McGovern campaign.

HART. Larry O'Brien's role was very clearly spelled out —orally and in writing—when the announcement was made of his position as campaign chairman. He was principal ambassador to elements of the regular party. Members of the press, for one reason or another, chose not to respect that statement, but it was accurate. Larry O'Brien made no effort to run the campaign.

DEES. There will never be another campaign like the McGovern campaign. Any critical strategic meeting could be attended by anybody. The Republicans could have gotten information just by sending a volunteer over to walk into any meeting that happened to be going on any time.

OTTEN. Jeb Magruder is smiling; it looks like they did.

DEES. It was truly a democratic campaign. Gary Hart's door was never locked to anybody—though maybe it should have been. We had a lot of interplay.

BILLY JOE CAMP (press secretary for Wallace). Let me add one thing here, though it relates back to the Wallace campaign in the primaries. The McGovern campaign didn't have a monopoly on decision-making problems. There was disagreement in the Wallace campaign while we were working in Indiana, Tennessee, and North Carolina. Those of us traveling with the Governor felt that we were in real good shape in both Tennessee and North Carolina and would do well to spend a minimum of time there. We wanted everything for Indiana, where we thought we needed the work. Others thought we needed the work in Tennessee and North Carolina and didn't want to spend time in Indiana. In our case, I think if the traveling crew had prevailed, we would have won Indiana.

OTTEN. Some people have charged that at the local and state level, McGovern people were really not seeking out the support of people who had been working for the other candidates, or not really welcoming it when it was offered. Was this happening?

HART. It's wrong to generalize about almost anything in politics, and that's a generalization. There are states where all elements of the Democratic Party worked very well together. It had to do with the chemistry of the state, the traditions, the people, what other races were going on, and so forth. There were other states where it didn't work so well. Frankly, there were some very important states where the so-called McGovernites, the people who had been in our campaign prior to the convention, spent too much time courting fairly ineffective regulars—people who had no power, who could not deliver a bottle of milk, and yet had some title or status and felt that they should be courted. You can make the mistake both ways. As a general rule, I'd have to say that the McGovern campaign around the country made at least a reasonable effort, in some places a very strong effort, to work with and seek the support of all sorts of Democrats. I cannot say that that happened uniformly.

CHESTNUT. In Minnesota, that was particularly true, and this was a state where, obviously, there was a strong feeling for Hubert Humphrey. A young man by the name of John Reuther, who was the McGovern coordinator, did an excellent job of bringing all elements of the Democratic Party together. I think the Minnesota vote is reflective of his efforts.

STEWART. Half of the Muskie staff joined up with the McGovern camp, as I recall.

KEEFE. If there was a failing on the part of the McGovern people generally, it was that they failed to understand that after the convention they were the establishment of the Democratic Party. They didn't take advantage of operating from that posture, which they clearly could have done. For the most part, McGovern people had been the outsiders looking in, and they failed to realize that now they were the insiders. They were hesitant to give direction to people who had been the establishment.

OTTEN. What about the war issue at this point?

DAILEY. We never thought that the President would be on the right side of the war issue in January, but it turned out that way in the election. It began to turn for us while the war was still right up at the top of the list of people's concerns. In November of '72 the President's position on the war issue was perceived as being very different from what it was in January. I think things began to turn with the mining of the harbor in Haiphong and the President's toughness. The more the McGovern side tried to say that the President was in *favor* of the war, the more it worked to our advantage. The electorate at that point had pretty well decided that the President had done just about everything he could do, short of crawling, to end it, and they began to support his position.

OTTEN [to Jeb Magruder]. What did your polls show as to the impact of the announcement that "peace is at hand"?

MAGRUDER. I think what Pete Dailey says is absolutely correct. The polls were very good on the Vietnam war issue. At no time during the four years of his Presidency —and we had done polling through the Republican National Committee for the whole four-year period—was President Nixon ever considered to be at fault for that war. No matter how much the other side tried to say that it was our war, it never became our war in the public's mind and that gave us a tremendous edge. Aside from the small percentage of people in the peace movement, the public did not perceive us as being the people who created the Vietnam war; and the President was perceived, particularly after May, as being the most reasonable person in trying to solve the problem that he himself had not created. The Democrats never got that monkey off their back. I don't think the public ever forgave the Democratic Party for that war.

CADDELL. We spent a lot of time [for McGovern] looking

at the Vietnam war as a voting issue and a non-voting issue. From May on, in terms of the war, the President was doing pretty well overall. His actual job rating on the war was not particularly good, except in comparison with others. However, the thing that surprised me was that the people who were defecting from Nixon in the period from July to September tended to be defecting on the war. Lou Harris was running a series of agree-disagree questions on statements about George McGovern. One of them was, "McGovern was wrong to say that he would go to Hanoi and beg for the release of U.S. POW's." I thought for sure that would be a 70 per cent agree statement right there, but it came out 46 per cent agree, 39 per cent disagree. So we went back and looked at that problem. People were really ready to get out, even if it meant a President had to do something drastic. But the reaction to the statement that "peace is at hand" was more negative—people thought it was a political ploy. [To Jeb Magruder] I understand your surveys showed the same thing.

OTTEN. Besides the war issue, how accurately did the public by November perceive McGovern's positions and Nixon's positions on the major issues? Was it accurately perceived where they stood, and if not, where was the gap?

MAGRUDER. As much as Gary Hart and his troops would like to say that the issues were not important, we [in the Nixon campaign] felt very strongly that the public understood where the President stood on key domestic issues right down the line. We found tremendous response in our polls to the concept of bringing the government back to the people, through revenue-sharing for example; and I think there was a feeling on the part of the public that the welfare program was just one great disaster. We feel very strongly, I think, that the public is not happy with the product of thirty years of social legislation. I think they want social legislation, but they want it to be effective, and so far it hasn't been effective. We have continued to say that in our reorganization efforts, in our programmatic efforts. In the campaign we did very well on the issues near the end, up from our low point in January of '71. We kept getting better on the issues because the public perceived our position as being much more the centrist position in this country, something that they could accept and live with. I do think they perceived McGovern's position as being unacceptable to the vast majority of Americans.

HART. I don't think the public at large ever really understood George McGovern or his basic political posture. The public was confused by misstatements about McGovern's positions in the late primaries; it was further confused by statements made by other Democrats at the convention. I'll go to my grave thinking that this election was decided on the issue of who was competent, who had those characteristics of leadership that people generally think should be in the White House. Thirty million of us felt that George McGovern had those characteristics and was much righter on the issues than Nixon. But many people misunderstood. Jeb Magruder's statement just now about welfare was a classic and proves my point. George McGovern proposed the so-called $1,000 payment or something like that to end the thirty-year welfare mess —it wasn't an expansion of it, it was an end to it. This was a position which the President himself had basically taken some time before and, as with some other positions, had backed off from. And the same position was taken by some very respectable economists.

Where we erred was not on the basic positions themselves, but in the way that they were presented. I'm not saying that we [in the McGovern campaign] should be relieved of responsibility—we made some very serious mistakes in the way we presented some of these controversial issues. But I don't think the American people ever got to the substantive issues themselves. They judged by what seemed to be confusion around McGovern and decided not to take a chance on putting him in the White House. Does the average voter sit down and say, "Now, let's see, do I agree with Nixon or McGovern on welfare? Do I agree with Nixon or McGovern on defense spending?" It's very visceral. I don't think the voters got down to anything that concrete in this election.

MAGRUDER. I must say that it doesn't seem that you picked up anything from what came out of the election. You may be absolutely correct that George McGovern really wanted to do what the President wanted to do about welfare, but rightly or wrongly the $1,000 welfare program was perceived as a giveaway program. You never were able to articulate it correctly, and the public perceived that program as a giveaway and they did not want continued government giveaways.

HART. You keep using the word "perceived"—and that's my point.

MAGRUDER. It's your responsibility as a candidate to articulate. If you really believed in the program, as you say you did, you had the responsibility to articulate it, and you failed.

HART. We failed, but that was not a mandate on the issue.

MAGRUDER. It surely was, because people perceived of you as being over on the left side of that issue to the point where they were against you.

HART. That may be a poor campaign. It doesn't mean the issue was wrong.

MAGRUDER. No, it means that you weren't able to articulate that issue. The conception that the public had of your welfare program and of your defense program was that they were very left-fringe.

WATTENBERG. I am very interested in this dialogue about what is perception and what is reality. As a writer, I have found that if you can't say it and you can't write it and you can't articulate it, then maybe it isn't so. [To Gary Hart] I'm suggesting that maybe your perception of McGovern—or McGovernism, or "new politics"—is beclouded in a forest-trees kind of way. You believed that George McGovern stood for A, B, C, and D, but what the American people thought he stood for might indeed have been closer to what he really stood for. I would say that what happened substantively in this election was that there was the equivalent of a referendum in this country. It was a referendum on the so-called cultural revolution that has been going on allegedly for four or five years in this country. It involved many, many facets—busing and defense and welfare and all sorts of things—and a perception of whether this country was doing pretty well or teetering on the brink of failure. If there was going to be an election on something in this country, this was a pretty good thing to have an election on. And the American people voted no on what the whole "new politics" movement was about.

HART. I didn't say we couldn't articulate those issues, I said we didn't.

WATTENBERG. Why didn't you? Maybe you couldn't. Maybe you just think you didn't, but you couldn't.

WEXLER. My own observation about this campaign is that there was little importance given issues, at least in the minds of the voters. There was always something else that was occupying them. The President may have spent a great deal of time on issues—but when he spoke about them, he spoke about them on the radio. The press received a press release that was already typed out, and some of the newspapers used it and some of them didn't. Senator McGovern spent a good deal of time talking about issues in all of his speeches, some of which got reported and some of which didn't. My perception of the entire campaign was that it had very little to do with substantive issues. I think the three important questions in this campaign were competence, trust, and who was Presidential. If anything created an impression and a feeling in this country, it was the very brilliant commercials done by Peter Dailey and his group on the President's trips to China and Russia. These created the aura of a President and a good internationalist, qualities that were important in this campaign, and people did remember them. But other issues were never perceived.

DAILEY. I wonder if another way to look at it is the role of the press in this whole area. It's almost as if the press is the spokesman for the public, particularly in an election with an incumbent. The press looks at the rest of the field and asks each one three things: first, whether he is tough enough to be the President, because it's a very demanding job; second, whether he is capable of managing this country, which is the most difficult managerial job in the world; and third, whether his plans for the direction of this country are better than those of the incumbent President. I think by the time the primaries were over, the press had pretty much said, "Well, okay, Senator McGovern is tough enough for the job, because he's been through this trial by fire." Then the questioning began, "Are you capable of running the country?" They never got past that question because of the Eagleton issue. The question was one of the capacity to govern.

HART. Precisely.

DAILEY. McGovern never got a chance to get past the second trial. He never got to discuss how his way of handling this country would be better than the incumbent President's.

HART. I couldn't have said it better myself.

MAGRUDER. I agree that the competence question was important, but the substance was still there. The contest was perceived as being between a centrist, moderate candidate who had shown ability to lead this country and a candidate of the new cultural revolution.

WATTENBERG. The nature of competence and trust is keyed to substance. *What* is he competent to do? It doesn't work in the abstract.

MAGRUDER. McGovern was associated with the gay libs, the welfare rights, the black militants, the women's libs, the pot-smokers, the long-haired college kids. Maybe that was incorrect, but that's how he was perceived, and that's substance because there is substance in those issues.

NAUGHTON. Is that argument over already? I've been wanting to ask Pat Caddell whatever happened to the McGovern Southern strategy.

CADDELL. In July in most Southern states, McGovern still had terrible recognition problems. We would find that 60 or 65 per cent of the people in places like North Carolina knew really nothing about McGovern. Our thought was that in some of those states there was a potential for McGovern, who had come out of the primaries perceived less as a radical than as a very quiet sort of guy. But whether or not McGovern would have any success in those states, if he could make a race there, his campaigning would force the Republicans to come in and spend some time there and hopefully run a campaign that would run adverse to them in the North. It was as much a strategic thing as anything else; but particularly in some of the states we had targeted, we thought there was potential. But by the time the Eagleton thing came about, we had basically written the whole thing off. We had to ditch it—we hadn't the time or the resources.

NAUGHTON. I'd like to try to get at what the impact was of labor's neutrality in the general election.

KEEFE. I don't know what its impact was, but I go back to the point that George Meany's specific constituency is his executive committee, and that the executive committee —its members and their unions—split three ways. A majority of them went for George McGovern; a substantial minority endorsed the President; and another handful stayed neutral. I think it would have been impossible under those circumstances for the leadership of the AFL-CIO, had it wanted to—and I won't suggest that it really wanted to, to get the kind of unity necessary to mount the kind of campaign that, for example, it did mount for Hubert Humphrey in '68. Mr. Meany's decision to stay out of it was based, I believe, on his feeling that he couldn't really weld the elements together, and that, had he tried, it would have only further emphasized the fact that they were split, and they never really would have gotten a constructive, unified labor campaign for McGovern off the ground.

I think that the unions that jumped in and supported George McGovern did so quite wholeheartedly and gave a best-effort kind of thing. It was a broad range of unions, certainly far beyond the number of unions that had supported Senator McGovern in the primaries or at the convention. The Textile Workers, for example, had been very strongly anti-McGovern, but in the fall campaign they did everything within their power to support the Democratic ticket. On the other hand, the unions that supported the President did likewise—I think they gave the President much more than lip service. So I think the problem was that the labor unions were just plain split on the question of who they should support for President, and the various elements gave their best efforts for whichever candidate. There was still a large group that did nothing, I think.

NAUGHTON [to Gary Hart]. From your perspective, how badly did those labor defections hurt the McGovern campaign? And why was there not a continuation, at least to the extent that there had been in the primaries, of the personal effort by Senator McGovern to woo workers—symbolically, at least—by making those factory visits?

HART. I'm not the best person to ask the first question because I don't have the background in Presidential politics. I can't compare '72 to other years. Bob Keefe or somebody else could tell you what it means at the local

level to have wholehearted labor support. I do know that
the labor committee for McGovern-Shriver was an active,
hard-working, committed, Democratic group of labor
people from the top down, and they did a tremendous job
for us in most states. Again, the biggest mistake one can
make in politics is to generalize. Everything varies from
state to state, or city to city, or whatever. It depends on
people—it depends on the political circumstances. I spent
a year and a half of my life answering press questions
about how you can get the nomination without labor support. You just do it. You get some labor support, and
other people get some labor support. There are very few
monoliths in our society, and I don't think labor is one
of them. It may come closer than some, but I think '72
proved that you don't talk about labor as one group. What
help we got from labor was very good; I don't know how
to judge what we missed. We could have used some more.

What intrigued me about the fall campaign, as opposed
to the nomination race, was the degree to which logistics
conditioned the way McGovern campaigned. The size of
the press corps traveling with us conditioned the kind of
campaign we waged; we had to plan around what air-
ports we could land at and how long it takes to bus between places. We tried those factory appearances and
going into hospitals. But you gentlemen from the press
know what it's like to go into a hospital with a string of
150 reporters behind you—with all the pads and over-
coats and everything—knocking people out of bed. It
becomes a huge zoo, and you can't take it everywhere.
We wanted to do more campaigning in factories, but the
plant managers would say, "Stay the hell out of here, we
don't want you in here."

NAUGHTON. Those of us who were in those entourages
know that there were many occasions when we had to

stand outside a given building, while a small pool of press went in with the candidate.

STEWART. Muskie had to do that in New Hampshire because there was just such a crowd traveling with us that we were losing votes. When people are making shoes on piecework and there are some guys just standing around, they get upset. Finally, we went to plant managers and said, "Look, we just want you to say that you don't want all these people in there." And some of the managers were more than happy to help us out by saying that.

NAUGHTON. The point that I'm trying to get to is that in a one-on-one situation Senator McGovern seemed very successful in handling those same issues that proved to be problems with the electorate at large; and that if his one-on-one encounters had been conveyed on a fairly regular basis in the media, it might have had some impact.

HART. I would have liked to do that very much. But in laying out the block schedules for McGovern for the next week or month, I would keep getting instructions back from the road saying, "Forget about plant appearances; forget about the kind of campaign we did in some of the primary states, very effectively. We're getting too much heat from the press—they don't like the pool arrangement and they won't tolerate it."

OTTEN. Did labor's attitude complicate the image problem? Was the fact that McGovern couldn't bring labor into line another blow at his general competence and ability to govern?

HART. It may have underscored the divisions in the party

and kept reminding people that McGovern didn't have wholehearted Democratic support.

CADDELL. In view of people's general disaffection with politics and their image of unions, perhaps the best thing the McGovern campaign could have done would have been to cut loose and say that these union people didn't want us. This might have been an effective political thing to do in terms of imagery, if we could have manipulated it properly. We played with this idea. Perhaps it would have been too bold and impractical.

WATTENBERG. I think that some labor people perceived that such a feeling might exist in the McGovern campaign, and this was one of the reasons that Mr. Meany decided what he did. I was astonished earlier when Gary Hart said that he was surprised at the depth of feeling against McGovern on the part of the Humphrey people in California. He said his people knew they were going to get some opposition, but they didn't understand the vehemence and the depth of it. But insofar as labor people were concerned, I know there was a feeling that over the last three or four years, the McGovern wing—or the "new politics" wing, or whatever you want to call that part of the party—had been referring to them as racists, conservatives, imperialists, and geriatric labor barons. These were phrases that were commonly used. I'm not saying that McGovern said this; I'm not saying that Gary Hart said it.

HART. Who said it?

WATTENBERG. I don't have my telephone directory here. But a lot of people said it, and they were people who were generally associated with what I'll call "new politics." And when these people came around after the nomination and said, "Now, you racist, conservative, imperialistic, geriatric, unresponsive labor bosses, please endorse us," the answer was predictable. The main reason they were upset, I think, was that they felt they were better liberals than George McGovern ever was. They still feel this, and the struggle in the Democratic party right now is about the real nature of liberalism in the 1970's.

HART. If I could just clarify one point, I did not refer to the depth of feeling by the people who supported Hubert Humphrey; I referred to the depth of feeling by Hubert Humphrey himself.

WATTENBERG. Oh, I see; I'm sorry.

HART. I think that's very important, because the counterpoint is that George McGovern wasn't saying those things you described just now.

WATTENBERG. Yes, I know that McGovern wasn't saying those things.

WEXLER. I think that comparisons between '68 and '72 are quite irrelevant because George Wallace was not running in '72—which made a tremendous difference in the labor effort. In 1968 there was an enormous effort made by the rank-and-file of organized labor to reduce the Wallace vote.

KEEFE. That was because in '68 that was where the disaffected labor vote was going. This time it was going to Nixon.

WEXLER. Exactly. But the point is that this time, even

though there was a tremendous effort on the part of the leadership of the labor group for McGovern-Shriver, the rank-and-file did not go in and simply vote Democratic. They split their tickets more than they've ever done in their lives; and whether the fact that George Wallace was not in the race was an element in this is something I suspect you will never know.

BRODER. What about the relationship of labor and the Republicans in the general election? [To Thomas Houser] Coming from Illinois, a major industrial state, you have been involved in campaigns in which labor has been pretty solidly lined up against you. What, if any, difference did it make that there was a policy of neutrality proclaimed this year?

HOUSER. I think it definitely helped the Nixon campaign. Apparently unlike the national scene, in Illinois I had the impression that most of the labor organizations remained neutral. A few went to McGovern and a couple went to Nixon, but the great bulk of them stayed out of it. Over the years locally the Democrats have received an awful lot of financing from the labor organizations, as well as support in the field, so I think in Illinois it made a considerable difference.

KEEFE. The principal unions in Illinois, in Chicago, are the Teamsters and Steel. Steel stayed out, and the Teamsters were supposed to be helping Tom Houser. In the Senate race, certain unions were supporting the Republican candidate.

BRODER [to Jeb Magruder]. Is there any price at all that you paid in terms of the campaign for the labor support that you got?

MAGRUDER. When you start with nothing, as we did in '68, anything is a great improvement. We [in the Nixon campaign] were very pleased with the support we got, not only from labor, but also from the Jewish constituency and the famous peripheral urban ethnics. From a policy standpoint, I'm sure we'll have an increased flexibility in our dealings with labor in the next four years. So if we've given up anything, what we've given up is the rigidity that possibly the Republican Party has had in the past relating to labor.

KEEFE. The Administration picked up some of its labor support on the basis of its individual industrial policies. For example, the maritime unions and the maritime industry are in lock step on legislative and administrative policy. The Administration has reacted very favorably to the interests of the maritime industry in the United States and has thereby attracted maritime labor on the basis of performance.

BRODER. Two of the names that have occurred least frequently in our discussion are the names of the Vice Presidential candidates—Spiro Agnew and Sargent Shriver, just to refresh your memories. Did both campaigns wall them up? If you think they had any effect at all on the campaigns, would you please describe what you think that effect was?

MAGRUDER. We felt that Vice President Agnew was one of our most effective surrogates. We used him very frequently; he was on the road during the whole period of the campaign. If you want to compare '70 with '72, which is what most people did, I think he approached the '72 campaign on a different rhetorical level—very consciously and very correctly—and felt much more comfortable. He was our major figure at fund-raising dinners, as well as our critical link with the regular party people.

BRODER. Why was the Vice President not included at all in the media campaign?

DAILEY. We didn't think that he had that much impact on the part of the electorate that we were trying to influence. We had the 43 per cent of the vote that was solid Republican, and we were trying to get the marginal Republican vote, the independent vote, and the movable Democratic vote. We felt that the Vice President was most beneficial to our efforts in the role that Jeb Magruder has described. Also, our basic effort was to stay with the President and not diffuse the issue. We thought that the issue was clearly defined, that there were two choices— the President (and I mean that distinction—not Richard Nixon, but the President) and the challenger, the candidate George McGovern. We wanted to keep the issue clearly defined that way.

NAUGHTON. To follow that up, was there any difficulty persuading the President to stay off the road?

MAGRUDER. No difficulty at all. I think there was an early decision that the strategy would be to have the President remain as the President as long as it was practical. He campaigned in fifteen or so states only in the last three weeks. We thought that was the appropriate approach, and I think he felt very strongly himself that it was.

DAILEY. I'd only amend that by saying that it is obvious that any man who had been in office and in politics as long as the President had would have loved to go out and, in the Harry Truman sense, "give 'em hell." But his own personal desires were one thing and running for re-election was another, and he was fully behind the decision.

MAGRUDER. We analyzed the Democratic platform and saw some loaded sticks in there that would have been beneficial to us. But we already had a campaign strategy laid out that we thought was going to be effective, and we didn't see a need to introduce elements that were not likely to affect the outcome. We had two or three key issues, and we didn't believe in changing our strategy in mid-stream because of other ancillary factors.

BRODER. What was Shriver supposed to do?

HART. He was a super campaigner. In terms of energy and conviction and excitement and so forth, he was superb to the degree that a lot of people wondered why he wasn't selected [by McGovern] in the first place or at least given more consideration. He would go practically anywhere and work as hard as you wanted him to work, but he had been out of politics for a while and had to educate himself almost overnight on the currents that were going on in American politics. Occasionally he tended to evidence a 1960 type of attitude about where the voters' heads were at.

KEEFE. Ben Wattenberg says those were Shriver's best speeches.

HART. Ben thought they were very advanced.

BRODER [to Patrick Caddell]. As far as you can tell, from your perspective [as McGovern's pollster], did either of the Vice Presidential candidates have any effect on the election?

CADDELL. Not really. Initially, I was a little surprised that Agnew was kept on the Republican ticket. In a lot of states, when we had very early run him with the President against a ticket, he would move some of Nixon's very soft support away from him. Agnew would cost Nixon a couple of points by shaking away some liberal, moderate, suburbanite Republicans. But during the campaign, the Vice President picked up a little bit from a point that was not very high, so he made no real impact on the election.

BRODER. During our discussions here, almost everyone has related finances, success at the convention, speeches, debates, and so forth, to the results of the polls. Since almost everyone has criticized the credibility of these polls, why is there still so much importance attached to them?

CADDELL. When you're a pollster for a campaign that's very far behind in the public polls, you find yourself in an interesting twilight zone as to what you believe about polls. Everyone follows polls because everything in American life is geared to the question of who's going to win— whether it's sports or politics or whatever. There's a natural curiosity. But there is a distrust of polls in terms of just horse-race numbers. That is usually the least important information that you can get.

BRODER. I'm not sure in my own mind that there is really a question about the credibility of the polls. Is there a question?

KEEFE. They were on the beam, weren't they?

WATTENBERG. They were right on the money.

KAMPELMAN. Except for the Field poll, which we really have to raise a question about. But other than that, I think there's no credibility question.

HART. When the members of the press would ask, "What do Caddell's polls say?" I would answer, "Well, his surveys are telling us such-and-such." A distinction constantly has to be made between polls—that is, horse-race numbers—and surveys—voter attitudes. The disillusionment with the polls that we [in the McGovern campaign] and other people felt lay in the use of the polls throughout '70 and '71 and '72 to predict who would be the Democratic nominee. That's where the polls fell flat. They can't factor in intensity.

OTTEN. But there obviously is a difference, isn't there, between polls in the primaries and the final election?

CADDELL. The polls done right before the election usually were very good. But the problem came when you started early, without the factors of recognition and campaigns, and tried to make predictions. Most people who do public-opinion polls for newspapers do them in the last twenty-four or forty-eight hours; the likelihood of being wrong then is very little. We [Cambridge Survey Research] had clients in state races, in incumbent-challenger situations, who, going into September, were thirty points behind in the polls. But we knew that they had the potential to win. The public polls very rarely get into a discussion of what's underlying the numbers, what the potential is, who might be moved, and so forth.

KEEFE. One of Pat Caddell's competitors has written a book that should be required reading of all newspaper people—Tad Cantril's book on polls [Albert Cantril and

Charles Roll, *Polls: Their Use and Misuse in Politics*]—
which tries to explain to people like reporters, who don't
understand it, what it's all about.

5
The Press
in the
Campaign

JAMES M. PERRY (*National Observer*). Our discussion here suggests that the voters may not have been very interested in Vice President Agnew, but members of the press damn well were. I suppose you could go back to the [1969] speech in which particularly television journalism was attacked for having an alleged leftward bias. In a recent column in *Newsweek*, Dick Dougherty [McGovern's press secretary] guesses that 90 per cent of the reporters covering George McGovern voted for him. I'm not sure that's correct—I think it was considerably less than that—but Dougherty ends up by asking why they didn't write it that way if they were that much for him. Finally he suggests that what we need is more advocacy journalism. We wonder whether the press, in fact, does have an ideological bias, to the left or any other direction. It would seem that initially the press ignored McGovern entirely and went to Muskie, who was supposed to be the centrist. Then we rediscovered McGovern and found him to be one of the great geniuses of our time, along with his agents—Gary Hart, Frank Mankiewicz, and the rest. Then we decided finally that McGovern and his people were bumblers. We went full circle on McGovern and everyone else. I think the best thing is to let you all beat us over the head if you like, except of course the four of us who are here.

MAX M. KAMPELMAN (adviser to Humphrey). I would certainly challenge anybody who would try to state that the answer to the problem of the press is advocacy journalism. The problem, it seems to me, is the reverse. I sense that the tendency toward advocacy journalism is there—both on the air and in the print media. And even though frequently that advocacy happens to be on my side, I think it's a disservice to our democratic institutions. I don't like it; it's an easy temptation.

But there's another problem, which is exemplified by the nature of the press bus in a campaign. They're all together and there's a crowd up ahead, for example, and somebody looks up and says, "That's a helluva big crowd," and everybody says, "Yes, it's a big crowd." If this fellow had stood up and said, "What a lousy crowd," everybody would have said, "Yes, it's a lousy crowd." It's a natural thing to reflect what you hear among your colleagues because you certainly know they're not biased—you respect their professionalism. But I think there is a herd instinct in journalism, and it is reflected in the kinds of things you're talking about. It's interesting to me that Jim Perry described what "we" did. There was a kind of uniformity —going to Muskie, ignoring McGovern, going to McGovern, and completely, consistently ignoring Humphrey throughout the whole campaign. A professor at Johns Hopkins got some graduate students in political science to study four or five newspapers, including the *Washington Post* and the *New York Times*. Through a complicated mechanism, they judged column-inches, size of headlines, favorable and unfavorable summary evaluation. From January to June [of '72] there were really appalling figures in terms of Humphrey. There were covers on *Newsweek* and *Time* and on *Life* of McGovern; no covers of Humphrey during that whole period. It's a herd instinct, and I think it's a problem.

JAMES M. NAUGHTON (*New York Times*). How did the study factor in the subjective judgment of what is new in the news?

KAMPELMAN. They did not try to evaluate that. But, as a matter of fact, it's going to be very hard for me to be persuaded that somehow there was a great deal more new about what Muskie and McGovern were saying than about what Humphrey was saying. Also, you're injecting something else here, which is the whole definition of news, which I think is disturbing. You fellows write a story by starting with a lead which is supposed to be an attention-arresting beginning to a story; and, in my judgment, you've begun the process of distortion right there.

GARY W. HART (campaign director for McGovern). A defense of the press. We were so convinced sometime in '71 that Muskie was getting all the press and that McGovern was getting none that we commissioned one of our volunteers to spend a tedious number of days at the Library of Congress measuring column-inches. We were planning to get a room full of press people then and just let them have it. Much to our chagrin, as it turned out, the totals were within a fraction of the same. It is very easy in a campaign to feel subjectively that your man isn't getting the coverage when, factually and statistically, he is.

On the other hand, I'll have to support Max Kampelman about the so-called pack journalism. Of course, you have to distinguish between the electronic media, the print media, the editors, the columnists, the reporters. The people who write political columns in this country are, by and large, dead wrong—the so-called columnists. The people who report politics are, by and large, excellent. But there are the lazy ones who want to see what Johnny

Apple [of the *New York Times*] is going to say and what Dave Broder is going to say and then write their stories. I have literally seen reporters gather around Johnny Apple as he files his lead on the phone, and then go back to their typewriters and type their stories. If Johnny Apple says that George McGovern made a "surprisingly strong showing" in Iowa, that is going to appear in all kinds of papers, just because they heard him say it. That's too bad.

ANNE WEXLER (Democratic voter-registration director). I'd like to hear a little bit from the members of the press about their feelings on covering the Nixon campaign, and what it was like to cover a candidate that in fact did not campaign.

PERRY. We couldn't cover Nixon, so we all rushed out and covered Agnew. It was a sorry solution to the problem. I think a lot of reporters believe that covering a campaign means to jump on the campaign plane and go along with the candidate and listen to the same speech and measure the crowd he had that day. I did once go with Nixon, and Ron Ziegler [Nixon's press secretary] conned us all by saying that the crowd in Atlanta was something like a million; I measured the square feet of the space where the crowd had gathered, and found that the most you could have gotten in there was 75,000. That's the kind of thing we were doing—going along and saying how wonderful the crowds were.

NAUGHTON. The first point that I'd like to make is that we did cover the Nixon campaign 365 days a year. We covered it in China, we covered it in the Soviet Union, we covered it whenever we wrote about the President and his activities. But my second point is that in covering Nixon, either as President or as campaigner, we did not get as close to him as we may have gotten to McGovern in the general-election campaign. We didn't get at him; we didn't irritate him; we didn't draw him out. That was something over which we discovered we had very little control, in part because of the strategy of the Republican campaign. When George McGovern announced, he made a point of being open and, as a consequence, invited the kind of attention that we eventually got around to giving him. I don't know that there would have been any way to avoid giving him that attention.

RICHARD H. STEWART (press secretary for Muskie). I'd like to take exception and give an example of one instance which I was amazed at, frankly, in terms of the White House press coverage. There was a statement by a member of the White House staff who said that he thought the press in the White House asked soft questions and that he didn't see any great need for press conferences.

JEB S. MAGRUDER (Committee for the Re-election of the President). That was John Ehrlichman's statement.

STEWART. And it was just a few days later that the President held his first televised press conference after the Watergate disclosure. That press conference was kind of a jocular give-and-take between the President and the press—everybody was happy and everybody was kidding with the President. It was a helluva press conference, from the President's point of view. Not one person in the White House press corps had the guts to ask Nixon a question about Watergate, which was paramount in everybody's mind at that time.

PERRY. You hear all the time these days that print has

lost its influence and doesn't have that much impact on a campaign—that what is important is electronic. Do any of you who ran campaigns have thoughts on the question of print versus electronic?

ROBERT J. KEEFE (consultant to the AFL-CIO). Walt deVries [political analyst] has published a lot of work in that area. He thinks that print is a major influence, but his studies do not show it to have the influence of electronics—at least in his target groups.

PETER H. DAILEY (The November Group—Nixon). It's obvious that television is the dominant element today. The average television set is in use in a house six hours a day.

BEN J. WATTENBERG (adviser to Jackson). When you try to work the press on behalf of a candidate, you find that the way to get the video coverage that you want is to get the print coverage that you want. In other words, video people take their cue from what the commentators, the reporters, the guys traveling, write—whether Jackson is a conservative or a liberal, whether Humphrey is an old politician or a new politician, whether McGovern is the wave of the future or the wave of the past. It is very difficult to work the TV network guys themselves because so many of the decisions are made by some faceless people up in New York. Whereas you can get to Dave Broder by picking up the phone. It's a different process really.

KAMPELMAN. And these fellows in New York are reading the *Washington Post* and the *New York Times.*

RICK G. STEARNS (deputy campaign manager for Mc-

Govern). A lot depends on the quality of the paper and how it is perceived by the community. The McClatchy papers in California must be worth 200,000 votes in the Central Valleys. I have seen people walk into polling places in Fresno and Sacramento carrying recommendations clipped from their papers. And I think one reason we lost Fresno County in this election was that the McClatchy papers did not endorse McGovern—which came as somewhat of a surprise since it was the first time in my memory that they had not endorsed the Democratic nominee. Another aspect that ought to be mentioned is the extent to which the press conditions campaign decisions. I would guess that we subscribed daily to eighty or ninety newspapers from around the country, and these were our main sources of information about what was happening. What the candidate said in Seattle or what he said in Portland was probably more determined by newspapers than by any other single set of information that we were receiving, other than the advice of our local campaign managers.

WATTENBERG. I think that this year we saw the advent of something very salutary in political journalism—increased attitudinal reporting. You can't cover a candidate by going out and looking at the crowds; the real story, of course, is what's going on in the minds of the voters. The *New York Times* really made a departure with Jack Rosenthal's work on the Yankelovich studies. And Dave Broder and Haynes Johnson [of the *Washington Post*] did structured attitudinal interviews. Although I didn't always agree with the results, and people tended to buy some notions that weren't wholly valid, I think basically the development in the press was very good.

As for what Max Kampelman said about the bias of the press—in the Jackson campaign we felt that early on we were blacked out of coverage. We felt this was partly because the press people were leaning to the left, which may or may not have been true; but the view I ultimately came to was that any such bias is superseded by another one. We saw it first with Muskie, when they built him up and then tore him down, and then with McGovern, when they built him up and tore him down; they have the bias of the piranha fish—they will go after anything that bleeds.

DAILEY. I think one thing that has to be considered is the fact that for George McGovern and for many of the people involved in his campaign, this was their second or maybe their first effort. You've got to realize that this was President Nixon's fifth Presidential campaign, and you can't go through that many campaigns without having developed certain understandings and disciplines.

CHARLES GUGGENHEIM (media adviser to McGovern). A voter once remarked to me about a candidate I was helping that "to know him was to dislike him." This election may have been a case in which George McGovern's appearances on television hurt us more than they helped us. And I think if Richard Nixon had been on television news as much as George McGovern, the Democrats would have gained votes. Having come out of five Presidential campaigns, Nixon must have realized this. I imagine that the President might have said, "Well, look, I'm on television in China; I'm on television in Moscow; I don't want to be on television talking to George McGovern." I think we have to understand that more does not mean better, that more does not mean we're going to win, that more may mean less.

Another point: we should recognize the effect that the press has on our decisions on where we go and how we operate. *Newsweek* did a survey that showed the most widely read column in the United States is Jack Anderson, closely followed by Art Buchwald, or it may be in reverse —but only 4.3 per cent of the people who read newspapers read those columns. Again, I don't think a day went by in the McGovern campaign when someone didn't get absolutely livid about what somebody was saying in a column that was read by only 1.5 per cent of the people in this country, and this influenced the election because it influenced us to go out and do something or react to something or get upset with something. But we have to put these things in perspective. The real events are so much more important.

PERRY. What about the contention that the press has a bias toward the left?

MAGRUDER. I think we [in the Nixon campaign] felt very comfortable with the news coverage of this campaign. The one thing which surprised us was that the press didn't zero in on us earlier and start to realize what was really going on in our campaign. We were very pleased because we did not want to get our strategy out on the line early, but I think some enterprising people could have found out more about our direct-mail activity and our really unusual use of the telephone. I thought this was just a lack of aggressiveness on the part of the press. On the whole we were pleased, though of course, as you know, we think there is advocacy journalism to some extent in the Eastern liberal establishment axis. I think that it's more prominent than it should be in the *Washington Post* and in the *New York Times*. But that's a point of view.

PERRY. Are you suggesting that if the press had zeroed

in on your direct mail and your telephone banks there would have been an adverse result?

MAGRUDER. No, I just think it was a news story that was missed early by the press; I don't think it would have had a negative result. I think it might have given the opposition more opportunity to gear up, but maybe not. In our case, we made effective use of the information we had on the McGovern organization to get our troops going. We really pounded home to them the fact that George McGovern had a very strong, tough-minded organization. We had a problem of apathy with our troops, and this helped us tremendously in gearing them up to work.

HART. I'd like to ask the reporters their opinions on whether the McGovern campaign was too open. Were we too available?

PERRY. It was the most garrulous staff that I've ever seen—they lined up to talk to you.

HART. I guess that answers my question. Wait until next time.

NAUGHTON. I doubt seriously if I can improve on that answer, but I would like to say that Jeb Magruder raised the question of enterprise in the political press corps in trying to determine what may have been going on in the Republican campaign. Access is, of course, very important to enterprise. It was very easy to obtain access to key people in the McGovern campaign, and this was not true on the other side.

MAGRUDER. That's really not true. Your guy Bob Semple used to float in and out, and he would come over and say, "I've got a real problem—I'm handling the White House and I'm supposed to handle you and I really can't take the time." I'd say, "Well, that's fine, Bob, nice seeing you," and Bob would come in once every four months. That's really what happened in the case of the *New York Times*.

NAUGHTON. But I would like to suggest that anyone familiar with both headquarters could easily have noted a contrast between the McGovern and the Nixon campaign offices, simply in terms of ability to enter any given office. It was much more difficult, time-consuming, and frustrating for those who were covering your campaign to get at people with any degree of ease. I wasn't covering you, but I'm aware of other people's complaints.

MAGRUDER. In your case, it wasn't until September or October that Linda Charlton was evidently assigned to the Nixon campaign. She was all over the place, seeing everybody. We gave her access to everything, and she wrote some very good stories. But that was very late in the campaign, and the stories could have been written in June.

NAUGHTON. Another part of the problem is that we have been conditioned for so many years to assume that the campaign exists where the candidate is. We have not spent nearly enough time talking, first of all, to the voters, who are, after all, going to make the decision, and secondly, to the technicians in the campaign. I think that's changing; I think it changed to a large extent among a number of media people this year and will, no doubt, change considerably in the future, if we're allowed to get in.

MAGRUDER. The guy who had the best stories consistently on what I call the internal workings of the Nixon campaign was Lou Cannon of the *Washington Post*. He continually scooped the other newspapers with very accurate information on our programs and was really the first one to get into the surrogate program in any depth.

DAVID S. BRODER (*Washington Post*). That was a compliment to my colleague, but I must say that I think it's somewhat disingenuous to argue that there was not a difference in the matter of access to the two campaigns. The difference was pervasive at every level. You mentioned your telephone banks. I recall a year ago in New Hampshire running into a very charming lady from Minnesota who was up there running your phone-bank program. She was somewhat disconcerted at being recognized and said, "It's off the record that I'm here." And I said, "Well, that's a little difficult. Instead of that, why don't you give me your own version of what this campaign is doing here with your phone operation?" She said, "I cannot do that." I think she meant that quite literally. And it was, as we all know, quite a different situation at the Doral Hotel [in Miami] at the Republican convention and at the Democratic convention.

MAGRUDER. We agreed that that was a mistake. I think we felt that we were overly security conscious because of demonstration problems. We agree with you there, and we have said so publicly.

BRODER. But of all the disparities between the campaigns that have been mentioned here, I would guess that the most consequential, in terms of the outcome, was the disparity in access to the two candidates. I compliment you, from your point of view, on the degree of control that you maintained over access to the President. In effect, the only things that we were able to report about the President's campaign were those things which he selected to make available for reporting. This goes to a question that we haven't really discussed here—and it's probably beyond the scope of this meeting—as to whose campaign it is. The whole assumption here is that the campaign is in the control of the candidates and their managers. I would suppose, as reporters, that it would be our institutional bias that the campaign, in one sense or another, belongs to the public. This was an attitude that I think we found very little reflected in the Nixon campaign this year.

DAILEY. It gets back to whether or not there really are two candidates, and to whether or not the President, by his performance in office for three and a half years, isn't already providing far greater access than the candidate. By being President, he is campaigning in a sense; his performance in office is really being judged. It's all out there.

STEWART. But he can't be questioned on his performance the way the candidate is who is in the field every day with the traveling press corps. The fact of the matter is that the press people did not have the same opportunities to parry with the President that they did with Senator McGovern or Senator Muskie or Senator Humphrey or Senator Jackson. I just don't think that this is in the best interest of the country. By staying in the White House, I think the President made the right decision in political terms, but not in terms of the good of democratic institutions.

MAGRUDER. The Nixon campaign certainly always had a relatively controlled press policy. We always were accessible in campaign headquarters, but under controlled conditions. We wanted interviews to be scheduled through the press office so that we would have some knowledge of output. You may disagree with that policy possibly, but I don't think there is any reason why, in running a campaign, we shouldn't be able to control the output of our own employees. Much of what they might say could be very inaccurate because, with only a partial knowledge of things, they could get into all sorts of areas that they really don't know anything about. We tried to give the press people a broad-gauged look at the campaign so that they would get the story as accurately as possible. I think in this case that less, not more, was probably best from all points of view. [To David Broder] It's true that you would have a hard time talking with an employee up in New Hampshire in a casual situation, but you would not have had difficulty in talking about that same telephone bank with the proper people.

HART. Jim Perry made it very explicit that he thought that people in the McGovern campaign talked too much. Dave Broder seems to be suggesting some beneficial aspects of being open. Where do you draw the line, in case some of us ever do this again? In two and a half years, I don't remember ever calling a reporter and asking to get together with him, or inviting a reporter to lunch. On the other hand, I didn't turn too many of them down. Where do you draw the line?

PERRY. I think that's your problem. The point I was making was that there was a lot of self-serving going on within McGovern's staff. One person would whisper to you about how badly this other person was doing. It struck me that there were some disloyal people involved in that campaign.

HART. So it wasn't quantity so much as it was what people said?

PERRY. Yes. And a lot of it was minutiae of one kind or another that didn't go to the heart of what the campaign was about. It just seemed like almost adolescent behavior on the part of some people.

JACK L. CHESTNUT (campaign manager for Humphrey). These things become problems in a campaign if the campaign manager doesn't set some rules and guidelines for people about who can talk to the press in certain areas. In a campaign, many of your employees are very temporary, and in some instances you don't have much knowledge of their background or their capabilities. They have only limited information in any particular area, but they're questioned on the broad range of the campaign and expected to give an opinion. Then you see, "A well-placed source in the XYZ campaign says so and so," and you may get an image that is almost impossible to overcome. It's one of the management problems that you have in a campaign; and if you don't establish these rules, you particularly leave open an opportunity to those who are disloyal, to those who are seeking additional positions of power within the structure of the campaign and will use this as a device.

MAGRUDER. I think there's a natural desire, when questioned by the press, always to have an answer. A person who doesn't know the answer to a question may make up an answer, and his answer may become a major news story even though it's absolutely incorrect.

STEWART. Quite frequently I found in some of the less responsible papers that somebody would be quoted as a

Muskie source, and it would turn out to be some eighteen-year-old kid out of high school who was spending a couple of days in the campaign and was overwhelmed to be asked a question by a guy from the media. The ego thing is so strong that people can't help saying something, and they say the glibbest thing they can think of so that it will get into print. The comment is never attached to a name, yet when the public reads it, they make the general assumption that the quote is from somebody who really knows what's going on.

ALAN L. OTTEN (*Wall Street Journal*). There are good reporters and there are bad reporters, just as there are good academicians and bad academicians, and good lawyers and bad lawyers, and even good campaign tacticians and bad ones. But the basic thing, it seems to me, is the old and perfectly obvious and trite point that you kill the messenger bringing the bad news. Jeb Magruder said the press was great this year because we were kicking hell out of McGovern, but we weren't so good last year when we were kicking hell out of Nixon, and we weren't so good again when we were kicking Nixon on Watergate. Dick Stewart thought we were great when we were saying Muskie was the front-runner, but he didn't like it when we said Muskie cried. The McGovern people liked it when we said McGovern was up, but they didn't like us when we said he screwed up on Eagleton. Humphrey people didn't like us when we said he was running all over the country making a million promises a day. The press wasn't making those promises; the press didn't pick Eagleton; the press didn't tap phones, if in fact anybody did; the press didn't cry. I think it's very easy to pick on little things and get away from what was really basic and continuing throughout the campaign.

WATTENBERG. But everybody that I've known who has ever worked on a political campaign—right, left, or center —comes up with the same basic viewpoint—that what you read in the media isn't what's happening. It's a fairy tale. It's distorted. I think most of us know members of the press who are good, honest, loyal, wonderful people, but there's something in the mechanism of having to write a story, of having to file daily, of having to find news where sometimes there may not be very much news, that produces a picture for the public that does not coincide with the reality of either the candidate or the campaign.

NAUGHTON. I think this discussion has been very interesting and has, among other things, once again proved what I regard as a truism, which is that there are no two groups in American society which are more paranoid than politicians and the press.

6
Looking
to '76

JAMES M. NAUGHTON (*New York Times*). You may recall that Art Buchwald summed up the 1972 election by saying that Richard Nixon still came across as the man trying to sell a used car and George McGovern appeared to be the one who had bought it. Let us, like those generals who never seem to learn from how the last war was fought badly, attempt to draw some conclusions about this campaign, in terms of what it may mean in 1976.

DAVID S. BRODER (*Washington Post*). There are two or three specific questions that have been raised, the implications of which people might want to address themselves to as they make their comments. One is the question of financing: does the experience first of the Goldwater campaign on the Republican side and now of the McGovern campaign on the Democratic side suggest that an increased role for small contributors may tend to skew the nomination process in favor of candidates of ideologically extreme positions? A similar question is raised by the rules of reform that took place last time in the Democratic Party and the delegate selection changes that will be taking place next time in the Republican Party. Do these changes tend to skew the process in favor of the activists of an ideological extreme? The other question refers to the Democratic experience this time, but it may have implications for the Republicans four years from now, when they may have a contest for the nomination. Do the ideological differences that turned up in the Democratic Party presage some sort of basic political realignment?

JEB S. MAGRUDER (Committee for the Re-election of the President). I think everybody in our party realizes that we have an opportunity, not necessarily to turn the Republican Party into a majority party, but at least to turn more voters into independent voters and ticket-splitters. If we can do this and then put up the right kind of candidates, fund them correctly, and give them the proper management, we can do well despite our relatively small numbers as a party. This would be the minimum. Most people that I know in our party, in the White House and so on, feel that we should try to develop a broader based effort which will include some of the people who historically have not voted for Republican candidates, like the blue-collar workers, the Jewish constituency, the Mexican-American constituency—the groups that we did very well with last time. Some of these people have already made their initial effort at voting for a Republican, and we think it will be easier next time. I think it's important for us to try to build on this; and since we hold the executive for the next four years, I think we have an opportunity to do so. It is critically important that we put up the kind of candidates that can win; if we do, we can do very well, even though we're a minority party. If we put up poor candidates, we will lose. This may not be the time for a realignment of the parties—I think parties are going to have a tough time becoming the factor they used to be in the '20's and '30's. But we can build a base on which we can win national and state elections on a continuing basis. We do have this opportunity, and I think you'll see us continuing to try to build that coalition.

J. PHILIP REBERGER (Republican National Committee). I think Jeb Magruder quite accurately described the situation, and I'd concur 100 per cent. I must say that I was surprised at the Republican convention at the intensity of the conservative wing of the party and their efforts to tone down the reforms. Traditionally, and I think Barry Goldwater is a primary example, the activist wing of the Republican Party is the conservative wing. I don't personally believe that the liberal members of the party could secure the nomination for a very liberal candidate. Tom Houser and I were talking about this earlier today with regard to Senator Charles Percy [of Illinois]. He was saying how good a candidate Senator Percy might be in 1976, but that he would have a very difficult time getting the nomination through the Republican Party process.

As for reforms in our party, I hope they come about but I don't see a drastic realignment of the power structure within the party if they do. I don't know about the ability of the McGovern people to raise money through the small donors. But Goldwater did this in 1964, and I think the base of the small donors that he got through the television appeals of Governor Reagan and himself allowed the Republican Party to exist through 1966 and go into the 1968 campaign with money that they wouldn't have had otherwise. They had no place else to go; they used that Goldwater list and they survived. Ray Bliss was able to put together an organization that the Republican nominee could ride on to victory in 1968.

As for the 1972 election, we in the Republican National Committee were generally quite pleased that John Mitchell and Jeb Magruder met with our key political people early on in 1971 and that we were included in the

organizational decision-making process. We also produced a weekly newsletter that served two purposes. It
was our communication vehicle to keep our donors and
members out in the grass-roots area informed of a very
partisan view of the President's record and the party's
stands; but also quite often *Monday* made news in the
press all by itself, standing on its own. We were pleased
to play a fairly major role in the Presidential campaign,
as we haven't done in previous years.

RICK G. STEARNS (deputy campaign manager for Mc-
Govern). When we talk about the issue of the party system in this country—at least in terms of Presidential
elections—we are really addressing the question of
whether or not the Democratic Party will survive as an
electioneering organization. I can remember as a student
being impressed with the quaint alarm the founding
fathers expressed at the phenomenon of "factions." That
really is what we have in the Democratic Party. We are
not any longer a unified national party. We are a loose
and uneasy coalition of two factions that had their origins
in internal dispute over the war in Vietnam. Since 1968
the fight within the party has become institutionalized
to the extent that healing the breach will be a difficult
process. We have to recognize that the Democratic Party
is essentially a party of incumbency, and unfortunately
we are an incumbent party that has been put out of
power, with only the shreds of issues and programs. I'm
sure Ben Wattenberg will disagree with me, but I think
that our factions are really differentiated more by style
than by serious difference over real issues. In the intel-
lectual leadership of the two factions, one group thinks
the party can best cope with the 1970's by retreating to
the 1950's, while the other group thinks that any idea
that was rejected by the New Deal can be resurrected

now, labeled new again, and put forward as a program for the future.

At one point, the Byzantine Empire was governed by factions called Blues and Greens, which sponsored chariot races at the Hippodrome. These groups took on a political life. No one quite understood their origins or what divided them, but everyone recognized the intensity of the hostility that these two crowds developed after years of competing with one another. That is the point that the Democratic Party has come to. Institutionalized factions threaten to destroy the Democratic Party as a national party. If the Democratic Party is going to survive its history since 1968, it's going to have to concentrate less on fighting and more on thinking. In particular, it must think about the kind of program that we're going to carry to the public in 1976.

ROBIN SCHMIDT (campaign manager for McCloskey). I have nothing to add to what Jeb Magruder and Phil Reberger said, except maybe to reiterate my feeling that a liberal Republican candidacy is out of the question in 1976. And I guess I'd like to register my personal regret that the McGovern and McCloskey campaigns in '72 had so little effect on the war.

RICHARD H. STEWART (press secretary for Muskie). It struck me in my own experience with Muskie in this particular year that there were passions on the left and there were passions on the right, as exemplified by McGovern and Wallace, and there was in fact no room in the middle in the primaries for the centrist candidate. And in large measure, the money opened up on both the right and the left because of passions. If you can win primaries only by being perceived to be on one fringe or the other, because only those people who are passionate are going to come out and vote in primaries, then you have a problem when you face the general election. I don't know that it should be a great surprise that the public won't accept candidates, generally speaking, who are perceived as being on the left or the right.

The Democrats have lost some of their traditional voting strength, and I think Richard Nixon, unlike some of his predecessors who spent a lot of time building their own personal constituency and not building the party constituency, is working to build the Republican Party. I read the other day that he's going to put labor people in second-echelon positions throughout the government. I think he's trying hard to keep the voting blocs that he won this time. And I think Nixon probably will do a better job of it than Lyndon Johnson or Dwight Eisenhower did, because they didn't care and I think Nixon does. I think this is a problem that the Democrats are going to have to face.

BEN J. WATTENBERG (adviser to Jackson). I was very interested in Rick Stearns's analysis of Byzantium and the days of the Blues and the Greens. I think that there is a split in the Democratic Party—between the Redskins and the Dolphins, or the Blues and the Greens—but there is surely a split. I have been attempting to gauge what the McGovern people here feel about what happened this year. Gary Hart said that he thought up until the very end that McGovern would win. And we've heard that the convention was really terrific, and that people in America thought it was a wonderful show. We've heard that McGovern lost because of a lack of competence. And we've heard that one of Sargent Shriver's problems was that his head was back in the 1960's. As a Democrat who'd like to see this party win in 1976, I think the keystone to restructuring this party has to be a recognition that this party lost in 1972 because the American people did not agree with what it stood for or what its nominee stood for.

This is not to say that this party cannot win with a liberal candidate. I think that there is a great area of agreement between the Blues and the Greens on issues of health care, economics, civil rights, civil liberties, the environment, aid to cities—all of these 1960's liberal issues. The belief in these liberal issues, which Gary Hart thinks is a flaw in Shriver's head, I would say is a great strength—the 1960's was a time when we elected Presidents and changed the country for the better. This is a valuable consensus and one, despite what Mr. Magruder says, that the American people have not rejected. There is a liberal constituency out there that can be appealed to, and that a candidate can represent. I would go back to what Richard Scammon and I said in our book [*The Real Majority*]—that you can be economically and pro-grammatically extremely liberal in this country, but that when you slop over into areas of social-issue liberalism, it's death on wheels. I think that we learned this in '72 on issue after issue—on busing, on amnesty, on pot and permissiveness—the whole series of things that, rightly or wrongly, became identified with the "new politics." And therein is a lesson.

ANNE WEXLER (Democratic voter-registration director). Jeb Magruder said that the Republican Party intended to concentrate on ticket-splitters and independents and would try to develop good candidates in order to build a majority in this country. I think that the same applies to the Democratic Party. I think that there is no longer in this country any institutional loyalty to political par-ties. I think the campaigns of both '72 and '70 proved that. At this point in time, because of the great increase in independent voters, there is no majority political party, and that is something that the Democratic Party must address itself to in the next four years.

In addition, I think that the Democratic Party, and probably the Republicans as well, should begin to consider the direction in which the entire Presidential selection process is moving. In 1972 we had twenty-three primaries; and if the country is going to continue to move in the direction of more state primaries, I think people should be looking at whether or not a national primary is a feasible idea. The selection of candidates for national office by primaries, where there are some real questions about the size of the turnout and about the kind of people who vote, is something that must be looked at by both parties in the next four years.

In addition, I think a lot of Democrats are not aware of the new rules that were passed at the '72 convention. We started a lot of trouble for ourselves in '72 with some of the new rules we passed because a lot of them have to do with changes in state laws. We passed a rule that there must be proportional representation in every state as far as delegates to the '76 convention are concerned. We passed another rule that there can be no more unit-rule primaries, so you can't have a primary like the one in Maryland where whoever wins the preference poll gets all the delegates, even though delegates may have run pledged to other candidates. We also passed a rule that no Democratic primary can have crossover voting. In the next four years we have a rather significant job to do in trying to implement these rules, and it's not going to be easy.

In addition, I think we're going to have to look very hard at some of the reforms that were passed in 1972. I certainly don't approve of going backward, but I think this is something that should concern Democrats in the next four years. I think probably the other thing that should concern us all is the fact that parties as institutions are definitely on the way out.

PATRICK H. CADDELL (Cambridge Survey Research—McGovern). I'm not so much interested in the party struggles as I am in what has been going on in the country. There have been changes going on, and some of them are not particularly positive. It has been a traditional fact of American life that people have always believed that their country was getting better, that they were the chosen people, that history had never really been visited upon them in the sense of their losing anything, that the future was going to be better than the present, and that the present was always better than the past. But those of us who have been listening to the American people this year have been struck by the fact that they no longer believe that things are getting better; they now think that things are getting very much worse.

We go on talking about the great struggle between the two parties and within the parties, but people in general don't think that those parties particularly affect them. And beyond that, they think the government doesn't care about them, that it lies to them, that it does nothing to improve their lives, and, most importantly, that it doesn't seem to affect the country. A new study by the Potomac Associates has found that there's a tremendous desire for basic change in the structure of the country. I think perhaps we have been out of touch with the American people, and unless we do something for all these people who feel that the system doesn't work for them—and I'm not talking about the kids or intellectuals, but about people who make $10,000 a year and move to the suburbs—then at some point we're going to have to pay the piper.

JACK L. CHESTNUT (campaign manager for Humphrey). I think one thing that we should have learned from the 1972 campaign is that we must nominate a candidate with whom the broad spectrum of the Democratic Party can more clearly identify. We also have to gain, I think, a greater respect for the importance of the office of the Presidency, and recognize how important it is to the Democratic Party to elect a Democratic President. We must understand the awesome power that this office has as a force for social good, and the long-term effect it has on individual rights and justice. We are willing to argue about degrees in terms of ideology, but that ideology isn't important unless we obtain the office. I once had a football coach who told us that you can't score if you can't get into the game, and if you can't learn to play as a team, you can't get into the game. We haven't been in the game for the last four years, and we're not going to be in it for the next four. I think that in 1968 the intolerance of the left of the Democratic Party had much to do with the defeat of Hubert Humphrey; in 1972 the intolerance of the middle and the right had much to do with the size of the defeat of George McGovern. If we continue to operate this way, with this degree of intolerance within our own party organization, and fail to operate as a team, we're not going to elect our candidate in 1976.

PETER H. DAILEY (The November Group—Nixon). I agree with Anne Wexler that, at least at the Presidential level, a party label on a candidate is of very little consequence any more. Labels only really appeal to hard-core segments on either side. Ever since the '72 campaign got under way, I have been in awe of the power of the incumbent and marveling at the magnitude of the job that faces a challenger to an incumbent President. The process in '72 was more of a referendum than an election, and we really can't take very much that we learned this year into '76 because then we'll be back to having two candidates again instead of a President and a candidate.

Finally, in spite of all the credit that Phil Reberger and Jeb Magruder and I and others would like to take for influencing the election, for swinging the winning margin of votes, I think basically we would all say that the President did it himself. He was at 60 per cent in the preference polls in September before we did anything to effectuate a campaign, and I think his stewardship of the office got the vote—even if it sometimes came from people who said, "I'd rather take a devil I know than a devil I don't."

MORRIS S. DEES, JR. (direct-mail chairman for McGovern). I'm not sure of the long-range effect of what I learned in this campaign, which was the value of the small donor to political parties and political campaigns. It's interesting to hear Phil Reberger say that Goldwater's small donors were used to keep the Republican Party alive until Nixon could get his $10 million in undisclosed contributions. And had Muskie not had some Nixon money in New Hampshire, I wonder where he would have been. With the new financial-disclosure law, it's questionable whether large contributions are going to come from people who are not ideologically concerned with issues. McGovern got a lot of money from people who are antiwar or anti this or that or the other, who are idle rich or very rich or some other kind of rich, but this is not the usual Democratic money that you get.

I notice, looking over the Republican contributors, that they had a lot of $3,000 and $6,000 contributions from officers in large corporations. I wish Billy Joe Camp was still here to talk for Wallace, but I think the financing of the Wallace effort in national politics has been almost solely by smaller donors. There were a lot of rumors in

Alabama that H. L. Hunt [Texas oil producer] gave Wallace a lot of money. All he ever gave him, and I really do know this personally, was two autographed copies of some book he wrote, and he sent those without postage and they had to pay the postage. I know all this because I've been very close to the Wallace organization—they keep their names on a computer that I used to own in Montgomery. But I think that the new disclosure law is going to cause small donors to be critically important.

One thing I did learn in the campaign—and I think the Republicans probably learned it long before we did—is that copy does count. We learned this a long time ago in the business field. I don't know if McGovern's eight-page letters worked in the Harvard atmosphere, but they worked out there in the grass roots. That copy was important to us in getting our money. I don't know whether this can translate to a centrist candidate—consider that the national magazines like *Life* and *Look* have failed because they cannot attract subscribers and advertisers, whereas the special interest magazines have gone on.

Maybe McGovern was a special interest cause, like Goldwater and Wallace, and only such a cause could attract the special interest donors that made it successful. But I hope that this isn't the case. The Democrats now have a roster of over a million small donors through the telethon and McGovern's list and the Democratic list, and I believe that this could be turned into something maybe larger than the Republicans' small donor program. I think that we could, very practically, have two million contributors in the next Democratic campaign if the right techniques are used.

CHARLES GUGGENHEIM (media adviser to McGovern). I'd like to say first of all, in case no one else wants to say it, that this has been a great experience for me and I think for a lot of us. I think too often in the democratic process we see our adversaries as people with horns, who couldn't possibly be as intelligent and as honest and as forthright as ourselves. I think there's a great lesson to be learned around this table that that is not true, and it's a lesson we ought to carry into our next campaign.

Thomas Jefferson said that the ultimate wisdom really lies with the people. And though I can't help feeling that maybe the American people did not exercise their ultimate wisdom, I think there are many reasons to believe that the American people really did know who the candidates were and what they believed. I don't think there was anything in the process, anything in the mass media, that distorted to any important degree who Richard Nixon was or who George McGovern was and what they would try to do in office. I don't think the process as we saw it open up in front of us, with its lies and distortions and understatements and overstatements, really turned the American people's mind away from what was really happening and who was who and what was what. We may disagree with how they took those facts and finally executed them into votes. But the thing we can all be very proud of, and I think get very excited about, is that through this jungle, this traveling circus, this menagerie of facts and everything, people did get to hear and see and feel most of everything that was going on—certainly more than any other people in the history of man. I think that's very, very good.

I'm disappointed perhaps on the outcome of the war issue, and I'm also disappointed that maybe the process does not allow an incumbent President to come out and be faced with issues and problems. The founding fathers instituted the election process as a cleansing process, one where things could be brought out and discussed and the people could every once in a while take new inventory. I don't think we had a chance to do that in this election. I think the incumbency of the President, whether he be Democratic or Republican, does not permit that. I think the process has to be changed to make that necessary, and if it is not, I think we are going to have some dangers there. I hope that next election we can improve some of the things that we've been discussing so that the people at this table and the people not at this table can get involved in a process which I think ultimately cannot leave anything but pride in all our hearts.

GARY W. HART (campaign director for McGovern). It seems to me three questions have emerged at this conference, and they are the same three that emerged from the election. First, did Richard Nixon create a new majority? Second, was this election decided on the crucial issues of the day? And third, did George McGovern represent a potentially viable political mainstream in this country or was he merely a fringe candidate?

I'll come back and give my answers to those questions after answering the further question of whether or not George McGovern could have won. I think he could have. He was a long-shot candidate who had to do everything right and get almost all the breaks. We had to have an absolutely unified party. We had to be able to articulate the issues that he was concerned about simply enough and clearly enough so that people understood them. We had to have for all practical purposes no political problems to solve—certainly not a problem like the Vice Presidency. We had to run a flawless campaign operation, which is rarely done. President Nixon had to make a few mistakes, that is to say, he had to come out and campaign. And finally, the perception of George McGovern, which is really the combination of all these things, had to be a very good one. The key word, it seems to me, that's been used here has been "perception." We failed to create the proper perception.

In my judgment the answers to my three original questions are as follows: Nixon did not create a new majority; this election was not decided upon the crucial issues of the day; and George McGovern does, in fact, represent a potentially viable political mainstream position in this country. In my judgment the mood of the country is progressive. I don't know whether that is the same thing that Ben Wattenberg means by 1960's liberalism; maybe it is. What Pat Caddell was saying about people of this country being in a mood for change, not in a mood to retrench or stand still or back away from the problems of this country or the world, is absolutely right.

If there has been a failure this political year, on the part of both Democrats and Republicans, it has been a failure of leadership, of courage, of telling the American people what they need and want to hear. That's a plague on both our houses, but the Republicans are more guilty than we are because they have the power of the White House. The problems this country faces are not so much substantive as they are structural and institutional. And if the institutions don't change, then the people will change them. That's what most of us are concerned about.

ROBERT J. KEEFE (consultant to the AFL-CIO). Four years ago, in the analyses that were made of the '68 election, there was much written and much said about the United States entering an age of one-term Presidencies. It was contended that the problems of the country were such that it would be impossible to solve the problem of managing the problems and at the same time maintain a viable political base on which to be re-elected. I didn't quite agree with that then, and I think the President has since demonstrated that, in addition to all its other awesome powers, the awesome political power of the Presidency is such that it limits the opportunity of a contending party or contending candidate to unseat an incumbent President. When 1972 arrived, the Democratic Party had an opportunity to secure the power of the White House, but it was a limited opportunity, and the President took advantage of his power to further limit it.

We had some downside risks as a party [in '72] and I think the downside risks were avoided. The downside risk of paramount interest to me was that we could very easily have lost the power of the Congress. We didn't lose the power of the Congress; in fact, in an ideological sense, we not only maintained the level of Democratic support but increased it slightly. A second downside risk was that we could have lost some of the gains that we, as a party, had made in the off-year elections in 1970 in the South. The South in 1970 sort of came back to the national Democratic Party, and we could have very easily blown that; that we didn't was, I think, in large part the result of the activity of Governor Wallace. We won't really know about this until the next couple of elections—the off-year election in '74 and then '76.

Whenever I review the influences on the nominating process, I'm always distressed that the impact of finances is so great. The candidate's ability to fund himself seems to be more important than a lot of other factors in determining who is nominated; you have to have enough money at the right times in order to become viable. I don't know how this problem will be solved, but I think it will have a tremendous effect on the future of the country unless it is solved.

Our party will spend a lot of energy and talent looking at itself for the next couple of years, and I think that's good. I'm impressed by the lack of argument about what was good and what was bad in the party reforms. I think that, unfortunately, we will have to run an election under the new rules to determine what was progress and what wasn't. In the discussions that I have with both the Blues and the Greens, I'm impressed that they see the strengths and weaknesses pretty similarly. So I have some optimism that the re-examination process won't have the kinds of emotional conflicts it might have been expected to have. I think the worst thing we did to the electoral process was to make it more expensive. But on the whole, I think that the Democrats came out of the election with minimal loss. A last comment: I was concerned that this conference might be somewhat like a meeting I attended when I was in college of the Burlington Liars' Club, and it hasn't been that. And I think we're all the better that it hasn't been.

NAUGHTON. Without attempting or presuming to speak for the Institute of Politics or for the Nieman Foundation, or for that matter for any future candidate who may benefit from any wisdom generated by this conference, I would like to say that I think these discussions have been remarkable. My hope is that whatever mistakes all of us make over the next four years, we will be given an opportunity to come back and offer alibis and explanations.

Appendixes
and Index

Appendix A
Some Campaign Dates

1971

January 18   *Senator George S. McGovern* (Democrat, South Dakota) announced that he was a candidate for the Presidency.

February 19   The recommendations of the McGovern Commission on Delegate Selection and Party Structure were accepted by the Democratic National Committee.

July 9   *Congressman Paul N. McCloskey* (Republican, California) declared his intention of seeking the Republican nomination for President.

July 15   *Senator Harold E. Hughes* (Democrat, Iowa) stated that he would not seek the Presidency.

September 24 *Senator Fred R. Harris* (Democrat, Oklahoma) announced that he would be a candidate for the Presidency.

October 12   Following his wife's major surgery, *Senator Birch Bayh* (Democrat, Indiana) said that he would not seek the Democratic nomination for President.

October 26   Former *Senator Eugene J. McCarthy* (Democrat, Minnesota) announced that he would be attempting to gather convention delegates.

November 10   Citing lack of funds, Senator Harris announced his withdrawal from the competition.

November 19   *Senator Henry M. Jackson* (Democrat, Washington) formally declared his intention of seeking the Presidency.

December 17   Senator McCarthy said that he intended to be a candidate in the Massachusetts primary.

December 28   New York *Mayor John V. Lindsay,* after having switched to the Democratic Party in August, announced that he would be seeking that party's Presidential nomination.

December 29   *Congressman John M. Ashbrook* (Republican, Ohio) declared his intention of entering the New Hampshire and Florida primaries in order to present a conservative alternative to President Nixon.

1972

January 3   *Senator Vance Hartke* (Democrat, Indiana) announced his intention of entering the New Hampshire primary and perhaps others.

January 4   *Senator Edmund S. Muskie* (Democrat, Maine) announced that he was a candidate for the Presidency.

January 7   *President Richard M. Nixon* declared that he would be seeking re-election.

January 10   *Senator Hubert H. Humphrey* (Democrat, Minnesota) announced for the Presidency.

January 13   Alabama *Governor George C. Wallace* declared his intention of entering the Florida primary.

January 18   *Congressman Wilbur D. Mills* (Democrat, Arkansas) requested removal of his name from the primary ballot in Florida, while allowing it to remain in Wisconsin and Nebraska.

January 25   *Congresswoman Shirley Chisholm* (Democrat, New York) declared that she would seek the Democratic Presidential nomination.

February 21   President Nixon arrived in Peking for an eight-day visit.

February 22 *Senator Edward M. Kennedy* (Democrat, Massachusetts) requested removal of his name from the primary ballots in Wisconsin and Nebraska.

Governor Wallace announced that he would enter the Maryland primary.

February 26 Senator Muskie appeared at the *Manchester Union Leader* building in New Hampshire to counter charges made by publisher William Loeb.

February 28 Senator McGovern listed the sources of his campaign contributions since the announcement of his candidacy in January 1971.

March 1 Congressman McCloskey revealed his campaign contributors to date.

March 3 Senator Kennedy requested removal of his name from the primary ballot in Oregon.

March 7 *New Hampshire primary*: Senator Muskie, 46 per cent of the Democratic vote; Senator McGovern, 37 per cent. President Nixon, 68 per cent of the Republican vote; Congressman McCloskey, 20 per cent; Congressman Ashbrook, 11 per cent.

Mayor Lindsay announced the sources of his campaign funds.

March 10 Citing a lack of money to continue in competition, Congressman McCloskey announced his withdrawal from active campaigning.

March 14   *Florida primary*: Governor Wallace, 42 per cent of the Democratic vote; Senator Humphrey, 18 per cent; Senator Jackson, 13 per cent; Senator Muskie, 9 per cent; Mayor Lindsay, 7 per cent. President Nixon, 87 per cent of the Republican vote.

Senator Humphrey announced his campaign contributors.

March 21   *Illinois primary*: Senator Muskie won 63 per cent of the Democratic vote, with opposition only from Senator McCarthy in the preferential race.

March 26   Senator Hartke announced his withdrawal.

March 27   Senator Muskie announced the sources of his campaign funds.

April 4   *Wisconsin primary*: Senator McGovern received 30 per cent of the Democratic vote, followed by Governor Wallace with 22 per cent, Senator Humphrey with 21 per cent, Senator Muskie with 10 per cent, Senator Jackson with 8 per cent, and Mayor Lindsay with 7 per cent.

Mayor Lindsay withdrew from the Presidential race.

April 7   New disclosure laws on campaign contributions went into effect.

April 25 *Massachusetts primary*: Senator McGovern received 52 per cent of the Democratic vote; Senator Muskie, 22 per cent.

Pennsylvania primary: first primary win for Senator Humphrey, with 35 per cent; Governor Wallace, 21 per cent; Senator McGovern, 20 per cent.

April 27 Senator Muskie announced his withdrawal from active campaigning in the primaries, but did not release the delegates he had already won.

May 2   *Indiana primary*: Senator Humphrey, 47 per cent; Governor Wallace, 42 per cent; Senator Muskie, 12 per cent.

Ohio primary: Senator Humphrey, 42 per cent; Senator McGovern, 39 per cent; Senator Muskie, 9 per cent.

Senator Jackson withdrew from the primaries.

May 4   *Tennessee primary*: a victory for Governor Wallace, with 70 per cent; Senator Humphrey, 16 per cent.

May 5   It was announced that the Republican convention in August would be moved from San Diego to Miami Beach.

May 6   *North Carolina primary*: Governor Wallace, 50 per cent; a distant second, former North Carolina Governor Terry Sanford.

May 9   *Nebraska primary*: Senator McGovern, 41 per cent; Senator Humphrey, 35 per cent.

            West Virginia primary: Senator Humphrey, 67 per cent; Governor Wallace, 33 per cent.

May 15   An assassination attempt on Governor Wallace in Maryland left him critically injured.

May 16   *Maryland primary*: Governor Wallace, 39 per cent; Senator Humphrey, 27 per cent; Senator McGovern, 22 per cent.

            Michigan primary: Governor Wallace, 51 per cent; Senator McGovern, 27 per cent; Senator Humphrey, 16 per cent.

May 20   Senator McGovern received the endorsement of Senator McCarthy.

May 22   President Nixon arrived in Moscow for a week of talks with Soviet leaders.

May 23   *Oregon primary*: Senator McGovern, 50 per cent; Governor Wallace, 20 per cent; Senator Humphrey, 12 per cent.

            Rhode Island primary: Senator McGovern, 42 per cent; Senator Muskie, 21 per cent; Senator Humphrey, 21 per cent.

May 28   The first of three debates between Senator McGovern and Senator Humphrey was broadcast over national television.

June 6   *California primary*: Senator McGovern, 44 per cent; Senator Humphrey, 39 per cent. According to California's primary rules, the victory gave Senator McGovern all 271 convention delegates.

     New Jersey primary: Senator McGovern.

     New Mexico primary: Senator McGovern, 33 per cent; Governor Wallace, 29 per cent; Senator Humphrey, 26 per cent.

     South Dakota primary: Senator McGovern.

June 9   Senator Muskie announced that he was still a Presidential candidate.

June 17   Arrests were made of five intruders in the Watergate headquarters of the Democratic National Committee.

June 20   *New York primary*: Senator McGovern.

June 29   A ruling of the Democratic credentials committee against the California primary law resulted in Senator McGovern's loss of 151 convention delegates.

July 10   The Democratic convention began its proceedings, and the 151 disputed California delegates were restored to Senator Mc-Govern.

July 11 — Both Senator Humphrey and Senator Muskie withdrew from competition.

July 12 — Senator McGovern was nominated as the Democratic Presidential candidate.

July 13 — *Senator Thomas F. Eagleton* (Democrat, Missouri) was named Democratic candidate for Vice President.

July 19 — The AFL-CIO executive committee voted against endorsing a Presidential candidate.

July 22 — *Vice President Spiro T. Agnew* was named as President Nixon's choice again for 1972.

July 25 — Senator Eagleton revealed his history of psychiatric treatment.

July 31 — Senator Eagleton relinquished the Democratic nomination for Vice President.

August 8 — *R. Sargent Shriver* was named by the Democratic National Committee as their Vice Presidential candidate.

August 9 — Former Secretary of the Treasury John B. Connally was named head of the Democrats for Nixon.

August 21 — The Republican convention began its proceedings, and subsequently nominated

President Nixon and Vice President Agnew as the candidates of the party.

September 3 President Nixon's re-election campaign was formally opened.

September 15 Two former White House aides were among the group of seven men indicted by a federal grand jury in connection with the Watergate case.

November 7 President Nixon was re-elected overwhelmingly, winning all states but Massachusetts. The popular vote: President Nixon, 61 per cent; Senator McGovern, 38 per cent.

Appendix B
Some Campaign Statistics

OFFICIAL 1972 PRESIDENTIAL PRIMARY RETURNS

Following is a list of official presidential primary returns as supplied by secretaries of state. Two primaries, in Alabama and New York, were strictly delegate selection contests and are not included in the tallies.

State	McGovern	Humphrey	Muskie	Wallace	Others*	Total Democratic	Nixon	Ashbrook	McCloskey	Others*	Total Republican
California June 6	1,550,652	1,375,064	72,701	268,551†	297,550	3,564,518	2,058,825	224,922	—	175	2,283,922
Dist. Col. May 2	—	—	—	—	29,658	29,658	—	—	—	—	—
Florida March 14	78,232	234,658	112,523	526,651	312,490	1,264,554	360,278	36,617	17,312	—	414,207
Illinois March 21	3,687†	1,476†	756,914	7,017†	445,745	1,214,839	32,550†	170†	47†	802	33,569
Indiana May 2	2†	354,244	87,719	309,495	—	751,460	417,069	—	—	—	417,069
Maryland May 16	126,978	151,981	13,363	219,687	56,122	568,131	99,308	6,718	9,223	—	115,249
Massachusetts April 25	325,673	48,929	131,709	45,807	65,638	617,756	99,150	4,864	16,435	956	121,405
Michigan May 16	425,694	249,798	38,701	809,239	64,641	1,588,073	321,652	—	9,691	5,400	336,743
Nebraska May 9	79,309	65,968	6,886	23,912	16,062	192,137	179,824	4,996	9,011	801	194,632
New Hampshire											

OFFICIAL 1972 PRESIDENTIAL PRIMARY RETURNS—continued

New Jersey June 6	—	—	—	—	76,834	76,834	—	—	—	—
New Mexico June 6	51,011	39,768	6,411	44,843	11,260	153,293	14,067	—	3,367	3,035	20,469
North Carolina May 6	—	—	30,739	413,518	377,153	821,410	159,167	—	8,732	—	167,899
Ohio‡ May 2	480,320	499,680	107,806	—	124,524	1,212,330	692,828	—	—	—	692,828
Oregon May 23	205,328	51,163	10,244	81,868	59,423	408,026	231,151	16,696	29,365	—	277,212
Pennsylvania April 25	280,861	481,900	279,983	292,437	39,658	1,374,839	153,886†	—	—	30,915	183,794
Rhode Island May 23	15,603	7,701	7,838	5,802	920	37,864	4,953	175	337	146	5,611
South Dakota June 6	28,017	—	—	—	—	28,017	52,820	—	—	—	52,820
Tennessee May 4	35,551	78,350	9,634	335,858	33,328	492,721	109,696	2,419	2,370	4	114,489
West Virginia May 9	—	246,596	—	121,888	—	368,464	—	—	—	—	—
Wisconsin April 4	333,528	233,748	115,811	248,676	196,721	1,128,584	277,601	2,604	3,651	431	286,444
TOTAL	4,053,453	4,121,372	1,830,217	3,755,424	2,221,817	15,982,363	5,344,064	311,543	132,731	46,081	5,835,569

*Includes write-ins and votes for "none shown."

†Write-in votes.

‡Vote total is highest amount received by any at-large delegate on a particular slate.

Source: 1972 Congressional Quarterly Almanac, p. 1059.

1972 DELEGATES FROM NON-PRIMARY STATES

Listed below are the results of conventions in 32 states and territories that did not hold primaries to choose delegates to the 1972 Democratic National Convention at Miami Beach . . .

State	Uncommitted	Chisholm	Humphrey	Jackson	McGovern	Mills	Muskie	Sanford	Wallace	Total
Alaska	1	—	3	—	6	—	—	—	—	10
Arizona	5	1	1	—	10	—	8	—	—	25
Arkansas	—	—	—	—	—	27	—	—	—	27
Canal Zone	0.50	—	—	—	2.50	—	—	—	—	3
Colorado	5	1	6	—	24	—	—	—	—	36
Connecticut	18	—	1	—	26	1	5	—	—	51
Delaware	6.50	.65	—	—	5.85	1	—	—	—	13
Georgia	26	5	3	1	14	—	—	—	3	53
Guam	—	—	1.50	—	1	—	0.50	—	—	3
Hawaii	15	—	—	—	2	—	—	—	—	17
Idaho	3	2	1	—	8	—	3	—	—	17
Iowa	10	1	—	—	18	—	17	—	—	46
Kansas	18	—	—	—	17	—	—	—	—	35
Kentucky	—	—	—	—	10	—	37	—	—	47
Louisiana	16	—	2	—	23	—	—	—	3	44
Maine	—	—	—	—	—	—	20	—	—	20
Minnesota	2	8	33	—	21	—	—	—	—	64
Mississippi	3	—	—	—	22	—	—	—	—	25
Missouri	53	—	—	—	20	—	—	—	—	73
Montana	2.50	—	—	—	14.50	—	—	—	—	17
Nevada	2	—	3	.75	5.25	—	—	—	—	11
North Dakota	2.10	—	4.20	—	7.70	—	—	—	—	14

1972 DELEGATES FROM NON-PRIMARY STATES—continued

Oklahoma	26	—	—	—	13	—	—	—	—	39
Puerto Rico	1.50	—	0.50	—	5	—	—	—	—	7
South Carolina	17	—	5	—	7	1	2	—	—	32
Texas	33	—	21	—	34	—	—	—	42	130
Utah	8	—	—	—	11	—	—	—	—	19
Vermont	—	—	—	—	9	—	3	—	—	12
Virginia	10	1	3	—	35	—	2	2	—	53
Virgin Islands	—	—	—	—	3	—	—	—	—	3
Washington	—	—	—	52	—	—	—	—	—	52
Wyoming	7.15	—	1.10	—	1.10	.55	1.10	—	—	11
	291.25	19.65	89.30	53.75	375.90	30.55	98.60	2	48	1,009

Source: National Journal 4:1090 (July 1, 1972).

POPULAR AND ELECTORAL VOTE FOR PRESIDENT FOR 1972 AND 1968

State	1972 Electoral Vote Nixon	1972 Electoral Vote McGovern	1972 Popular Vote Nixon	1972 Popular Vote McGovern	1968 Electoral Vote Nixon	1968 Electoral Vote Humphrey	1968 Electoral Vote Wallace	1968 Popular Vote Nixon	1968 Popular Vote Humphrey	1968 Popular Vote Wallace
Alabama	9	—	728,701	256,923	—	—	10	146,923	196,579	691,425
Alaska	3	—	55,349	32,967	3	—	—	36,428	34,501	9,887
Arizona	6	—	402,812	198,540	5	—	—	255,970	166,742	45,066
Arkansas	6	—	445,751	198,899	—	—	6	186,547	183,317	236,504
California	45	—	4,602,096	3,475,847	40	—	—	3,409,554	3,187,364	482,162
Colorado	7	—	597,189	329,980	6	—	—	409,262	336,272	60,691
Connecticut	8	—	810,763	555,498	—	8	—	569,942	661,595	78,931
Delaware	3	—	140,357	92,298	3	—	—	95,479	88,471	28,285
District of Columbia	—	3	35,226	127,627	—	3	—	31,012	139,556	—
Florida	17	—	1,857,759	718,117	14	—	—	886,804	676,794	624,207
Georgia	12	—	881,496	289,529	—	—	12	365,722	333,062	535,389
Hawaii	4	—	168,865	101,409	—	4	—	91,440	141,300	3,465
Idaho	4	—	199,384	80,826	4	—	—	164,029	88,835	36,058
Illinois	26	—	2,788,179	1,913,472	26	—	—	2,137,239	2,008,319	385,058
Indiana	13	—	1,405,154	708,568	13	—	—	1,057,784	806,259	243,030
Iowa	8	—	706,207	496,206	9	—	—	616,776	477,445	66,258
Kansas	7	—	619,812	270,287	7	—	—	468,172	299,890	87,453
Kentucky	9	—	676,446	371,159	9	—	—	458,905	395,097	190,493
Louisiana	10	—	686,852	298,142	—	—	10	259,715	317,929	537,045
Maine	4	—	256,458	160,584	—	4	—	164,560	212,950	6,232

POPULAR AND ELECTORAL VOTE FOR PRESIDENT FOR 1972 AND 1968—continued

Michigan	21	—	1,961,721	1,459,435	—	21	—	1,330,749	1,567,310	320,344
Minnesota	10	—	898,269	802,346	—	10	—	620,687	807,122	66,948
Mississippi	7	—	505,125	126,782	—	—	7	88,214	149,419	414,402
Missouri	12	—	1,154,058	698,531	12	—	—	807,635	785,908	205,129
Montana	4	—	183,976	120,197	4	—	—	130,119	109,218	18,548
Nebraska	5	—	406,298	169,991	5	—	—	303,968	163,531	42,604
Nevada	3	—	115,750	66,016	3	—	—	71,961	58,999	20,071
New Hampshire	4	—	213,724	116,435	4	—	—	154,903	130,589	11,173
New Jersey	17	—	1,845,502	1,102,211	17	—	—	1,325,465	1,264,206	262,164
New Mexico	4	—	235,606	141,084	4	—	—	168,473	129,451	25,602
New York	41	—	4,192,778	2,951,084	—	43	—	2,980,420	3,356,999	349,205
North Carolina	13	—	1,054,889	438,705	13	—	—	619,434	456,968	490,609
North Dakota	3	—	174,109	100,384	4	—	—	138,667	94,319	14,244
Ohio	25	—	2,441,827	1,558,889	26	—	—	1,785,318	1,692,213	468,591
Oklahoma	8	—	759,025	247,147	8	—	—	449,697	301,658	191,731
Oregon	6	—	486,686	392,760	6	—	—	403,491	355,875	49,151
Pennsylvania	27	—	2,714,521	1,796,951	—	29	—	1,991,784	2,203,946	368,275
Rhode Island	4	—	218,290	191,981	—	4	—	115,929	239,497	14,967
South Carolina	8	—	477,044	186,824	8	—	—	260,558	196,889	211,754
South Dakota	4	—	166,476	139,945	4	—	—	147,438	117,505	13,209
Tennessee	10	—	813,147	357,293	11	—	—	467,232	350,041	421,044
Texas	26	—	2,298,896	1,154,289	—	25	—	1,227,199	1,267,317	581,717
Utah	4	—	323,643	126,284	4	—	—	238,637	157,072	27,052
Vermont	3	—	117,149	68,174	3	—	—	85,128	70,449	4,953
Virginia	11	—	988,493	438,887	12	—	—	595,607	443,873	322,203
Washington	9	—	837,135	568,334	—	9	—	520,491	561,675	85,713
West Virginia	6	—	484,964	277,435	—	7	—	306,601	373,382	72,022
Wisconsin	11	—	989,430	810,174	12	—	—	809,997	748,804	127,835
Wyoming	3	—	100,464	44,358	3	—	—	70,093	44,893	11,059
Total U.S.	520	17	47,165,234	29,168,110	302	191	45	31,304,992	30,994,354	9,825,459

Source: The 1973 World Almanac, p. 40, for 1968 figures; The 1974 World Almanac (forthcoming) for 1972 figures.

Index